CELEBRATING HOMER'S LANDSCAPES

CELEBRATING

Yale University Press New Haven and London

J.V. Luce

Homer's LANDSCAPES

TROY AND ITHACA REVISITED

Published with assistance from the Mary Cady Tew Memorial Fund.

Designed by Sonia Scanlon.
Set in Monotype Bembo by Ink, Inc., New York.
Printed in the United States of America.

Library of Congress Cataloging-in-Publication
Data
Luce, John Victor, 1920–
Celebrating Homer's landscapes: Troy and
Ithaca revisited/J.V. Luce.
      p.   cm.
Includes bibliographical reference and index.

ISBN 0-300-07411-5 (cloth: alk. paper)
1. Trojan War—Literature and the War.
2. Homer—Knowledge—Geography.
3. Literary landmarks—Turkey—Troy (Extinct
city) 4. Literary landmarks—Greece—Ithaca
Island. 5. Excavations (Archaeology)—Turkey—
Troy (Extinct city) 6. Homer. Iliad. 7. Homer.
Odyssey. I. Title.
DF221.T8L83   1998   939´.21—dc21
98-3859

A catalogue record for this book is available
from the British Library.

10   9   8   7   6   5   4   3   2   1

To the memory of my father, who taught me the Greek alphabet at the age of five and was with me on my first visits to Troy and Ithaca

CONTENTS

MAPS

PREFACE

Robert Wood (1717?–1771) was born in Ireland and developed a keen amateur interest in classical antiquity. In 1750 he visited the Troad in the company of two friends, and his pioneering survey of the area is appended to his famous *Essay on the Original Genius and Writings of Homer*, which was published a few years after his death. In this epoch-making work of Homeric scholarship he speaks of "the humble duty of bearing testimony, as an eyewitness, of the poet's veracity," and that phrase sums up the animating spirit of my own topographical researches.

More than a century later Walter Leaf, in his classic study *Troy* (1912), gave it as his considered opinion that "no case of a local inconsistency, not a single anatopism...can be brought home to the *Iliad*." This is a judgment with which I fully agree, and I believe that it can also be extended to cover the picture of Ithaca given in the *Odyssey*.

Evidence for the accuracy of Homer's topography counteracts a pronounced trend in Homeric criticism that has developed in the last quarter of the twentieth century. It is currently fashionable to regard the Homeric accounts of landscape and locality as "poetic constructions," with the implication that much of the detail is fictional and imaginary. It is my hope that the text and illustrations of this study may serve as a counterpoise to this trend. The book is written in the firm belief that "truth to life" is Homer's paramount concern in local description.

It has been my good fortune to make many stimulating, if brief, visits to Troy and Ithaca as a lecturer on Swan Hellenic cruises. I have also supplemented these visits by some more extended expeditions, in the course of which I have walked all over Ithaca and seen nearly all the locations in the Troad named in the *Iliad*.

I was able to draw on the photographic expertise of Mr. Brendan J. Dempsey, who supervises the Photographic Centre in Trinity College Dublin, and I wish to express my thanks to him for much useful advice, and for the care and interest he has taken in the preparation of my illustrative material for publication.

The book's inception owed much to the friendly interest of the late Professor John Herington; and the wide-ranging scholarship of Professor George Huxley has always been at my disposal when help was needed. I must also express my gratitude to Professor Manfred Korfmann for the kind welcome he extended to me when I visited Tübingen, and for the pains he took to ensure that I was brought fully up to date on the work of the Troia Projekt.

Professor Korfmann has written feelingly about the cultural significance of the *Iliad*, and about the archaeological importance of Troy and its surroundings. He has also shown himself acutely aware of the threat to the area posed by incipient speculative development. Long-standing Turkish proposals for turning this key section of the Troad into an historical national park have received his active support, and it is a pleasure to be able to record that late in 1996 the scheme was approved by the Turkish government. The landscape is still little changed from Homer's day, and if this book helps in any way to conserve the precious but precarious integrity of an historic region of world importance, it will not have been written in vain.

Ithaca has its share of visitors—it is quite easy to reach from Corfu or Patras—but retains the charm of comparative seclusion. I like to recall that Byron spent a few last happy days there before plunging into the fevered cauldron of Hellenic politics at Missolonghi. The following passage from a memoir by his friend Trelawny catches the spirit of the visit: "The grey olive-trees, bright green fig, and rampant vine that grew above our heads, screened us from the sun; the fresh breeze from the sea, with the springs of purest water gushing out of the rocks, soothed the Poet's temper. He turned out of the path to look at a natural grotto, in a grove of forest trees, and said: 'You will find nothing in Greece or its islands so pleasant as this. If this isle were mine—I would break my staff and bury my book.'"

Ithaca is indeed an isle where the air is full of voices—Homeric voices—and it is easy to agree with the much-travelled Odysseus when he said that he could see no land more sweet. If any of my readers are moved to visit it, may I suggest that they take a copy of the *Odyssey* with them. There can be no better place to read it.

The translations in the present work are my own, as are italics, unless otherwise acknowledged.

John V. Luce   June 1998
Trinity College
Dublin

You sing the saga of the Achaeans so well and finely . . . as though you

had been there yourself, or heard it from one who was.

—Odysseus to the bard Demodokos (Od. 8, 489–91)

THIS BOOK SURVEYS IN DETAIL what Homer tells us about Troy and Ithaca, and examines how landscape and locality are woven into the texture of the *Iliad* and the *Odyssey*. I shall attempt to demonstrate, in opposition to much current scholarly opinion, that Homer was well informed about the terrain in both regions, that his account provides an authentic setting for the action in both epics, and that he does not arbitrarily invent landmarks to suit his poetic purposes. My aim, in short, is to provide a comprehensively illustrated vindication of the overall accuracy of Homeric topography.

The bardic tradition, supplemented and enriched by his own travels, provided Homer with a mass of topographical information. If, as many scholars think, he was composing and reciting his epics between c. 750 and 700 B.C., we can say that by this time the Troad and the site of Troy itself had been colonised by Aeolian Greeks. The island of Ithaca had also become an important staging post on the route to the new Greek cities of southern Italy and Sicily. Local knowledge shared between bard and audience will have acted as a constant control on the reliability of his scenic descriptions. Homer will have had little scope and less incentive to distort or falsify the geography of what had become well-known regions of the Greek world. As a result the action of the *Iliad* has been given a setting that is remarkably faithful to reality on the ground, and the same is true of the *Odyssey* in respect to Ithaca and adjacent parts of Greece.

It is a major contention of this study that authenticity in scene setting is one of Homer's paramount concerns. Only very rarely does he allow himself to make a slight displacement of natural features in order to streamline or enhance the flow of the narrative. Such topographical licence, I maintain, is minimal, and does not lay the poet open to the charge of arbitrary invention. My discussion of notorious cruxes like the hot and cold springs near Troy or the island of Asteris in the Ithaca channel should help to bear out the truth of this assessment.

In general, Homeric indications of location or direction can be shown to be in close accord with the lie of the land. Topographical precision is particularly evident in the *Iliad* in the accounts of journeys made by gods or men. Here it seems to be the rule that Homer always specifies the starting point, the route, and the destination, and the journey can be followed on a map with the aid of these indications. Confirmation of this pattern will be found in the accounts of the journeys of Chryses, Poseidon, Hera, and Priam.

In regard to the *Odyssey,* a distinction must be drawn between the far-flung Wanderings of Odysseus narrated in books 9 to 12 and his movements within Ithaca itself. Charting the Wanderings is a hopeless quest. Some of the narrative colouring may derive from sailors' reports about west Mediterranean waters, but once Odysseus reaches the land of the Lotus-eaters, he has essentially sailed off the map into regions imagined rather than known. Only in fancy can one follow him to the land of the Cyclopes or the islands of Circe or Calypso. Ithaca, on the other hand, was a known part of the Greek world, and his comings and goings there can be precisely determined in accordance with textual indications (see Chapter 7). The same, I argue, is true of the journey of Telemachos to the Peloponnese and back.

Homeric topography was something of a battleground in antiquity and has been debated in immense and intricate detail over the past two centuries. The reader might be excused for supposing that nothing new could be said on such a well-worn topic as the environs of Troy. But in fact recent geophysical investigations have transformed our understanding of the Trojan plain. Since 1977 bore-holes have been sunk to a considerable depth in many parts of the plain, and the cores of sediment recovered have been analysed with a view to determining its profile since the last Ice Age. The scientific data prove that the extensive floodplain that we see now has been built up by sedimentation during the past ten thousand years or so, with the sea retreating and the delta being steadily advanced by river action. The precise position of the shoreline at the time of the Trojan War, say about 3,250 years ago, has not been finally determined, but most, if not all, of the plain that now extends northwards from Troy to the Dardanelles (Hellespont) is the product of alluviation since c. 1250 B.C.

This new information about the growth of the plain requires believers in Homeric authenticity to make a detailed reappraisal of the course of the battles described in the *Iliad,* and I attempt this in Chapter 5. The thrust of the new scientific information tends to vindicate the accuracy of certain traditional material embedded in the *Iliad.* This material relates particularly to the mustering of the Trojan forces in defence of their city and to the line of their advance into the plain and across the river Scamander to attack the Greek camp. A number of passages that were previously hard to interpret have become much more comprehensible. This outcome lends support to the view that the *Iliad* reflects the strategy and tactics of an actual campaign.

Just as geophysical surveys have given us a better grasp of the surroundings of ancient Troy, so estimates of the size and importance of the city itself have been radically transformed by the current excavations. Troy must now be viewed as one of the major strongholds and trading centres of Asia Minor in the Late Bronze Age. The Achaean enterprise in laying siege to such a place is correspondingly magnified, and the Homeric picture of a great war is far less open to the charge of poetic exaggeration.

The strength of one's belief in the historicity of the Trojan War depends on one's estimate of the overall reliability of ancient Greek tradition and its particular embodiment in the poetry of Homer. This major issue for ancient historians and classical philologists will not be argued in any detail in this study. I am content to follow Herodotus and Thucydides, and the ancient world in general, in their acceptance of the Trojan War as a highly significant event in early Greek history. There is good hope that the progress of archaeology and the further study of Hittite archives will throw increasing light on the date and historical context of such a war. In the meantime one can do worse than follow Homer. It is certainly a tenable hypothesis that the nucleus of the story and the names of the main participants were embodied in heroic songs composed at the time of the events. Comparative study shows that this commonly happens in cultures like that of the Achaeans, dominated by warrior aristocracies. Tacitus, for example, reports that Arminius's defeat of the Roman legions under Varus in A.D. 9 became at once a theme of song among the Teutonic tribes. There is every reason to suppose that something similar happened with the story of Troy. In recent years the researches of philologists and archaeologists have tended to converge in support of the view that Homer was heir to a substantially valid tradition transmitted down the centuries by a succession of oral bards who were the generally faithful custodians of Greek folk memory in an illiterate age. The detailed conclusions of this study are intended to lend support to this position.

The topography of Ithaca is on a somewhat different footing from that of Troy. Here one does not have to take account of any major geophysical changes. The lineaments of the island still called Itháki (or Thiáki) remain as they were in ancient times. The island was never the scene of any major historical events or military campaigns. In the Late Bronze Age it was a minor kingdom on the margins of the Mycenaean world. But it *was* part of that world, and archaeological investigation in the twentieth century has provided enough evidence of a Mycenaean presence on the island to lend credibility to the saga of Odysseus as it appears in the *Iliad*. In the Catalogue of Greek forces (Il. 2, 631–37) he is listed as the ruler of an island kingdom who brought a small fleet of twelve ships to join the confederate Greek expedition. In the campaign that followed, his personal qualities as a leader of men gave him an importance out of proportion to the forces under his immediate command, and, according to the tradition, he played a major part in the final capture of Troy by masterminding the ruse of the Wooden Horse. He then sailed for home, but in the course of this voyage, as Homer tells it in the *Odyssey,* he was blown off course by a storm and found himself transported to a wonderland of ogres and witches, where his adventures are the stuff of folktale and fiction rather than saga.

When Odysseus returns to Ithaca, the story takes on a different flavour. The fantastic gives way to the realistic, and we are plunged into an exciting and very human tale of plot and counterplot, of disguise and stratagem, of superior numbers defeated by courage and enterprise. All ends happily when the heroic protagonist recovers hearth and home from the clutches of the rapacious Suitors. As with the Wanderings, the story line must be read as fiction. But there is a crucial difference in the setting. We are no longer in Fairyland but in a recognisably real island that had long been a well-known part of the Greek world. Here topographical study does seem in order.

Because of its geographical position, Ithaca was always a natural staging post on the ancient sea route from the Gulf of Corinth to the south of Italy and Sicily. Rather than venture out across the large open expanse of the Ionian Sea, ancient skippers preferred to follow the coast and island route as far as Corcyra (Corfu), and then cut across the Straits of Otranto to the heel of Italy. This was the route followed by Mycenaean explorers and merchants in the Late Bronze Age, and it was certainly the route taken in the early eighth century B.C. by the pioneers of western Greek colonisation. The merchant adventurers of Euboea came this way as they sailed westwards to found the earliest Greek colony on Pithekoussai (Ischia) off the Bay of Naples. They took the alphabet with them, and one of the very few examples of written Greek from the eighth century has been found in that colony. It is also noteworthy that a similar example of alphabetic writing—a few lines of hexameter verse scratched on a pot and dated c. 700 B.C.—was found in Ithaca.[1] It may be significant in this connection that Homer mentions Euboea as one of the remotest destinations reached by his fictional Phaeacian mariners (Od. 7, 321–24). This could be a reference in reverse, as it were, to the actual voyages of Euboean mariners in Homer's lifetime.

The paradox of Ithacan topography is that the island is described in remarkably accurate detail as part of a largely fictional story line. I have long felt that the best way to account for this paradox is to regard Homer as a pioneer in the genre of the historical novel. Just as a modern exponent of this genre will go to immense pains to get the settings correct in every detail, so, I believe, Homer visited Ithaca and familiarised himself with the terrain. That such a journey would have been possible for him is clear. Conviction that he made it will, I think, come only to those who take the trouble to visit the island themselves. The case for eyewitness knowledge on Homer's part has often been made and as often denied. I hope that the evidence presented and discussed in Chapters 6 and 7 may help to reinforce its claim to credence.

All modern exponents of Homeric topography have to take account of ancient contributions to the problems that still dog the enquiry. Intensive scholarly study of the Homeric epics became a feature of Alexandria in the first half of the third century B.C. when Zenodotus of Ephesus, the first head of the museum and library established by the Ptolemies, collated earlier texts to produce a pioneering recension of the *Iliad* and the *Odyssey*. The work that he initiated culminated a century later in a major critical edition of Homer by Aristarchus of Samothrace, rightly regarded as the prince of ancient scholars. We know that his line-by-line commentary included discussion of topographical problems. He also published separate monographs, one of which dealt with the location of the Greek ship station at Troy, a question that is still the subject of much discussion. Unfortunately, only scattered fragments of this editorial work survive, preserved mainly in the marginal notes in Byzantine manuscripts of Homer.

The museum was essentially a research institute, staffed by scientists as well as literary scholars. The work of Eratosthenes of Cyrene, librarian in the second half of the third century, spanned both disciplines. His researches included work on the history of comic drama, but his most remarkable achievement was in the field of mathematical geography, where he calculated the circumference of the earth to within a few hundred miles of the true figure. Eratosthenes is rightly revered as the first systematic geographer, and his work included a highly sceptical treatment of the Wanderings of Odysseus. Although none of his books is extant, the general line of his critique of Homer as a geographer is clear enough from later references, particularly in Strabo.

Strabo (c. 64 B.C. to A.D. 21), a Greek from Amaseia in Pontus, is a key figure in the history of Homeric topography in the ancient world. The seventeen books of his treatise *Geographica* are extant, and in them he touches on many of the matters that form the substance of the present study. In particular, he has much to say about Homeric Ithaca and Homeric Troy. But Strabo, it must be said, is better at articulating problems than at providing solutions. In the case of Troy he relied on the published fieldwork of others, and did not himself visit the Troad. As for Ithaca, he may have seen the island from shipboard on a journey from Greece to Rome, but he does not appear to have gone over the ground in any detail. Strabo has a broadly philosophic approach to geography and displays some appreciation of the geological changes that can occur over a long span of time. He was aware, for example, of the changing dimensions of the floodplain at Troy. But in general he can be characterised as widely read rather than widely travelled, and his skills are those of a compiler rather than an original thinker. Not the least of his merits is that he names and quotes his sources in considerable detail, thus enabling us to see something of the history of the problems he discusses.

Strabo regarded the Homeric poems as the fountainhead of Greek geography, and much of his first book is devoted to defending Homer's reputation against the criticisms of Eratosthenes. Eratosthenes, he tells us, took the view that Homer's function as a poet was to entertain, not to instruct. It was, in his view, misguided to look for geographical information in the epics. In particular, he thought it a waste of time to look for locations like the Cave of Polyphemus or Circe's island, because Homer's account of Odysseus's Wanderings was purely fictional. In a crushing witticism he remarked: "You will find the island of Aeolus when you find the cobbler who sewed the bag for the winds."

Eratosthenes was surely right to hold that the landfalls in the Wanderings cannot be precisely located on the map. But it is also undeniable that the Greeks who colonised Italy and Sicily from the late eighth century onwards thought that they were returning to an area that Odysseus had visited. The findings of modern archaeology supply a credible basis for this belief insofar as they show that Mycenaean Greeks did indeed explore the waters of the Tyrrhenian Sea and that they set up trading posts from the Gulf of Taranto to Sardinia in the period from c. 1400 to 1200 B.C. It is therefore a reasonable supposition that some memories of these Bronze Age voyages were embodied in Mycenaean poetry and so transmitted to Homer by the bardic tradition. The westward voyage of Odysseus would form a counterpart in saga to Jason's eastward quest for the Golden Fleece. Both stories have been heavily overlaid with folktale motifs, but they may not be totally divorced from physical and historical fact. In support of this line of thought one might plausibly find some basis for the episode of Scylla and Charybdis in the currents and whirlpools that still make passage of the Straits of Messina quite difficult for small boats. One could also point out that the inhabitants of Georgia still peg sheepskins in their rivers to catch particles of alluvial gold.

In his handling of the Wanderings, Strabo rejected the abrasive scepticism of Eratosthenes, as well as the extravagant view of Crates of Pergamum that the landfalls of Odysseus awaited discovery in the unexplored outer ocean. Insofar as he envisaged a *general* setting for the Wanderings in the central or western Mediterranean, his view represents a fair attempt to steer a middle course between the Scylla of scepticism and the Charybdis of credulity.

Strabo, I believe, was also right to dissent from Eratosthenes' too sharp distinction between "entertainment" and "instruction." A similar dichotomy is still evident in the approach of those modern critics who emphasise that Homer is a poet, not an historian, and who go on to question his value as a source for the Trojan War. Aeschylus's *Persians* and Shakespeare's *Julius Caesar* show how creative genius can dramatise history without losing touch with reality.

Outright scepticism about the historicity of Homer is a modern phenomenon resulting, I suspect, from a too narrowly aesthetic approach to the epics. Thucydides, a very hard-headed handler of evidence, took account of the whole broad sweep and thrust of Greek tradition and had no doubt that Agamemnon was an historical figure. He quotes Homer for the extent of Agamemnon's empire and fully accepts that Agamemnon led a Greek expedition against Troy, though he does allow that Homer, "being a poet," may have exaggerated the numbers involved (1, 9–11). The sceptic does not, in my view, pay enough attention to the role of poetry in early Greek society, especially in the preliterate period. An ancient poet working in the oral tradition did not have the absolute freedom of a modern poet. Homer, as a professional bard, was the mouthpiece and custodian of Greek heroic tradition, and this, not artistic creativity, was his primary role.

The heroic tradition was embodied in a great mass of orally transmitted poetry far wider than the *Iliad* and *Odyssey*. Artifacts evidenced by archaeology, and early linguistic forms documented in Linear B, show that the roots of this poetic inheritance run well back into the Bronze Age and reflect the sophisticated organisation of the Mycenaean world between 1400 and 1200 B.C. Then, for reasons not fully understood, Greek civilisation went into a severe decline from c. 1100 B.C. on. A Dark Age set in, and the art of writing was lost until the adoption of the Phoenician alphabet early in the eighth century. But the tradition of a great past was preserved in the collective consciousness of the whole Greek world, and more specifically in the trained memories of individual bards. Paradoxically, illiteracy was a safeguard rather than a threat to the authenticity of the tradition. The illiterate memory is capable of amazing feats of retention and recall. In the absence of written records the bards performed a social function in voicing and transmitting the valued traditions of the whole community. Their audiences would welcome suitable embellishment but would not tolerate arbitrary falsification.

These general considerations about the presentation and transmission of historical facts in a preliterate culture apply also to topographical information. It is currently fashionable to appraise Homeric topography in terms of "poetical construction." The tone of much recent comment has been set by Agathe Thornton's firmly phrased statement: "The actual physical nature of the Trojan plain studied by Cook in great detail, both archaeologically and topographically, is not the principle or order constituting the arrangement of localities referred to in the Iliad. Homer's Trojan plain is a poetic construction with its own peculiar character and order."[2] Thornton's phrasing suggests a sharp antithesis between fact and fiction, between a real plain and an imagined plain. There is also, I think, the implication that topographical study should be confined to the actual plain and should not, as it were, trespass on the sacred turf of Homer's demesne.

The spirit of Thornton's approach seems to be reflected in much of the topographical discussion in two recent major works of Homeric scholarship. In the Cambridge *Commentary* on the *Iliad*, for example, we find Bryan Hainsworth taking the view that "except in the most general terms the epic geography of the Troad is clearly a poetical construction."[3] Similarly, Stephanie West, in her introduction to books 1 to 4 in the recently published Oxford *Commentary* on the *Odyssey*, argues that the poem contains a great deal of "topographical vagueness and inaccuracy."[4]

The assumption that poetic creativity has absolute licence to disregard geographical fact appears to underlie such comments. This may appeal to a modern aesthetic, but, as argued throughout this work, it is not the way to approach Homer. Homer expressed his creativity in the deft ordering and forceful presentation of a complex mass of saga material, in the development of character through dialogue, and in the embellishment provided by extended similes. It was his forte to invent speeches, not places. Where landscape and locality were concerned, he aimed at fidelity to fact. This fidelity was partly guaranteed by the aptness of traditional formulae like "beetling Troy" or "rugged Ithaca" but also, as I shall argue, underpinned by personal observation.

Anyone who envisages Homer as an eyewitness of the scenes he describes must at once confront the objection that Homer was blind. The tradition of the "blind bard" was well established in the ancient world, resting ultimately on a passage in book 8 of the *Odyssey*, where the depiction of blind Demodokos singing to a rapt audience in Phaeacia has the feel of a self-portrait. Homer does not, however, say that Demodokos was blind from birth. Indeed, the phrasing he uses may well suggest loss of sight in later life: "The Muse loved him greatly, and mixed good and evil in her gifts. She deprived him of sight, but kept enhancing the sweetness of his singing" (Od. 8, 63–64). The view that Homer, like Milton, went blind in midcareer is found in the oldest and fullest ancient *Life* of Homer, attributed (wrongly) to Herodotus. This, says the author, happened in the Ionian city of Colophon as the result of an eye infection contracted during a visit to Ithaca.

1.1 A head of Homer (from the collection of Lyde Browne, Esq.). This illustration featured as the frontispiece in Robert Wood's *Essay on the Original Genius and Writings of Homer* (London, 1775).

How trustworthy is this information? It is fashionable to preface any discussion of "Homer" (that is, the epics) with the statement that we know nothing about Homer (the man). Scepticism about the possibility of a *detailed* Homeric biography is indeed inevitable when one looks at the wide variety of dates and birthplaces given in the seven ancient *Lives* that are extant. Homer (fig. 1.1) lived before the rise of historical enquiry, and the details of his life were not destined to be accurately recorded. This fact, coupled with his fame, encouraged various cities to claim him as their own, a rivalry pilloried in the sarcastic couplet:

> *Seven cities claimed Homer dead*
> *Through which the living Homer begged his bread.*

One way to narrow these uncertainties is to subject the Homeric corpus to the closest possible scrutiny, and some of the findings of this approach come now to be considered. A recent, and remarkable, stylistic analysis of the *Iliad* and *Odyssey* compared their linguistic usage with that found in the works of

Hesiod and the remains of other early Greek poetry in the same mode. On the basis of carefully ordered statistics, the author feels able to date the *Iliad* to c. 735 B.C. and the *Odyssey* to c. 725 B.C.[5] This is a plausible result reached on the basis of an objective method. It supplies a firm basis for the view advanced on other grounds by various scholars that Homer is a figure of late eighth-century Greece. He seems, for instance, to have been touched by the excitement of the Greek colonial expansion that was beginning to gather momentum at the time, and he definitely antedates the rise of Greek lyric poetry that was well under way by the middle of the seventh century.

The superlative crafting of the epics and their homogeneity of style strongly suggest authorship by a single individual of rare poetic genius. This "unitarian" view of Homer was taken by Aristotle and by the ancient world generally. It has been opposed in modern times by the "separatist" or "analyst" school, whose members regard both *Iliad* and *Odyssey* as well-edited compilations of previously separate ballads or lays. The unitarian approach is now in the ascendant and is certainly the one adopted in this book.

Such salient characteristics of the Homeric style as stock epithets, formulaic phrases, type scenes, and word-for-word repetitions indicate that the poems were composed in the oral mode for public recitation. This in turn implies that their author was an early member of the class of professional bards whose prominent role in the Greek city states is well documented from the seventh century on. To fulfil his function in Greek society such an individual had to travel extensively, attending festivals to take part in competitions and reciting his repertoire wherever a suitable audience could be found. A wandering bard would naturally seek the patronage of ruling families, and Homer may have been court poet to some aristocratic house, enjoying a status like that of Phemios or Demodokos as depicted in the *Odyssey*. In this connection, the Aeneadae of the Troad, whose dynasty receives unusually favourable mention in *Iliad* 20, 307–8, have come into serious consideration.[6]

One other general inference may be made from the *language* of the poems.

The predominantly Ionic character of the Homeric dialect suggests that the composer lived and worked mainly within the boundaries of Ionia.

The above deductions are consistent with some scattered but important testimony found in major Greek writers of the Classical age. Herodotus does not venture an opinion on Homer's birthplace but says very firmly: "I consider that Homer and Hesiod lived four hundred years before me *and not more*" (2, 53; my italics). If the *floruit* of Herodotus is taken to be c. 450 B.C., that would put Homer and Hesiod back in the ninth century. Herodotus's finding has the merit of linking Homer and Hesiod—they may well have been near contemporaries—but it was probably based on a rather high estimate of the average length of a human generation as forty rather than thirty years. For this and other reasons Herodotus's dating is now thought to be too early, probably by about a century. Alphabetic writing was not known in ninth-century Greece but had come fully into use by the end of the eighth century. The preservation of the epics in the form given them by Homer would hardly have been possible without the aid of writing. But Herodotus has the merit of being the first to work out a possible dating for Homer, especially if we can reduce his four hundred years to something nearer three hundred. His emphatic "and not more" indicates that he was combatting contemporary opinion that put Homer back nearer the time of the Trojan War. Such impossibly early datings survive in the traditional *Lives*.

Like Herodotus, Aristotle made a special study of Homer and his work. He concurred with the view, found also in a fragment of Pindar, that the city of Smyrna was the scene of Homer's birth and early upbringing (fig. 1.2). He also says that Homer was honoured in Chios, "though it was not his native city," thus indicating his belief that Homer changed his domicile.[7]

The Chian connection also receives support in other early sources, and it is particularly notable that the association of a highly regarded blind poet with Chios is attested in the Homeric *Hymn to Apollo* (165–73). In a famous and beautiful passage, a chorus of Delian women is told to proclaim the undying poetic fame of "the blind man who dwells in rocky Chios." Was this Homer?

1.2　A view of the site of Old Smyrna (Bayrakli) in the northern suburbs of Izmir.

Thucydides thought so (3, 104), taking the *Hymn* to have been composed by Homer himself, but stylistic analysis of the *Hymn* as a whole makes this attribution unlikely. Still, the passage in question could date from the first half of the seventh century. If so, it may well have been a tribute to Homer composed by one of his followers or successors in the field of epic recitation. The existence of a group known as *Homeridae*—sons or followers of Homer—is well attested. They were said to have carried on his work in Chios, and this evidence is consistent with speculation that the *Hymn to Apollo* contains the earliest reference to Homer and his reputation as a master composer of heroic poetry.

What then of his blindness? The powerfully visual nature of Homeric description has always impressed critics and translators. As a good example one might take the description of Hector's infant son who "shrank back wailing into the bosom of his nurse," terrified at the sight of "the horsehair plume that nodded terribly from the helmet's crest" (Il. 6, 467–70). An ancient editor commented that the scene was "as if painted in a picture."[8]

Would such artistry be possible in a poet who had never seen the external world? Alexander Pope's poetic soul strongly rejected any suggestion that Homer could have been blind from birth. In the *Essay on Homer* prefixed to his translation of the *Iliad* (fig. 1.3) he wrote: "He must certainly have beheld the Creation, considered it with a long Attention, and enriched his fancy by the most sensible knowledge of those ideas which he makes the Reader see while he but describes them." The visually enriched "fancy" of which Pope here speaks is perhaps most evident in Homer's masterly use of extended similes. Linguistic analysis has shown that such similes constitute the latest and least traditional part of the text. It is therefore reasonable to suppose that they were composed by Homer himself rather than inherited as a stock part of a tradition that probably already included such visually memorable phrases as "rosy-fingered dawn" or "wine-dark sea."

One or two examples will help to make the point. Early in the *Iliad*, when the various contingents of the Achaean host pour out from their encampment to muster in battle array, Homer compares them to "thronging flocks of geese or cranes or long-necked swans, that gather in the Asian meadow by the streams of the Kaÿstrios." The extended simile then continues (Il. 2, 459–63): "Hither and thither they fly, rejoicing in their wings, and as one flock wheels and settles noisily in front of another, all the grassy plain resounds with their clamorous cries."

Anyone who has ever watched marsh fowl on the move will confirm the vividly accurate quality of Homer's description. It gives a very strong impression of having been studied from life, an impression supported by the unusually

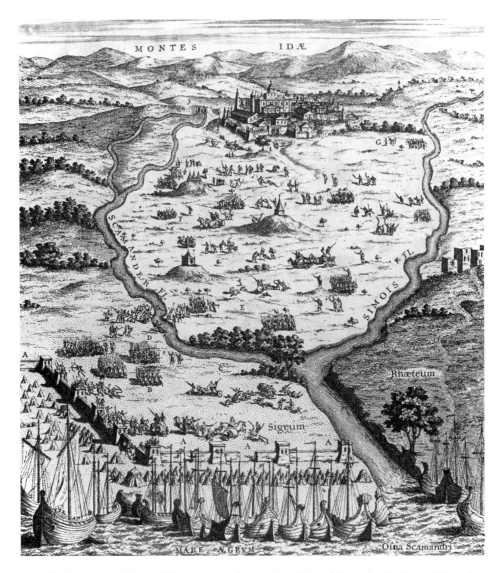

1.3   The Greek camp in front of Troy as pictured in the first edition of Alexander Pope's translation of the *Iliad*. Troy is situated, much as later proposed by Lechevalier and Choiseul-Gouffier, at the inner edge of the plain on the foothills of Ida. Robert Wood was scathing about the whole conception, pointing out that the printer reversed the block, which wrongly puts Cape Rhæteum (Rhoeteum) on the right (west) and Sigeum on the left.

precise location of the scene by the banks of a named river. The Kaÿstrios still makes its way to the sea through its spreading floodplain (the "Asian meadow") to the west of ancient Ephesus (fig. 1.4). Homeric similies are normally quite general in their phrasing, and only rarely are they tagged in this way with a topographical reference. In view of all this it is tempting to suppose that the simile embodies a personal memory of what the poet saw on a visit to Ephesus. Attendance as a performer at the festival of the Ephesia would supply a plausible motive for such a visit.

In much the same way we may deduce a visit by Homer to the great early Ionian folk gathering on Delos. The evidence is contained in a passage of the *Odyssey* where Odysseus is complimenting Nausikaa on her youthful beauty. He says that he views her with delight and awe, and compares his feelings to those he experienced on a previous occasion when he observed (Od. 6, 162–63) "the young shoot of a palm tree springing up on Delos beside the altar of Apollo." The botany is said to be somewhat faulty because only mature palm trees are tall and slender, but Nausikaa will not, I think, have taken the comparison amiss.

Many more examples might be quoted of powerfully vivid visual imagery in the Homeric epics. I conclude that loss of sight in midcareer is the best way to explain both the quality of the poetry and the strong tradition of the blind poet. The story in the pseudo-Herodotean *Life* may well have arisen from a similar process of reasoning. I like to think that this hypothesis may find support in another remarkable simile in which the rapid movement of the goddess Hera as she flies from Ida to Olympos is compared to (Il. 15, 80–82): "the darting intellect of a much travelled man, one who forms this thought in his sagacious heart: 'Oh to be there, or there!' and is filled with longing." "As quick as thought" has become a cliché, but the comparison here is far from hackneyed. The simile stands out as very unusual in Homer because of its psychological and introspective quality. It is perhaps not overfanciful to detect in it also a note of frustration, such as might have been felt by a much travelled bard who had lost his sight.

There is evidence that Greek lyric poets travelled extensively in the earlier part of the seventh century B.C. Terpander, a native of Antissa in Lesbos, is

1.4 A view over the floodplain of the Kaÿstrios River taken from the citadel hill of Seljuk about two miles to the east of Ephesus. This is Homer's "meadow of Asia," scene of the marsh-fowl simile of *Iliad* 2, 459–63.

recorded as having won a musical competition in Sparta at the festival of the Carneia in 676 B.C. Arion of Methymna (also in Lesbos) was on a voyage from Italy to Corinth when he was thrown overboard and (as legend averred) rescued by a dolphin and brought ashore in the southern Peloponnese.[9] Similar travels by Homer, a generation or so earlier, would have been perfectly feasible. Indeed, a professional bard's need to travel if he is to enhance his reputation is quite strongly suggested by a passage in the *Odyssey* where Homer lists the "divine bard" with other itinerant professionals like seers and doctors and remarks (17, 382–86): "Such men are welcome visitors in men's houses over the wide surface of the earth." The detailed topographical study that follows is written in the firm belief that Homer was just such a traveller and that his eagle eye and well-stocked mind gave him an accurate and comprehensive grasp of the landscapes in which his epics are set.

From thence all Ida was in view and the city of Priam.

—Il. 13, 13–14

TWO **THE TROAD**

HOMER REPEATEDLY INVOKES the aid of the Muses "who dwell on Olympos," and they afford him access to the councils of the gods held there by Zeus. With their inspiring aid, he gains a more than human insight into the divine motivation behind the events of history and becomes a privileged observer of the Trojan War. By the same token, he is able to soar in imagination to present a "god's eye view" of the geography of Priam's kingdom. In an age when maps were unknown he shows a remarkable ability to select and describe the salient features of the landscape in their proper physical alignment. He can, as it were, contemplate the Troad from on high, and when he embodies the results of such mountaintop vision in his poetry, he manages to catch something of the comprehensive clarity of a modern satellite photograph.

Two notable examples of such elevated vision come at the beginning of the thirteenth book of the *Iliad*. Zeus, as we were told in an earlier book, has been watching the progress of the great battle on the Trojan plain from the top of Mount Ida (Il. 11, 183). He has just seen Hector smash his way through the outer fortification of the Greek camp, and the Trojans are close to the ships. Satisfied with the progress of his plan to humiliate Agamemnon and bring honour to Achilles, Zeus relaxes the intentness of his surveillance and lets his gaze stray upwards and onwards in the same line of vision (Il. 13, 3–6):

> Zeus turned away his glittering eyes, and let his gaze stray
> far off to the land of the horse-herding Thracians. Next
> he descried the warrior Mysians, and after them the noble

Hippemolgi ["mare milkers"], whose food is milk, and
finally his gaze rested on the Abioi, most just of men.

The vision coheres well with geographical realities. Zeus has been looking
down from Mount Ida to Troy in a northwesterly direction. If this line of sight
is continued across the sea it intersects the coast of Thrace (map 1). Homer
shows himself well aware of this fact by specifying that the "land of the horse-
herding Thracians" comes first into Zeus's purview. The warlike Mysians can
be located farther north in what is now Bulgaria. The habits of the Hippemolgi
indicate that they are nomads roaming the plains of Scythia, north of the
Danube. Finally, his eye rests on the "Abioi, most just of men," who are to be
imagined as denizens of a "Utopia of the far North."[1]

The depiction of the panorama is as notable for what it omits as for what it
says. There is no mention of snowy mountains, broad rivers, or boundless
steppes. Instead, our attention is firmly focused on the tribes who inhabit the vast
landscape, and on their specific activities: Thracians herding horses, Mysians
fighting at close quarters, nomads living on yogurt, and the distant Abioi manag-
ing their affairs in exemplary fashion. In this respect the passage serves as a para-
digm for all Homeric landscape painting. The scene is accurately envisaged, but
its primary function is to provide a theatre for human action.

Zeus's gaze has wandered far afield, but not so that of Poseidon, to whom
Homer turns next. Poseidon has been keeping a close and anxious watch on the
fighting from "the topmost peak of wooded Samothrace." We are told that he
has come up from his watery domain to this lofty vantage point "because from
thence all Ida could be clearly seen, and clearly visible too was the city of Priam
and the ships of the Achaeans" (Il. 13, 10–16). Poseidon is waiting for a chance
to intervene on the Greek side, and his line of sight, like his intention, is dia-
metrically opposed to that of Zeus.

The rugged island of Samothrace stands well out in the northern Aegean,
some forty-five miles northwest of Troy (fig. 2.1). Roughly halfway between it
and the mouth of the Dardanelles lies the larger island of Imbros (Turkish

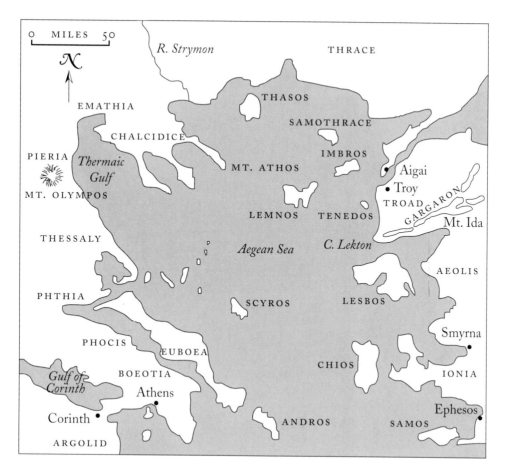

Map 1. Aegean Greece: The World of Homer

Gökceada). Imbros is itself quite mountainous, and its positioning would seem to block off all possibility of seeing the plain of Troy from Samothrace. So thought the Victorian traveller William Kinglake as he studied maps before journeying to the area. But after a visit to the Troad he knew better, as he relates in a memorable passage in his *Eothen* (1844): "Well, now I had come: there to the south was Tenedos, and here at my side was Imbros, all right, and according to the map; but aloft over Imbros—aloft in a far-away heaven—was Samothrace the watch-tower of Neptune!" Mount Fengari, the main peak of Samothrace, rises to 5,250 feet and is high enough to overtop Imbros, even at a distance of more than forty miles. So there *is* a direct line of sight from its summit to Troy—and also, of course, to the lofty and spreading massif of Ida beyond.

Kinglake's words catch the exciting and memorable quality of what I call the "Samothrace view" (fig. 2.2). Not every traveller to Troy will have the good fortune to see it, particularly on a late spring or summer visit, as even a small amount of haze in the atmosphere blots it out. But once seen it will never be forgotten. The glimpse of the towering pyramid of Fengari, faintly blue on the horizon behind the spreading flank of Imbros is indeed, as Homer might say, a "marvel to behold." Anyone who has experienced it will be irresistibly drawn to follow Kinglake in his inference that Homer himself must have stood where he stands, and seen what he sees, so telling is this "beautiful congruity betwixt the *Iliad* and the material world."[2]

One may also be led to reflect that the hard-pressed Achaean warriors for whom Poseidon felt such sympathy must often have seen the selfsame view in the course of their ten-year campaign. The view is particularly impressive when the westering sun begins to move behind the islands. Beyond a broad expanse of water their mountain ridges are sharply etched against a bright horizon, drawing the eye on to the remotest verge of vision. Homer hints at just such a landscape in one of his most haunting lines (Il. 1, 157): "the shadowy mountains and the echoing sea." In its context in the opening book of the *Iliad* the line has a melancholy ring to it, not a little reminiscent of Matthew Arnold's "Dover Beach" and the "grating roar" of wave-flung pebbles that brings "the eternal note of sadness in." The words are uttered nostalgically by Achilles as he thinks of the waste of waters and the many rugged islands that now separate him from "fertile Phthia." And he concludes his angry address to Agamemnon with a threat of final disengagement (Il. 1, 169–71): "Now I shall set out for Phthia, for it is much better that I should return home with my beaked ships, and it is not my intention to remain here in dishonour, topping up a full draught of wealth and riches for you." It is easy to imagine that war-weary Achaean Greeks must often have

2.1   Poseidon's watchtower: the island of Samothrace, seen from the southeast.

2.2   The "Samothrace view" seen from the Sigeum Ridge. Mount Fengari (5,250 feet) is dimly visible rising behind the spreading flanks of Imbros.

entertained similar thoughts as they saw the sun set behind the island stepping-stones that pointed the way back to hearth and home.

Having viewed the battlefield, Poseidon feels intense anger against Zeus and decides to intervene at once on the Achaean side. Now Homer "zooms in," as it were, on Troy and its immediate surroundings. He brings Poseidon rushing down from the craggy summit of the mountain, shaking the long ridges and the woodland as he goes. With four gigantic strides he reaches Aigai and his glittering palace in the depths of the sea (Il. 13, 17–22).

Aigai was a common name in Greek lands—at least four places of that name are recorded—and the identification here is uncertain. Ancient comment on the passage indicates a preference for an Aigai in Euboea, but a visit there would have taken Poseidon very far from the direct route to the Troad that seems implicit in the context. Richard Janko in the *Oxford Commentary* (ad loc.) tends to evade the problem in his statement that "we should not seek its location too seriously." George Huxley has made the important suggestion that we should look to the Thracian Chersonese, where an ancient lexicographer, Stephanos of Byzantium, locates an Aigai. This would suit the context well because the Chersonese (the Gallipoli peninsula) lies between Samothrace and the Troad and is also close to Imbros and Tenedos, which are the next places mentioned by Homer.[3] With "seven league boots" Poseidon would have no trouble in covering the intervening forty miles in four paces.

At Aigai, Poseidon mounts his chariot and drives over the waves to a sea cavern midway between Imbros and rugged Tenedos (Il. 13, 32–33). These indications serve to pinpoint the area of the Aegean just west of the entrance to the Hellespont, a destination suitably close to the Greek camp. Poseidon's onward progress is described in four surging lines that incidentally capture the feeling of elation felt by most seafarers at the sight of dolphins round their ship (Il. 13, 27–30): "He set out to drive across the water, and the sea creatures came out on all sides from their dens and gambolled around his path, recognising their lord. The ocean parted before him in delight. Easily onwards flew his horses, nor did the bronze axle of his chariot dip beneath the waves."

Let us leave him as he goes ashore to encourage the Achaean champions, and let us return to further consideration of Poseidon's overview of the Troad from the top of Samothrace. Significantly, this has two focal points: in the foreground "the city of Priam and the ships of the Achaeans," and in the background "all Ida" (Il. 13, 13–14). One could hardly have a more apt and succinct summary of the geography of the ancient Troad. The kingdom narrows to a point at its capital city, where the Aegean meets the Hellespont, and is bounded on the south and east by the spreading flanks of its chief mountain range (map 2).

When one surveys Homer's numerous references to Mount Ida, it becomes clear that he regarded the mountain with its spreading foothills as virtually synonymous with Priam's kingdom, and he was right to do so. The highest portion of the Ida massif (now called Kaz Dağ) lies some thirty miles southeast of Troy. The ridgeline there runs for four miles at an altitude of more than 5,000 feet, with the highest point at 5,820 feet. This summit ridge *can* be seen from Troy on a clear day, forming a distant but not dominating feature on the eastern horizon. But one gets a much more impressive overall view of the mountain from the south, when its great bulk is seen from across the Gulf of Adramyttium as one approaches the modern town of Edremit by the main road from Izmir. From here the long flank that runs west as far as Cape Lekton (now Cape Baba) appears to greatest advantage, rising steeply behind a string of sunny and well-sheltered holiday resorts on a "Riviera" coast. This flank of Ida constitutes the whole southern coastline of the Troad. It presents a ruggedly impressive spectacle and may receive special mention in the *Iliad*, for Homer uses the word *prumnoreia* (which occurs nowhere else in Greek) when referring to the lower slopes of Ida in this area (Il. 14, 307) (fig. 2.3).

The ancient city of Antandros (not mentioned by Homer) stood on a rocky crag towards the eastern end of this coastal strip. Virgil records the tradition that after the fall of Troy, Aeneas prepared a fleet there and set sail from its harbour "below the peaks of Ida" (*Aeneid* 3, 1–12). Just as Ida dominates the physical landscape of the Troad, so also it permeates the myth-history of the area. We learn from Strabo (13, 1, 5) that a mountain glen not far north of Antandros was

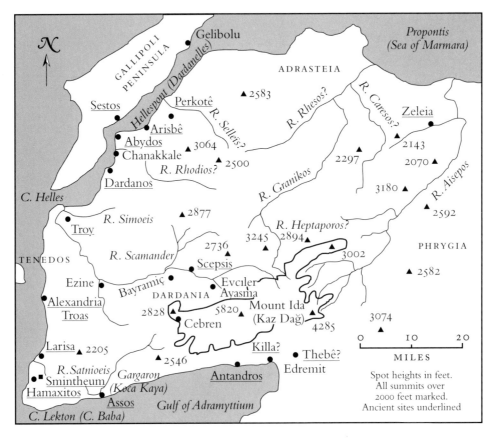

Map 2. The Troad: Mountains, Rivers, and Homeric Place-Names

pointed out by the locals as the place where Paris judged the goddesses. Paris's choice of Aphrodite as the winner set in motion the train of events that led to the Trojan War. Homer, too, associates Aphrodite with Mount Ida, saying that she lay with Anchises on the flanks of the mountain and that Aeneas sprang from this union (Il. 2, 820–21).

As a cousin of Hector, Aeneas belonged to a collateral branch of the Trojan royal family. He was ruler of the Dardanians, whose original territory, as Homer also says, had been located in "the foothills of many-fountained Ida" even

2.3   The lower slopes of the Ida range falling away to the Gulf of Adramyttium below the peak of Gargaron.

before "sacred Ilios had been established as a walled city in the plain" (Il. 20, 216–18). The foothills of Ida are thus intimately woven into the ultimate origins of the Trojan people, for the Dardanians took their name from Dardanos, a son of Zeus and the ancestor of the whole Trojan royal line as deployed in the Homeric tradition (see Appendix 1).

Ilos, grandson of Dardanos, was the reputed founder of Ilios (Troy) when he moved his capital down to the floodplain near the mouth of the Scamander. The older territory of Dardania lay higher up the river in its fertile upper and middle basins on the western flanks of the mountain (fig. 2.4). The area is easy to visit by car, for a good modern road runs across the plain from Ezine to Bayramiç and winds on up the valley to Ayasma, where one of the main tributary sources of the Scamander comes cascading down a rocky gorge. To me this western

2.4   A view of the main Ida massif from the west.

approach to Ida seemed even more beautiful than the "Riviera" coast to the south, and I would look no farther for Tennyson's "vale in Ida, lovelier than all the valleys of Ionian hills" where the fateful beauty contest was held (fig. 2.5).

Mount Ida is mentioned more than forty times in the *Iliad,* and the close connection of the mountain with the religion and daily life of the Trojans is repeatedly emphasised. Zeus has a "precinct and fragrant altar" on the peak called Gargaron (Il. 8, 47–48). Hector had been accustomed to make sacrifice there, as we learn from his final moments, when Zeus in pity recalls the many offerings that the hero made to him "on the peaks of many-folded Ida" (Il. 22, 169–71).[4] There is also a record of a much-respected priest of "Idaean" Zeus

2.5 The torrent at Ayasma, one of the principal sources of the Scamander. This illustration and fig. 2.4 answer quite well to Tennyson's romantic piece of scene setting at the start of his *Oenone*:

> *There lies a vale in Ida, lovelier*
> *Than all the valleys of Ionian hills . . .*
> *The swimming vapour slopes*
>   *athwart the glen*
> *Puts forth an arm, and creeps*
>   *from pine to pine,*
> *And loiters, slowly drawn. On either hand*
> *The lawns and meadow ledges midway down*
> *Hang rich in flowers, and far below them*
>   *roars*
> *The long brook falling thro' the clov'n ravine*
> *In cataract after cataract to the sea.*
> *Behind the valley topmost Gargarus*
> *Stands up and takes the morning:*
>   *but in front*
> *The gorges, opening wide apart, reveal*
> *Troas and Ilion's column'd citadel,*
> *The crown of Troas.*

being killed in the fighting (Il. 16, 603–7), and Idaios is the name of the Trojan herald (Il. 3, 248 et al.), as well as that of a minor hero who was the son of a priest (Il. 5, 9–11).

The summit of Ida serves as a command post from which Zeus observes and influences the course of the fighting. Seated "alone on Ida," as Hera vividly puts it (Il. 8, 207), he covers the mountain in cloud, thundering menacingly from the heights and sending his lightning flashing down to strike fear into Achaean hearts (Il. 8, 75; cf. 17, 594–95). In the final apocalyptic battle of the gods, Zeus thunders from above, while Poseidon shakes the earth from below, "and all the foothills of many-fountained Ida trembled" (Il. 20, 56–59). This passage marks the culmination of the tension and opposition between the sky-god Zeus and the sea-god Poseidon. All the Olympians are now locked in conflict, and the violence that is engulfing the human inhabitants of the Troad is powerfully symbolised in the earthquake that is here said to rock Ida to its roots.

The physical features of the great mountain emerge clearly enough from many allusions in the *Iliad*. In particular, four stock epithets serve to define its main characteristics. Homer calls it "well-wooded" (Il. 21, 449), and unlike many mountains in Greece it remains so to this day. Tracks used by woodcutters penetrate its recesses from every side, and timberyards are a recurring feature of its foothills.

When Agamemnon sends a fatigue party with mule carts to Ida to fetch wood for the funeral pyre of Patroklos, Homer provides a very sprightly description of the operation, and his account (Il. 23, 115–22) gives a vivid impression of the sort of landscape that may still be traversed in the foothills close to Troy:

> The mules went ahead, winding up and down, slantwise
> and crossways. And when they came to the flanks of
> many-fountained Ida, the men made haste to cut down
> oak trees with the long edge of their bronze axes. The tall
> trees tottered and came crashing down, and the Achaeans
> split the trunks and bound the timber on the mule carts.
> Then the mules dashed eagerly back to the plain, scoring
> the earth with their hooves as they made their way
> through the thickets of brushwood.

Today the forests, which are still very extensive, consist mainly of pine and fir, but stands mixed with oak and chestnut were noted by travellers in the nineteenth century. When I was exploring the ridge that runs to the east of Troy from Sarçalı village to Kara Tepe (Kallikolonê), I first passed through a broad glade stacked with timber (fig. 2.6) and then had to traverse a number of minor glens and ridges that lay between me and my objective. I thought feelingly of Homer's mules as I made my way up and down and across the slopes. The walking was on the whole easy enough, but there were occasional patches of quite dense undergrowth, just as Homer describes.

2.6   A timber yard on the plateau to the east of Hisarlik, near the village of Sarçalı.

It is a feature of descriptive landscape in Homer that different passages often interlock to build up an increasingly detailed picture of the same area. The wood-cutting expedition that traverses thickets on the lower slopes of Ida must be supposed to take place within reasonable reach of the Greek camp. In a previous and quite different context, the poet mentions woodland thickets that could hide an escaping warrior near Troy, and these are also placed on the foothills of Ida (Il. 21, 558–59).

The topography of the Agenor episode (Il. 21, 544–611) shows that Homer has a clear and comprehensive grasp of all the wooded terrain south and southwest of Troy. Agenor is a minor Trojan hero who is momentarily inspired by Apollo to take a stand against Achilles. They clash briefly, but then the god spirits Agenor away from the fight, taking his place and appearance in order to decoy Achilles away from the gates of Troy. Achilles duly chases the phantom into the countryside in a dummy run that foreshadows his later pursuit of Hector.

Achilles is thus diverted from his main objective, and the routed Trojans have time to gain the safety of the city walls.

The topographical indications are contained in two separate passages. In the first, Agenor is soliloquising about the courses open to him. He reflects that he could either join the rout back to Troy or attempt to escape in a different direction. In the end he decides that all flight would be futile because of Achilles' speed of foot. The alternative to flight *away* from the city is the important one from the topographical point of view. This is put as follows (Il. 21, 556–61):

> I might leave these Trojans to be pursued by Achilles, son
> of Peleus, and I might fly on foot in another direction
> away from the wall towards the Ileian plain, and so come
> to the foothills of Ida and take shelter in the thickets.
> Then in the evening I might wash off my sweat by
> bathing in the river, and so return to Ilios.

This is in fact the course taken by Apollo in the guise of Agenor, as described in a complementary passage (Il. 21, 602–4):

> Achilles pursued him closely across the wheat-bearing
> plain, turning him along the course of the deep-eddying
> Scamander, but Apollo deceived him by his crafty plan.

These two passages illustrate the principle of interlocking detail. The "Ileian plain" of the first is further described as "wheat-bearing," and the second informs us that the nameless river of the first is the Scamander.

The overall picture is clear. The pursuit heads south, away from Troy towards the line of hills where the Scamander breaks through to the Trojan plain. It therefore crosses the upper part of the plain on the right bank of the river, and so goes well away from the usual battlefield. This would be the driest part of the plain, and so the most suitable for wheat. Homer almost casually indicates his firm grasp of all this by throwing in the designation "Ileian," a unique epithet for a unique location (see map 5).

So Homer envisages the well-wooded lower slopes of Ida as lying within easy reach of both city and camp. This may still be seen to be the case. Pine-clad hills, the final offshoots of the great spreading mountain, rise on both sides of the defile where the Menderes debouches onto its floodplain, and scrub-covered slopes extend some way north on both sides of the river (fig. 2.7).[5]

It is hardly too much to say that Ida for Homer embraces and enfolds all of Priam's realm. His kingdom was, in the words of Apollonius of Rhodes, "the land of Ida" (*Argonautica* 1, 930), and the old king's final prayer in the *Iliad*, before he sets out on his mission to ransom his son's body, begins with a solemn invocation of "Father Zeus, most glorious and most mighty, who rulest from Ida" (Il. 24, 308). "Many-fountained" (Il. 8, 47 et al.) is the most evocative of the Ida formulae, and Cook notes that "springs are numerous and very chill in the high part of the mountain."[6]

The epithet "grassy," which occurs once only (Il. 11, 183), seems trite but is in fact more significant than might be thought. In context it refers to the summit ridge where Zeus is seated, thunderbolt in hand; and this portion of the range rises well above the timberline. The high open slopes still provide much valuable pasturage, and Cook reports that shepherds take their flocks there in high summer from villages as far away as the west coast. Grazing is also possible in the lower valleys, where flocks of sheep with their attendant shepherds may frequently be seen. This must be regarded as an immemorial aspect of life in the area. Homer reports that Achilles captured two Trojans who were pasturing sheep on the flanks of the mountain (Il. 11, 105, 112). Cattle are less common, but there are some herds in the area like those that Apollo was made to tend "in the glens of many-folded, well-wooded Ida" during his term of servitude to King Laomedon.[7]

Ida is also characterised as "mother of wild beasts" (Il. 8, 47 et al.) and merits the title still. In July 1750 Robert Wood, on a night traverse through the range, spoke of "the constant howling of jackals, and frequent brushing of wild beasts through the thickets."[8] One might remark that his experience is mirrored in a Homeric simile that portrays watchdogs listening uneasily to the sound of a

2.7 A view looking west from the wooded foothills bordering the southern end of the plain of Troy. The Menderes (Scamander) issues from a gorge to the left, and the line of the river may be seen in the middle distance. The Sigeum Ridge is on the horizon to the right.

"bold-hearted wild beast coming down from the heights through the brush-wood" (Il. 10, 183–85). Cook collected local reports of "hares, jackals, boar, badgers, deer, wild cats of some sort…bears in the main massif only, and leopards (kaplan) only on the west towards Ayvaçık." He himself heard jackals when staying overnight in the village of Gülpinar near the Smintheum.[9] On my last visit to Troy I was told about a guide at Ayasma under the main massif who takes visitors out to see wild game, including boar. The nobles of Troy must have hunted on Ida in the Late Bronze Age. Analysis of animal bones recovered in the current excavation has revealed that beginning in the period of Troy VI the bones of wild goats and good-sized deer occur among the larger mass of domesticated animals, and the jawbone of a lion is also reported. The Homeric *Hymn to Aphrodite* (lines 70–71) speaks of lions on the mountain, as well as wolves, bears, and panthers (leopards?).

The recurring phrase "on the flanks [or shoulders] of Ida" (Il. 2, 821; 11, 105; 21, 449, 559) should, I suggest, be read in close conjunction with the epithet "many-folded" (Il. 21, 449 et al.). Together they paint a vivid and accurate picture of the mountain's configuration. Long flanking ridges stretch out for many miles to the north as well as to the west of the highest summit, and the whole range is deeply folded into a multitude of spurs and glens. Strabo said that Ida is "like a centipede" (13, 1, 5). This may seem a bizarre comparison, but it is quite apt if one pictures the long spine of the mountain curving down from the Sea of Marmara to Cape Baba with numerous side-spurs projecting outwards like stumpy legs from a long segmented body (see map 2).

The spreading range, often referred to by Homer in the plural as "the Idaean mountains" (Il. 8, 170; 11, 196 et al.), forms the physical boundary of the Troad on east and south, and the chief rivers of the area flow from its high ridges. A glance at map 2 will show that the sources of the Scamander, Granikos, and Aisepos all lie close together.[10]

The epic tradition shows a good grasp of these basic geographical facts. The Trojan Catalogue in the second book of the *Iliad* lists Trojans from Zeleia who dwell "under the farthest foot of Ida" and "drink the dark water of the Aisepos" (Il. 2, 824–25). The Aisepos cuts through the final hills of the Ida range to flow into the Propontis (Sea of Marmara) and may be taken to mark the limit of Priam's realm to the northeast. Other Trojan principalities occupied the extensive plain of Adrasteia, west of the Granikos, and the coastlands bordering the Asiatic shore of the Hellespont. The names of their commanders together with the chief cities in due order from east to west are given in the Catalogue (Il. 2, 828–39).

We may next consider the sea borders of Priam's realm. Of these the Hellespont (now the Dardanelles) is the most prominent, receiving ten mentions in the *Iliad*. The name, meaning "Sea of Hellê," derives from the complex myth of the Greek king Athamas and his second wife, Ino. Ino proved a cruel stepmother to Phrixos and Hellê, the children of his first marriage to the cloud-goddess Nephelê. Ino engineered a call for the sacrifice of the children on religious grounds, but Nephelê provided a ram with a golden fleece to fly the pair to Colchis. Phrixos arrived safely, but Hellê fell off and was drowned in the strategic waterway that has never since ceased to figure prominently in stories mythical and historical.

The first two lines of the rousing old ditty "The British Grenadiers" may be quoted as an epitome of Hellespontine saga:

> *Some talk of Alexander, and some of Hercules,*
> *Of Hector and Lysander, and such great names as these . . .*

All four commanders had a close connection with the Hellespont. Herakles (Hercules), so the story goes, passed through the channel with the Argonauts, though he did not complete the voyage to Colchis. On another occasion he was in the area serving King Laomedon of Troy. But a quarrel arose, in the course of which he overran the city with a smaller force than that later brought by Agamemnon. This part of the Herakles saga is mentioned in the *Iliad* (see Chapter 4).

Hector's part in the later defence of the city under King Priam needs no elaboration, but Lysander's deeds in the area may be less known to the modern reader. Lysander was the able leader of the Spartan forces in the closing years of the Peloponnesian War. The long struggle reached its climax in the Hellespont when the Spartan fleet under Lysander finally broke the power of the Athenian navy at the battle of Aigospotamoi in 405 B.C. Aigospotamoi was an anchorage on the European shore not far north of the famous narrows anciently dominated by Sestos and Abydos and now controlled from the Turkish port of Chanakkale.

Alexander the Great claimed descent from Achilles and is reputed to have kept the *Iliad* always to hand on his campaigns. In 334 B.C. he opened his assault on the Persian Empire by transporting his army across the narrows, at the exact spot where Xerxes had built the bridge of boats for his own invasion of Greece in 480 B.C. Alexander himself proceeded down the European shore to Elaeus, a small Greek city near the tip of what is now the Gallipoli peninsula. There he sacrificed at the tomb of Protesilaos, who was reputed to have been the first Greek casualty on Agamemnon's expedition. As he crossed the strait he poured libations to Poseidon and the Nereids from a golden cup. Making sure that he was the first to leap ashore at a place traditionally known as "the harbour of the Achaeans," he made his way across the floodplain to Greek Ilion, then little more than a village. He made more sacrifices there, to Athena in her shrine on the historic hill and also to Priam, a gesture designed to avert the anger of the ancient ruler who had been so sacrilegiously slain at the altar by Neoptolemos, son of Achilles. Alexander then went on to confront a Persian army that had advanced into the Troad from Zeleia and had taken up a position on the eastern bank of the Granikos. There he won his first major battle on Asian soil and returned in triumph to Ilion to adorn Athena's temple with dedications and to elevate the town to city status with immunity from taxation.

We tend to draw a sharp dividing line between mythology and history, but ancient Greeks were not in the habit of doing so, and what we might regard as a mythical happening was normally given a precise geographical location.[11] Alexander acted in this spirit at Troy, and a standard modern *History of Greece* makes a good comment on what he did: "These solemnities on the hill of Troy are significant as revealing the spirit which the young king carried into his enterprise. They show how he was imbued with Greek scriptures and Greek traditions; how his descent from Achilles was part of his life, part of his inspiration; how he regarded himself as chosen to be the hero of another episode in the drama of which the first act had been illustrated by the deeds of that glorious ancestor."[12]

It was in this spirit, too, that many of the participants in the Gallipoli campaign approached the area in 1915. En route for Cape Helles with the naval division, Rupert Brooke wrote home to Miss Asquith from his troop transport: "I'm filled with confident and glorious hopes. I've been looking at the maps. Do you think...they'll make a sortie and meet us on the plains of Troy?" Some scraps of poetry that he was composing on the voyage survive in manuscript form, including the following fragment:

> *And Priam and his fifty sons*
> *Wake all amazed, and hear the guns,*
> *And shake for Troy again.*

2.8   The grave monument of Rupert Brooke on Scyros.

Brooke never reached his Troy, for he died of malaria on Scyros on April 23 (St. George's Day), 1915, and was buried in a beautiful and secluded olive grove in the south of the island (fig. 2.8). It is somehow fitting that he should rest on "steep Scyros," as Homer calls it, for the island had close associations with Achilles. He was said to have been hidden there disguised as a girl by his goddess mother Thetis in order to prevent his recruitment into the Achaean expeditionary force. But Odysseus discovered Achilles, who then willingly joined the Greek army. While on Scyros he fathered Neoptolemos by the princess Deidameia, and Neoptolemos was destined to be a key figure in the eventual capture of Troy. These events are not explicitly mentioned in the *Iliad,* but Achilles does mention that his "dear son" Neoptolemos had been reared in Scyros, and the poem also records that Achilles had once sacked the place (Il. 9, 668; 19, 326–27 and 332, with scholia).

In World War I the original scheme for forcing the Dardanelles was drawn up by Colonel Hankey, secretary of the Committee of Imperial Defence, who included the following gem in his *Memorandum:* "The Hellespont has always been the key to history. That is what makes the Trojan War the most modern of all wars and the *Iliad* the best manual for modern strategy." John Buchan, writing as a war correspondent with personal knowledge of the terrain, gave a more sober appraisal of the final evacuation of the Allied forces, but not even he could resist the Homeric parallels: "Across the ribbon of the Dardanelles, on the green plain of Troy, the most famous of the wars of the ancient world had been fought. If the banks of Scamander had seen men strive desperately with fate, so had the slopes of Achi Baba and the loud beaches of Helles. Had the fashion endured of linking the strife of mankind with the gods, what strange myths would not have sprung from the rescue of the British troops in the teeth of winter gales and uncertain seas? It would have been rumoured, as at Troy, that Poseidon had done battle for his children."[13]

Modern visitors to Troy will find that such thoughts follow naturally as they look across "the ribbon of the Dardanelles" to the British, French, and Turkish war memorials on Cape Helles (fig. 2.9). And the circle of myth-history is closed by the derivation of the Dardanelles itself from Trojan Dardanos and the later Greek city that bore his name on the banks of the Hellespont.

The town of Gelibolu also bears a Greek name—it was Kallipolis, "beautiful city"—and from there the Strait of the Dardanelles runs southwest for about forty miles until its waters enter the Aegean close to Troy. The strait is not as prominent as Mount Ida in the topography of the *Iliad,* but it has quite a strong presence, and Homer, as always, exhibits a good grasp of its main features. He twice calls it "strong-flowing" (Il. 2, 845; 12, 30), and this is indeed true of the immense body of water that streams through the mile-wide narrows at Chanakkale and holds its onward course past Cape Helles at a speed of from three to five knots. Such a current would not be thought strange off Atlantic coasts, but it is most unusual in the tideless Mediterranean.

Ancient sailors regarded the Hellespont as a river rather than a strait, and

2.9   A view from the steep northern flank of the escarpment of Hisarlik, looking across the floodplain of the Simoeis to Kum Kale and then across the Dardanelles to the British War Memorial on Cape Helles (top right).

this conception is embodied in the stock epithet, "broad," that Homer three times applies to it (Il. 7, 86; 17, 432; Od. 24, 82). "Broad" would be rather pointless as a description of an arm of the sea but is very much in order for a riverlike mass of water that flows constantly in the same direction and is between two and three miles wide at its point of entry to the Aegean. A third epithet, "fishy" (Il. 9, 360), is also apt enough, for its cold currents still teem with life, and the channel is much used by migratory shoals of tuna passing between the Black Sea and the Mediterranean.

2.10   The "broad" Hellespont seen from Cape Rhoeteum. The inlet at the mouth of the Kalafat Asmak (Strabo's "harbour of the Achaeans") is visible in the middle distance to the left. The Gallipoli peninsula lies in the background.

When Hermes is ordered by Zeus to escort Priam on his hazardous journey to ransom Hector's body, the god arrives "at Troy and the Hellespont" (Il. 24, 346). This explicit conjunction of the Hellespont with Troy is in accord with much modern thinking about the economic prosperity of the ancient city. Troy is often said to have grown rich from its dominating position at the outlet of the channel, which enabled the Trojans to exact tolls from passing shipping. For Homer, the Hellespont also lies in close proximity to the Greek camp, as is indicated by the thrice-repeated formula: "to the ships and the Hellespont" (Il. 15, 233; 18, 150; 23, 2). So the strait figures in the *Iliad* as a prominent feature of the landscape, and it still catches the eye of every visitor to Troy, particularly when the plain is viewed from the headland of Rhoeteum or the Sigeum Ridge (fig. 2.10).

Homer also knew that the Hellespont formed the frontier between the territory of the Thracians and the kingdom of Priam (Il. 2, 845). And it still retains geographical significance as a major waterway separating Europe from Asia. Its role as a political boundary is also touched on in the closing book of the *Iliad,* where Homer depicts Achilles in conversation with his royal visitor Priam. Musing on the mutability of human affairs, Achilles recalls Priam's former prosperity as ruler of a rich kingdom, bounded, as he says, on its seaward flank to the south by Lesbos, by Phrygia inland, and by the "boundless Hellespont" (Il. 24, 544–45).

The geography of this passage is well adapted to Achilles' perspective. The large island of Lesbos lies off the southwest corner of the Troad and is an impressive sight when viewed from the stretch of coast between Assos and Cape Baba (fig. 2.11). Achilles knew this region well. He had been on a plunder raid to Lesbos, presumably when Agamemnon himself led a force to subdue it (Il. 9, 664 with 9, 129). He had also himself sacked towns on the mainland to the north and northeast.[14] The mention of Lesbos completes the list of offshore islands visible from the Troad. Phrygia is a conveniently vague designation for the lands beyond the eastern limits of the kingdom. Achilles had not visited it but would have known of the Phrygians as Trojan allies (Il. 2, 862). As for the Hellespont, he knows it all too well in the vicinity of Troy, but here he is trying to view it in its entirety as the northwestern boundary of Priam's realm, and so he calls it "boundless" because he is uncertain of its upper limits. The vagueness is in Achilles' mind as subtly characterised by Homer, rather than in the term Hellespont as such, which in Homeric usage always designates the channel and not the open sea.[15]

The western limit of the Troad is marked by the somewhat featureless stretch of coast that runs almost due south for about forty miles from the mouth of the Hellespont to the bold promontory of Cape Lekton (fig. 2.12). Low headlands alternate with shingly beaches, and there are no really good harbours.[16] The most notable antiquities are the ruins of Alexandria Troas—which a number of seventeenth-century travellers took to be those of Troy—and the Apollo temple known as the Smintheum (fig. 2.13).

The site of the Smintheum was identified by Commander T. A. B. Spratt in

1853. It was partially excavated for the Dilettanti Society by the British architect R. P. Pullan in 1866. Pullan identified it as an Ionic temple of eight by fourteen columns, and renewed work in the 1980s by a Turkish team has shown that Pullan's findings were accurate. The temple has now been completely cleared and substantially restored and presents an impressive sight in its woodland setting below the village of Gülpinar (formerly Külâhli). In its present form the temple dates from the Hellenistic period, but the site was inhabited in prehistoric times, and it is now reasonably certain that it is the location of the ancient shrine of Apollo Smintheus, which figures prominently in the opening book of the *Iliad*.

Apollo, "son of Leto and Zeus," is the first god to be introduced in the poem, angry with Agamemnon, as Homer tells us, because the king had failed to honour his priest Chryses (Il. 1, 9–12). Chryses had come as a suppliant to ransom his captive daughter Chryseïs, who had been assigned as a prize to Agamemnon, and the king's initial refusal to comply with this request has caused Apollo to inflict a plague on the Achaean army. Under pressure from his peers, Agamemnon reluctantly allows Chyseïs to be returned to her father, but takes away Achilles' prize Briseïs in compensation, leading to the bitter quarrel that motivates all the subsequent action of the epic.

This complex narrative needed to be firmly located in the physical environment of the Troad, and it is instructive to see how deftly Homer proceeds to do just this. Faced with a similar task in *Troilus and Cressida,* Shakespeare opens his prologue with the blunt statement: "In Troy there lies the scene." Homer goes to work in a much more subtle fashion. Chryses, he tells us, "came to the swift ships of the *Achaeans*" to ransom his daughter, and in the opening speech of the poem he is made to pray that the gods might grant Agamemnon to "sack the city of *Priam* and return *home* safely." The location of "*home*" is then given in the king's curt refusal, when he tells Chryses that "old age will come upon her in my house in *Argos*, far from her native land."

So by line 30 the scene has already been set in the Achaean camp close to Troy, and we start to learn some topographical details about the Troad as we follow Chryses on his sad journey back to Apollo's shrine. His route is indicated

2.11   The island of Lesbos seen across the Gulf of Adramyttium from Assos (Homeric Pedasos).

2.12   Cape Lekton (Cape Baba) at the southwest corner of the Troad.

2.13   The Smintheum, a Hellenistic temple on the site of Homeric Chrysa.

in line 34: "He went grieving along the shore of the resounding sea"—in a direction, that is to say, south along the coast from the camp—and this route would take him past Larisa (Il. 2, 841) to the region where the Smintheum has now been restored (see map 2). His destination is skilfully implied in his invocation of Apollo and his prayer for vengeance on the Greeks: (Il. 1, 37–42):

> Thou who frequentest *Chrysa*, and rulest in might over
> *Killa* and goodly *Tenedos*, *Sminthean* lord, if ever I roofed a
> pleasing shrine for you, ... may your shafts make the
> Greeks pay for my tears.

2.14 *Est in conspectu Tenedos*... Virgil, *Aeneid* (2, 21). A view looking southwest from the Sigeum Ridge, from an area not far to the north of Beşika Bay. Yassi Tepe (Beşika Burnu), site of the ancient town of Achilleion, is the headland directly in line with the island. The tumulus to the left is Sivri (Beşik) Tepe.

Chrysa, Killa, and Tenedos stand out as the first local place-names of the Troad to be mentioned in the *Iliad*. The location of Killa, a minor place, is not known. Strabo placed it southeast of Mount Ida near the head of the Gulf of Adramyttium.[17] But the uncertainty about Killa in no way vitiates the above argument about Chryses' destination, for Killa, like Tenedos, is primarily named as a focus of Apollo worship, which was widespread in the Troad. Tenedos (now Bozcaada) serves as a signpost for the route taken by the priest, for it is a conspicuous island lying close to the west coast of the Troad, and its distinctive outline is visible from every point of that shoreline (fig. 2.14).

Both Chryses and his daughter take their name from Chrysa, and it is reasonable to suppose that Chrysa was the ancient (and Homeric) name of the Smintheum site. In the Hellenistic period there was still a place called Chrysa on the coast not far to the south.[18] In view of all this, it can hardly be doubted that Homeric Chrysa, with its Apollo shrine, was located at the now-visible temple site. Strabo thought it too far from the sea, but it lies less than two miles inland from the site of the ancient coastal town of Hamaxitus. Hamaxitus was founded from Lesbos c. 700 B.C., and its coinage carried the image of Apollo Smintheus. Its harbour was adequate for small boats. A "deep harbour" to which Odysseus brought Chryseïs back by ship is mentioned by Homer, and if this was at the Hamaxitus site, a fairly short walk up a convenient valley would have brought them to the shrine (Il. 1, 430–41).

A final glimpse of the Troad and its approaches, as seen through Homer's eyes, is afforded by his account of Hera's journey from Mount Olympos to Mount Ida. More than two centuries ago in the famous *Essay* that founded modern study of Homer, Robert Wood used Hera's journey to illustrate his thesis that when Homer's "persons are most ideal, his scene is not less real," and that his "celestial geography" is "happily connected with his Map of Troy."[19] Hera's object is to beguile Zeus into lovemaking and so distract him at least temporarily from active intervention on the side of the Trojans. Her seduction of Zeus is a major element in the plot of the *Iliad* and is described in extended and brilliant detail (Il. 14, 153–360), with the journey forming an important part of the narrative. Starting point and destination are clearly indicated, and the delineation of the route is achieved with the aid of no fewer than ten place names, all of which can be identified (see lines 224–30 and 280–93; also map 1). The route is undoubtedly circuitous, unlike that of Athena, who flies straight from Olympos to Troy (see Chapter 5). As Janko (*Cambridge Commentary*, ad loc.) suggests, it probably shows the influence of early Greek seafaring in that it avoids open water as much as possible. One should also bear in mind that Homeric narratives can differ markedly in tempo. In the Athena passage at the start of book 7 the narrative tempo is brisk; here its leisurely pace is evident from the devotion of seventy lines to a description of how Hera adorns herself before the journey even begins (Il. 14, 153–223).

2.15 "From Athos Hera winged her way over the surging sea" (Il. 14, 229). The peak (6,670 feet) is said to be visible from the Troad.

The slower tempo gives Homer scope to air his geographical knowledge. Hera starts from the summit of Mount Olympos and follows the coastline of Macedonia in a northeasterly direction, passing over the foothills of Pieria and the broad plains of Emathia. She then swings eastwards round the head of the Thermaic Gulf to cross the base of the Chalcidic peninsula in the general direction of the snowclad mountains of the Thracians. She is flying through the air (line 228), and from her lofty viewpoint the Brontous range and Mount Pangaion (with summits up to and over 6,000 feet) would be clearly visible beyond the river Strymon. She then changes course to follow the line of the Mount Athos peninsula (fig. 2.15) and flies out over the northern Aegean to her first touchdown at Lemnos. There she proceeds to enlist the aid of Hypnos, the god of sleep. This takes some time to achieve, and then the pair proceed together, leaving Lemnos and Imbros behind them (line 281), until they come to the westernmost extension of the Ida massif at Cape Lekton. Here they leave the sea and fly low over the wooded slopes of the range (lines 284–85; see fig. 2.12). Hypnos in the shape of a bird perches on a lofty fir tree, while Hera continues her flight until she reaches "the peak of Gargaron on lofty Ida," where Zeus is seated (lines 292–93), ready to respond to her amorous designs.

Cook is confident that the Classical Greek city of Old Gargara was located on the summit ridge of the peak now known as Koca Kaya (2,546 feet). Koca Kaya, meaning Great Rock, is the culminating point of the western extension of the Ida range. The mountain is crowned by a striking pinnacle of rock that one can easily imagine as the location of a peak sanctuary (fig. 2.16). Homer mentions an altar and enclosure sacred to Zeus on Gargaron and describes how Zeus drives in his chariot through middle air to seat himself on the summit peak and view Troy and the Achaean ships (Il. 8, 47–52). As Cook points out, the peak is clearly visible from Lesbos, and the name Gargaron must have been firmly attached to it from an early date by the Aeolian settlers of the area. There are therefore good grounds for supposing it to be the peak that Homer had in mind.[20]

It was in this belief that I set out to climb it on a hot May morning, grateful

2.16   The peak of Gargaron (Koca Kaya).

that the springs of "many-fountained Ida" still provide the wayfarer with plenty
of opportunities to slake his thirst. I was able to bring my car as far as the village
of Yesilyurt, a mile or so inland from the seaside resort of Küçük Kuyu. From
there it took me about two hours on foot to reach the summit. It was not a difficult climb, for there was a tolerable track all the way, but I had to follow a circuitous route around and over the flanks of "many-folded" Ida. From time to
time gay carpets of wildflowers covered the sides of the road (fig. 2.17), but I
did not, alas, see any of the beds of crocus and hyacinth that Homer had led me
to expect (Il. 14, 347–49). When I finally came to the foot of the final rock pinnacle, I was greeted by the barking of dogs from a wired-off compound, and a
uniformed official came out promptly to forbid photography. Zeus has been

2.17   A carpet of wildflowers on the upper slopes of Gargaron.

ejected from his traditional seat by the technology of modern telecommunications. I could not communicate meaningfully with this modern sentry, but after some minutes he relaxed enough to point out Mitileni (Lesbos) to the south. Tenedos was also in view. Visibility was not quite good enough for me to be absolutely sure that I could see as far as Hisarlik (Troy), but I could make out the foothills where the Scamander breaks through to the Trojan plain past Ballı Dağ and felt confident that I was high enough to have a clear line of sight over them to Troy and the Hellespont beyond. In clearer weather the next day I was able to confirm this by identifying the distinctive outline of the Koca Kaya ridge from the neighbourhood of Troy itself.[21]

3.1   The plain of Troy looking west from the Pergamos. The dark line of trees in the middle of the plain marks the course of the Scamander. The Sigeum Ridge appears on the horizon.

When they came to Troy and its flowing rivers

where Simoeis and Scamander join their streams . . .

—Il. 5, 773–74

THREE

THE PLAIN OF TROY
AND THE RIVERS

T HE PLAIN OF TROY is certainly not picturesque." Walter Leaf began his account of the Trojan landscape with these words, and one could hardly dispute the justice of his contention.[1] The celebrated plain is unrelievedly level and too extensive to be viewed as a whole. Its surroundings are also relatively featureless, consisting for the most part of low ridges of soft tertiary limestone from which all irregularity of outline has long since been eroded away (fig. 3.1). Placed in this open but scenically undistinguished landscape, the remains of ancient Troy occupy the extremity of a gently undulating plateau that runs out into the lower part of the plain from higher ground to the east. The tip of the final tonguelike projection has long been known to the Turks as Hisarlik, the "place of the castle," and here stood the Pergamos, or inner citadel, of "holy Ilios," Homer's preferred designation for the city of Priam (fig. 3.2). In the *Iliad* he calls the city Ilios on more than a hundred occasions, Troy on fewer than fifty. In most cases the two names are virtually synonymous, but "Troy" can refer to the whole territory of the kingdom as well as to the chief city.

The ground falls away steeply on the north and northeast of the Pergamos, and the ancient circuit of walls when viewed from this direction would have merited the Homeric epithet "beetling" (fig. 3.3). But from other directions Troy does not give the impression of having been a great or impregnable fortress. Visitors nowadays come by road from the east, where the approach is level and easy. If one looks to the left just before entering the main archaeological site, one sees a tree-dotted area that also formed part of ancient Troy. A

3.2   The Pergamos seen from the southwest. The lower town of Late Bronze Age Troy extended down across the slopes in the foreground.

3.3   "Beetling Ilios": a view of Hisarlik from the plain below the northwest corner of the mound. Schliemann's great trench runs diagonally into the hillside behind the bushes. Spoil from his excavation is heaped up between the bushes and the fence.

3.4   Hisarlik from the north, viewed from across the floodplain of the Simoeis, with the line of the river in the foreground.

broad apron of ground here extends southwards from the Pergamos for about five hundred yards, sloping gently downwards to the plain on three sides. Here stood the houses of the lower town, outside the great citadel wall but protected, as we now know, by a system of rock-cut ditches, wooden palisades, and in part, at least, by a stone-footed, mud-brick wall that ran back to join the inner circuit. The inner circuit of walls, still in part impressively visible, had a circumference of about six hundred yards. The total length of the recently discovered outer perimeter of fortifications was about one mile.

The highest point of the site is little more than a hundred feet above sea level, and from this modest elevation one can look westwards across the plain to the long low line of the Sigeum Ridge, beyond which lies the Aegean. The river Menderes (which must be identified with Homer's Scamander) is not visible from the Pergamos, but its course is marked by a straggling line of trees in the middle distance. Close under the citadel to the north a lesser stream, now

called Dümrek Su but anciently the Simoeis, flows in through its own small plain to join the main river (figs. 3.4 and 3.5). Only to the north, where the rivers enter the sea, is the prospect enlivened by the broad and glimmering expanse of the Hellespont.

The plain runs back from the shoreline in a long sweeping curve for nearly ten miles, and is on average between two and three miles in breadth. Even to the untutored eye it is obviously a floodplain built up over the millennia by the silting action of its rivers. It is large by Greek standards and has the additional virtue of great fertility. In the *Iliad* the name of Troy is seven times qualified by an epithet that literally means "with large clods," that is to say, with rich clay soil. In every case the context confirms what the epithet implies—namely, that Homer is here using "Troy" in an extended sense to cover the district, and particularly the plain, as well as the city. Troy's plain is indeed a notably large and

3.6 The fertile plain of Troy.

3.7 A herd of cattle coming up from the Trojan plain.

rich stretch of alluvium. Much of it today is intensively cultivated to yield crops of cotton, sunflower, maize, and wheat, and it also provides extensive pasturage for sheep and cattle (figs. 3.6 and 3.7).[2]

"It may be taken as certain," wrote Leaf, "that the coast-line did not in the Mycenaean age materially differ from that which now exists."[3] Alas for such certainties! Leaf followed Schliemann's lead in making this judgment, but it is now clear that their opinion was based on inadequate data. When Schliemann was excavating at Troy in the late 1870s, his scientific adviser Rudolf Virchow dug down into the plain north of Troy to look for marine deposits under the topsoil. Finding none he concluded that the plain must have reached its present extent during the Bronze Age, with all silt subsequently brought down by the river being washed away by the rapid Hellespontine current. But Virchow's trenches were too shallow, and his conclusion represented an ill-judged aberration from older and sounder views. Deep-coring has since produced evidence that the shoreline of the Hellespont was much closer to Priam's Troy than it is now.

From surveys made over the past 150 years or so, one can make a reasonably firm estimate of how rapidly the alluvium has accumulated during that period. The data show that between 1840 and 1940 the delta advanced by as much as 825 feet in places at the outlet of the main river channel (an average advance of a little more than 8 feet per annum). On a front of about 1½ miles the average advance over the past hundred years has been of the order of 4 feet a year.[4] If the delta had always progressed at this same rate (which is by no means certain), this would mean that at c. 1250 B.C. (an approximate date for the Trojan War) the shoreline would have been about 13,000 feet (2½ miles) farther south than it is now, with the area of the plain correspondingly reduced. There is still argument about the precise location of the shoreline at various dates in the past because the sea level, like the rate of alluvial deposition, may not have remained constant. But even on the lowest current estimate (about 2 miles), it is clear that the Achaean forces would have been too close to Troy for comfort had they attempted to encamp on the plain to the north of the city (see map 6). In any case, the maintenance of a permanent base there, with the troops in wooden huts and the ships drawn up nearly at sea level, would have been a virtual impossibility because the whole alluvial plain was, until recent flood-control measures, subject to frequent and total inundation in winter rainstorms.[5]

The implications of all this for the strategy and tactics of the Achaean attack on Troy will be developed in more detail in Chapter 5. The *Iliad* mentions Achaean forays into other parts of the Troad, but the Trojan plain is the setting for the main engagements. As a theatre for war its appeal is more to the imagination than to the eye. Byron responded to the historical importance of the landscape in a powerfully descriptive stanza in *Don Juan* (canto 4, 77):

> *High barrows without marble or a name,*
> *A vast, untill'd, and mountain-skirted plain,*
> *And Ida in the distance, still the same,*
> *And old Scamander (if 'tis he) remain;*
> *The situation seems still form'd for fame—*
> *A hundred thousand men might fight again,*
> *With ease; but where I sought for Ilion's walls,*
> *The quiet sheep feeds, and the tortoise crawls.*

Byron was writing at a time when the identity of the floodplain of the Menderes with the Trojan plain was fully accepted, but "Ilion's walls" had not been found, and the exact site of ancient Troy was the subject of fierce scholarly controversy (figs. 3.8–3.11).

Before 1790 travellers in the Troad like Richard Pococke and Robert Wood had made only vague and tentative suggestions about a possible site for Troy. But by the end of the century a detailed case was being made for the city's having been located on a hill known as Ballı Dağ. Ballı Dağ (sometimes referred to as the "false Troy") is situated at the inner or southern extremity of the plain. It rises steeply to a height of five hundred feet on the left bank of the Menderes, where the river runs through a picturesque gorge (fig. 3.12). The location dominates an important route from the interior of the Troad and is endowed with much more physical grandeur than Hisarlik. Moreover, the remains of an

A photographic evocation of Troy and its environs as pictured by Byron in *Don Juan*, canto 4, 77.

3.8 "High barrows without marble or a name . . ." Üvecik Tepe seen from the south.

3.9 "A vast, untill'd, and mountain-skirted plain . . ." A view over the plain from the western flank of Hisarlik. Part of the citadel wall, for which Byron "sought in vain," is visible in the foreground.

3.10 "Old Scamander . . ." The river remains.

3.11 "The quiet sheep feeds," grazing where the buildings of the lower city of Troy once stood.

3.12 Ballı Dağ, the "false Troy."

ancient circuit of walls and three barrows, taken to be heroic graves, could be discerned on its summit. It looked a promising choice for Troy.

Long before any excavation took place, what seemed to be a clinching topographical argument was found in the existence of a remarkable cluster of springs that bubbled up close to the base of the hill in the vicinity of the village of Bunarbashi (now Pınarbaşı). These springs, known by the Turks as Kirk Göz ("forty eyes"), were held to be those described by Homer in the *Iliad* (22, 145–56). Homer says that when Achilles was pursuing Hector outside the walls of Troy, the two heroes came to a place where "twin sources of the eddying Scamander spring up," and the poet further adds that one of the springs is hot and vaporous, while the other flows ice-cold even in summer. The narrative and topographical problems raised by this passage will be further discussed in Chapter 5. It is sufficient to say at this point that once attention was focused on the Pınarbaşı springs, it was inevitable that they should be used as a marker for the site of Priam's city. Homer seemed to place them close to Troy, and so it seemed logical to look for Troy close to them.

The discovery and identification of the springs as those described by Homer was first made in December 1785 by a French diplomat, Jean Baptiste Lechevalier, who was passing through the Troad on his way to Istanbul. Lechevalier was due to take up an appointment in the French embassy there, and this posting enabled him to make two further visits to the Trojan plain in September 1786 and March 1787, in the course of which he collected more data for his new theory of the site of ancient Troy. He went as a member of a team of scholars and antiquarians working under the direction of the French ambassador, Count Choiseul-Gouffier, whose *Voyage pittoresque de la Grèce* (1782) had already made its author famous. The count incorporated Lechevalier's findings in later editions of the *Voyage pittoresque,* failing, as Cook says, "to give Lechevalier the credit which was undoubtedly his due."[6] The prestige enjoyed by Choiseul-Gouffier's publications ensured wide currency for the equation of Ballı Dağ with Troy, and the theory is often credited solely to him. He certainly worked up its details with enthusiasm and considerable local knowledge, but the initial impetus was undoubtedly due to Lechevalier.

The outbreak of the French Revolution in 1789 prevented both Choiseul-Gouffier and Lechevalier from returning to France. Lechevalier travelled to Britain, where in 1791 he was given the opportunity to present his views on Troy to the Royal Society of Edinburgh. The lecture made a deep impression on the society, and Lechevalier's manuscript was translated and published in the same year by Andrew Dalzell, professor of Greek at Edinburgh, under the title *Description of the Plain of Troy.*

This publication gave the Ballı Dağ theory wide publicity in England, where it soon came under attack from Jacob Bryant, a Fellow of King's College, Cambridge, who had published a major *Analysis of Ancient Mythology* in 1774–76. Bryant was a pedant of a sceptical turn of mind, and in 1796 he produced a radical rebuttal of Lechavalier (and indeed of all attempts to find Troy) under the formidable title: *A Dissertation Concerning the War of Troy and the Expedition of the Grecians as described by Homer, showing that no such expedition was ever undertaken and that no such city of Phrygia existed.*

Bryant's *Dissertation* immediately elicited a reply in the form of an open *Letter* (1797) from an ex-Fellow of Jesus College Cambridge, Gilbert Wakefield. Wakefield affirmed that one who begins to doubt Homer will go on to doubt Christianity! A more solidly argued rebuttal was published the following year by J. B. S. Morritt, a scholarly amateur who, unlike Bryant, had toured the Levant. And so this Homeric battle rumbled on, with Bryant making a full reply to Morritt and his other critics in his *Observations* (1799). The interest generated by the controversy is reflected in a satirical poem, *Adieu to Troy,* that was in circulation at the time, and from which I quote the following somewhat laboured stanza:

> *Farewell, old Homer's Troy,*
> *The song of man and boy!*
> *How cruel are thy fates, how fickle!*
> *For ten long years to Greeks oppos'd,*
> *Then to corn-fields metamorphosed,*
> *And now mow'd down by Bryant's sickle.*[7]

Bryant died in 1804, but Byron remembered him and his scepticism with extreme distaste and years later penned a heartfelt and strongly worded outburst in his Ravenna Journal for January 11, 1821: "We *do* care about 'the authenticity of the tale of Troy'. I have stood upon that plain *daily*, for more than a month, in 1810; and if any thing diminished my pleasure, it was that the blackguard Bryant impugned its veracity.... Hobhouse and others bored me with their learned localities.... But I still venerated the grand original as the truth of *history* (in the material *facts*) and of *place.* Otherwise it would have given me no delight."[8]

It is easy to feel sympathy with Byron. His romantic respect for the historicity of Homer is to my mind well judged, and this book tries to demonstrate that "truth of place" is indeed a salient characteristic of Homeric poetry.

Byron disliked what he called "antiquarian twaddle" and was not much

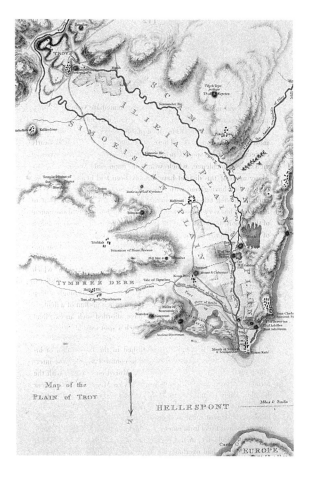

3.13 *Of Dardan tours let Dilettanti tell,*
I leave topography to classic Gell.
—Byron

The map of the Troad from William Gell's *The Topography of Troy and Its Vicinity*, 1804. The map follows Lechevalier and Choiseul-Gouffier in its identification of the site of Troy and the rivers.

concerned with the "false Troy" theory, whose main inspiration had been Lechevalier's discovery of the Pınarbaşı springs. The springs *are* a remarkable phenomenon, certainly the single most notable feature of the Trojan plain. Their output is copious, and they give rise to quite a considerable stream, now known as the Pınarbaşı Çay, which flows down the west side of the plain. In order to improve the drainage of this area, the stream was formerly diverted through an artificial cut to Beşika Bay, where it worked a mill. But the canal is now dry and derelict, and the stream continues its natural course until it joins the Menderes near the sea. Because Homer described the springs as "twin sources of the...*Scamander*," the sponsors of the "false Troy" theory proceeded—misguidedly, it must be said—to identify the minor stream of Pınarbaşı Çay with the Scamander and the much larger Menderes with the Simoeis. These unacceptable identifications are found on many nineteenth-century maps of the area (fig. 3.13).

The springs could have been regarded by Homer as sources of the Scamander because they rise near it and feed it. He may even have thought they were fed from it—rivers in Greece have a habit of disappearing underground and reappearing elsewhere. Either of these suppositions is adequate to explain the Homeric phrase, and both are found in ancient commentaries on the passage.[9] The Greek phrase need not be taken as implying that the springs are the *only* sources of the Scamander.

Springs large and small break out over quite a large area near the village of Pınarbaşı and are far more numerous than the pair described by Homer, but it seems that until about 1963 two major spring-fed pools were visible and that these were taken by nineteenth-century travellers to be Homer's "twin sources." With regard to the temperature difference, Choiseul-Gouffier stated in print that his "warm" source gave a thermometer reading of 81.5 degrees Fahrenheit, while the "cold" one was at 50 degrees. Whether he made the error himself or was misled by assistants who told him what he wanted to hear will never be known. At all events, for years afterwards the villagers of Pınarbaşı must have looked on with amusement, if not amazement, as a succession of learned visitors came to plunge thermometers into their springs. No one was ever able to confirm Choiseul-Gouffier's finding, and this is hardly surprising because it is now generally agreed that all the springs are tepid, emerging at about 63 degrees Fahrenheit.

It is now difficult if not impossible to check and correlate earlier reports and descriptions of the springs, because one of the principal sources has been harnessed for a local water scheme. In the course of this work the basin of the spring was largely filled in and covered with a pumping station. As one walks down to the springs from the village, the pumping station soon comes into sight on the left close to the track. Fortunately, it is possible to get a good impression

3.14 The broad shallow pool (Pool F) created by the Kirk Göz springs near the village of Pınarbaşı. The stream flowing from this pool is one of the main sources of the Pınarbaşı Çay. The water comes out from under the rock pavement in the foreground (close-up).

of the former appearance of the source there from a photograph published by Cook (*Troad*, plate 13a), and indeed Cook's whole account (pages 140–45) is essential reading for anyone now trying to make sense of the Pınarbaşı phenomenon. The spring now under the pumping house is designated as Pool C on the plan that Cook provides (141). It is likely (though not certain) that it was Choiseul-Gouffier's "warm spring."

The second large pool (Cook's Pool F) is still visible (fig. 3.14). To reach it one must walk nearly half a mile beyond the pumping station past a bare hillside on the left and, on the right, a verdant grove of poplars and the gardens and fields irrigated by the springs.

A comparison of plates 13a and 13b in Cook reveals that Pool C was not nearly as big as Pool F and that it probably had a deeper basin. This is confirmed in the crisp and clearly argued account by Col. William Leake, who visited the area early in the nineteenth century:

In one the water appears in a deep basin, which is noted among the natives for being often covered with a thick vapour like smoke; in the other place there are numerous rills issuing from the rocks, into a broad shallow piece of water, terminating in a stream which is joined by that from the smoking spring. As to the temperature of the water, the observations of travellers give various results. Some have observed a difference: according to others, it would appear that all being deep-seated springs, their temperature is the same at all seasons, or about 60 F. at their eruption from the ground; consequently they will all feel cold when the air is at 70 or 80, and warm when it is 40 or 50. But even in this case it is obvious that there will be a real difference between the heat of the shallow recipient of the springs, called the Forty Fountains, and that of the single deep pool. It seems sufficient to justify Homer's expression that a difference of temperature was believed, and that an occasional appearance of vapour over one source was observed by the natives.[10]

Leake is essentially saying that Pool C appeared to "smoke" in frosty conditions, when the broader and shallower expanse of water in Pool F had cooled closer to air temperature and so was not giving off visible vapour.

One may note that Lechevalier first visited the springs in December. The different configurations of the two main sources could lie at the root of the age-old perception that one source was hot and the other cold. Leake's conjecture about Homer's account gains in credibility when one observes that Homer says explicitly that one source flows out cold "in summer," and it is plausible to assume an implied antithesis with the other source smoking "in winter" (Il. 22, 149–52).

The "false Troy" theory was finally tested by excavation in 1864, when a German archaeologist, J. G. von Hahn, dug for about a month on the summit of

Ballı Dağ. He published a plan of the citadel and its fortifications and recovered sixteen bronze coins, all apparently dating from Classical Greek times. But he found no trace of any Bronze Age habitation on the hill. Subsequent work on the site, including digs by Schliemann in 1868 and 1882, also failed to produce evidence for any substantial occupation earlier than the Archaic period. Ballı Dağ can never have been Troy.[11]

Charles Maclaren has been acclaimed as the first modern writer to make a correct identification of the site of ancient Troy. The map that he published in his *Dissertation on the Topography of the Plain of Troy* (1822) correctly marks it at Hisarlik. Maclaren was a journalist who founded and edited the *Scotsman* newspaper, and thanks to his good Scottish education he knew his Homer. He shows a nice sense of humour in his preface, where he remarks: "It may be doubted whether a new topographical theory, however satisfactory, be likely to meet with a better reception than the project of a new Greek expedition." In fact, his work was ignored— he had not been to the Troad—and, despite much criticism from other writers, the "false Troy" theory held the field until the 1860s. By then Maclaren had visited the area, and his *Plain of Troy Described* (1863) appeared at a time when the claims of Ballı Dağ were about to be decisively weakened by the negative results of von Hahn's excavation and Schliemann was about to appear on the scene.

In his earlier *Dissertation* Maclaren claimed to be restoring ancient opinions rather than inventing new ones, and this, in fact, was what he did. His method was both sound and simple. Sensibly relying on "Homer's facts" rather than "Strabo's speculations," he affirmed (against Lechevalier and Choiseul-Gouffier) that the modern Menderes must be the ancient Scamander. He then quietly pointed out a clear indication in Homer that Priam's Troy did not lie in the foothills of Ida (that is, at Ballı Dağ) but in the plain (Il. 20, 216–18): "And he [Dardanos] founded Dardania, for sacred Ilios had not yet been built as a city in the plain."

But where in the plain? Again he found the answer in the text of the *Iliad* (5, 773–74): "But when she [Hera] came to Troy and its flowing rivers where Simoeis and Scamander join their streams…" Accepting Richard Chandler's proposal that the ancient Simoeis should be equated with the modern Dümrek

Su, Maclaren looked closely at maps of the plateau between the two rivers, particularly at the area where the ridge narrows to a point at Hisarlik. Speculation at the time was focusing on this area as the probable site of Classical and Hellenistic Ilion (which became Novum Ilium in the Roman period). It is not altogether clear whether Maclaren himself deserves credit for locating New Ilion at Hisarlik or whether (and how much) he was indebted to the work of previous investigators, including the Cambridge mineralogist E. D. Clarke.[12]

What is certain is that Maclaren must have known of the ancient body of opinion which held that Priam's Troy (though no longer visible) had stood on the same site as Greco-Roman New Ilion. This had been the view of Herodotus (7, 43) and of the inhabitants of the place, and was endorsed by Alexander the Great when he came to sacrifice to the Ilian Athena at the start of his Persian campaign. The identification had not, so far as we know, been called in question in the Greek world until local antiquarians disputed the claim in the Hellenistic period. Maclaren, then, finally assembled the pieces of his topographical jigsaw in the following definitive statement: "After a pretty careful consideration of the passages in Homer which refer to the position of the town, I am convinced...that the Troy of Homer occupied the very hill (Issarlik) on which New Ilium stood" (*Dissertation,* 179). It was a remarkable piece of deduction, and its success cannot but underline the value of Homer as a guide to the topography of the Troad.

Maclaren made good use of what Homer says about the rivers of the Trojan plain, and I proceed next to examine in more detail what is said in the *Iliad* about the Scamander and the Simoeis. It will become clear, I hope, that Homer has a good grasp of their essential features. In his list of the eight rivers of the Troad, the Scamander is the only one to receive an epithet, "divine" (Il. 12, 19–23). This marks it out as the most important river of the kingdom and helps to confirm its identity with the river now known as the (Kara) Menderes Su. Indeed, the names are recognisably similar. The Scamander is also the only river in Homer to have two names, one divine and the other human. "The gods," says Homer, "call it Xanthos, and men Scamander" (Il. 20, 74). There is no scholarly consensus about the significance of such dual nomenclature (which occurs in three other places in the *Iliad*), but one may note that *xanthos* is the Greek for "yellow," a suitable epithet for a turbulent stream, whereas *Skamandros* has no clear Greek derivation. This suggests, perhaps, that Scamander may have always been the local name, Xanthos a nickname given by Greek merchants or the invading army. Homer knows of another river Xanthos in Lycia (Il. 2, 877), though, so it may have been a name prevalent in Asia Minor in the Bronze Age.

The flow of the Menderes can dwindle away almost to nothing in the heat of summer, lending some credence to the report of Herodotus (7, 43) that Xerxes' army drank its pools dry. But in winter it becomes a formidable stream, filling its main bed, which in the lower plain is between two hundred and three hundred feet in width. Peter Forchammer noted that it is larger in proportion to the extent of the plain than is usual in the case of Grecian rivers.[13]

The course of the river from source to mouth measures between fifty and sixty miles. Its headwaters are nourished by numerous sidestreams that pour down from the steep northwestern flanks of Ida. The torrent at Ayasma, easily accessible by road through Bayramiç and Evciler, has long been singled out as the main source, largely because it is nourished by an impressively large volume of water that emerges from a cave in the steep side of its ravine. There is also a warm spring in this neighbourhood whose water is believed to have medicinal qualities.[14] But the Ayasma torrent is only one of a number of headwaters that flow out from the Alpinelike valleys of the area. By the time it reaches the site of ancient Scepsis, the Menderes is already an impressive river (fig. 3.15). From there it flows west through a broad and fertile valley that forms its middle basin, before turning northwards near Ezine to reach the gorge that brings it down past Ballı Dağ to the plain of Troy.

As Maclaren says: "The Scamander is seldom mentioned by Homer without some epithet expressive of its beauty, its grandeur, its preeminent importance among the Trojan rivers, or the special veneration with which it was regarded" (*Dissertation*, 42). It is indeed a "fair-flowing" stream, alternating rapidly between shallow glides and the deep whirling eddies emphasised in

Homer's system of stock epithets. Over much of its course, its bed and banks are unusually sandy, and this could explain the Homeric epithet *eioeis* (Il. 5, 36), said by the lexicon to be "of doubtful meaning." The derivation of the word is uncertain, but it could be connected with *eion,* meaning "seashore" or "beach," and certainly anyone who has walked the banks of the Menderes, particularly in the Trojan plain, will find no problem in ascribing "banks like beaches" to it (fig. 3.16).

Homer embodies the Scamander's divine pedigree in a thrice-repeated formula: "But when they came to the ford of the fair-flowing river, eddying Xanthos, begotten by immortal Zeus ..."[15] So in Homer's eyes Xanthos alias Scamander is a god and is listed as such among the gods supporting the Trojans (Il. 20, 40). This is recognised by Achilles, who addresses the river respectfully as "fostered by Zeus" (Il. 21, 223). Scamander was in fact held to be a son of Zeus rather than of Okeanos, but the epithet can also bear the sense of "rain-fed," which is appropriate for a river that streams down from the lofty massif of Ida, where Zeus gathers the storm clouds. Just as Zeus sends help to the Trojans from their great mountain, so his offspring brings down life-giving water to fructify their plain. Ida and Scamander lie at the heart of Homer's depiction of Trojan scenery, and in terms of physical geography they still constitute the essence of the Troad. Scamander, like Zeus, had his cult at Troy, and his priest Dolopion is said to have been greatly honoured by the Trojan people (Il. 5, 76–78). A cult practice in which animal sacrifices were made in the bed of the river is described in graphic detail by Achilles as he is about to slay Priam's son Lycaon on its banks (Il. 21, 130–32): "The fair-flowing silver-eddying river," he says, "will not be able to protect you Trojans, not though you sacrifice many bulls to it, and put horses down live into its eddies." Achilles' own battle with the river (Il. 21) will be the subject of further comment in Chapter 5. Here it may be pointed out that the power of the water is not finally subdued until Hephaistos, the god of fire, comes to the hero's aid. The scorching of Scamander prefigures the conflagration that will finally overwhelm Troy itself.

The river's close links with the wilder scenery of the Troad are further underlined for us when we read that a Trojan master-huntsman, who is said to

3.15   The fertile territory of Old Dardania in the middle basin of the Scamander (Menderes). The conical hill on the far bank of the river was the site of ancient Scepsis, home of Demetrios, the Hellenistic topographer on whom Strabo relied for much of his information on the Troad. The summit ridge of Mount Ida bounds the view on the right.

3.16   The sandy banks of the Scamander where the river emerges from its gorge onto the Trojan plain.

3.17 "Now running along the Simoeis to Kallikolonê" (Il. 20, 53). Homer's description of Ares' dash from the Pergamos to the hill is illustrated by this view, which looks east along the Simoeis in the foreground to the shapely dome of Kallikolonê in the background. The line of the river joins Troy to the hill, as Homer says.

have been taught by Artemis how to "strike down all the wild things that are nurtured in the wooded uplands," is called Scamandrios (Il. 5, 49–52).

The Scamander's intimate connection with the continuing but threatened life of Troy is also strongly symbolised in Hector's pet name for his infant son Astyanax. He calls the boy Scamandrios, as we learn in the moving scene where Hector and Andromachê meet on the walls of the city and talk for the last time. Andromachê has the baby with her, and there is intense tragic irony in Hector's prayer that his beloved little Scamandrios may grow up to become a great warrior prince of Troy, for we, like Homer's audience, know that the baby will suffer a violent death when the city falls.[16]

The river Simoeis is the minor partner of the Scamander, joining the main river as its last tributary before the sea. The two rivers converge in front of Ilios, enfolding the city in a joint embrace and enclosing a section of plain where some of the fiercest fighting takes place (Il. 5, 774; 6, 2–4). Homer appears to revert to the theme of bitter conflict in this area in his catalogue of the rivers of the Troad. The Simoeis is listed last, immediately after the Scamander, and Homer adds the comment that this was the place "where many shields and helmets fell in the dust, and fell also the race of semidivine warriors" (Il. 12, 21–23). The epithet *semidivine* occurs only here in Homer. As Hainsworth says, the usage confirms that the poet is not here "narrating events before Troy as a contemporary observer but commenting upon them from the standpoint of a later age."[17] This just observation encourages me to speculate that Homer may also have been in an archaeologising mood. Could he, as a visitor to the site of Troy, have heard stories of how the plough had turned up weapons and bones in the alluvium along the banks of the rivers close to the citadel?

Homer's topographical indications make it certain that the Simoeis is to be identified with the minor river that flows close under the northern flank of Hisarlik and is now called the Dümrek Su. This river takes its rise in a line of hills about eight to ten miles east of Troy. The main road from Chanakkale crosses the Dümrek immediately before climbing up to the plateau on which Troy stands, and the edge of the plateau forms an abrupt escarpment along the south bank of the river for most of its course.

The escarpment culminates in the shapely dome of Kara Tepe (Kara Your), which is commonly, and I believe correctly, identified with Homer's Kallikolonê, a name that means "beautiful hill."[18] Kara Tepe lies a little more than five miles east of Troy (see map 6), and this location agrees very well with Strabo's statement (13, 1, 35) that the distance between Kallikolonê and New Ilion was forty stades. Rising to a height of 670 feet, the summit stands out from its surroundings and forms an easily recognisable landmark in its immediate neighbourhood. Its association with the Simoeis is stressed by Homer when he says that Ares ran from Troy to Kallikolonê along the course of the river (Il. 20, 53) (fig. 3.17).

3.18   The view down to Hisarlik from the top of Kara Tepe (Kallikolonê).

Homer also says that the gods supporting the Trojans watched the course of the fighting "from the brows of Kallikolonê" (Il. 20, 151). Schliemann accepted the identification of Kallikolonê with Kara Tepe (which he calls Kara Your) but also endorsed the mistaken opinion of his friend and adviser Virchow that its summit is not visible from Hisarlik.[19] Indeed, Kara Tepe is hard to pick out as one looks east from Hisarlik, because its pine-clad slopes merge into the dark background of the higher Ulu Dağ range behind. But there *is* a direct line of vision between the two points, as Homer says, and I can testify from personal observation that the flat summit ridge of Kara Tepe provides an excellent platform from which to view the Pergamos of Troy and the surrounding floodplains of the Scamander and the Simoeis (fig. 3.18).

Kara Tepe is most easily reached from the village of Dümrek, whence a good track runs south to the foot of the hill. The ascent is steep, and the hill culminates in a long, narrow ridge rather than a single peak. This ridge runs for about two hundred yards from east to west and is between thirty and fifty yards

3.19 Worked blocks, the remains of some ancient structure, on the summit of Kallikolonê. Schliemann supposed that it might have been a temple of Ares.

in breadth. Falling away steeply on all sides, it does indeed provide the summit with marked "brows," as Homer says. Ancient remains have been excavated here, and worked blocks can be seen lying among the pine trees (fig. 3.19).

The Simoeis is a typical Mediterranean torrent, dwindling to the size of a minor brook from late spring on but capable of filling a surprisingly wide bed when in winter spate (fig. 3.20). When Scamander appeals to it for help in checking Achilles, the poet envisages it in full and powerful flood (Il. 21, 311–14): "Come quickly to my aid, and fill your streams with water from your springs. Stir up all your channels. Raise up a great wall of water, and whirl down tree trunks and boulders with a mighty roar." Down the centuries the Simoeis has built up a highly fertile alluvial plain in its lower reaches. Aware perhaps of its richness, Homer makes it provide immortal fodder for the horses of Hera's chariot (Il. 5, 777).[20]

Like the Scamander, the Simoeis also figures in Trojan nomenclature, giving its name to a minor Trojan warrior, Simoeisios, who is cut down in the

3.20   A ford over the Simoeis close to Dümrek village (on left). The extent of the winter flood channel is apparent.

bloom of youth by Ajax (Il. 4, 473–89). It was not unusual for ancient rivers to be associated with human fecundity, and in this episode we learn that Simoeisios was conceived by his mother "as she came down from Ida by the banks of the Simoeis when she had gone with her parents to watch the flocks." I was reminded of this pastoral vignette when I saw a shepherd resting his flock in a stand of pine trees close to the riverbank about a mile below the village of Dümrek. His dogs took exception to my approach, and I was unable to take a picture of the scene. When I returned to try to capture it some hours later, he and his sheep were nowhere to be seen. Shepherds still move freely in the vicinity of Troy, leading their flocks down pine-clad slopes in biblical fashion to feed and rest by "waters of comfort."

If ever Zeus allows us to sack the well–walled city of Troy . . .

—Achilles to Agamemnon (Il. 1, 128–29)

FOUR   TROY, HOMER, AND THE ARCHAEOLOGISTS

UCH STILL REMAINS to be discovered about Troy, but it may be taken as certain that the city named and described by Homer was located on the hill of Hisarlik. The determined sceptic may cling to the possibility that an alternative site still awaits discovery. But the whole area around the floodplain of the Menderes has been so intensively surveyed that the chances of this happening are virtually nil. And in favour of Hisarlik, the size, wealth, and long duration of the successive settlements revealed by excavation all combine to mark out the great mound as the Bronze Age capital of the Troad.

A major share of the credit for identifying the site beyond all reasonable doubt must go to the German businessman and amateur archaeologist Heinrich Schliemann. It was he who first uncovered the prehistoric remains hidden deep below the surface of the soil, and his discovery of a major hoard of treasure focused worldwide attention on his excavation. But what led him to Hisarlik? That part of the story is now better understood and deserves to be more widely known.

Schliemann conducted his first major campaign from 1871 to 1873, but he had previously visited the Troad in 1868. On that occasion he made some unproductive soundings on Ballı Dağ and convinced himself that it was an unlikely candidate for Priam's city. Uncertain how to proceed, he then had the good sense to make contact with an Englishman named Frank Calvert, whose family had long been resident in a commercial and consular capacity in the area. Calvert's part in the discovery of Troy has been overshadowed by the glamour and panache of Schliemann's well-publicised achievements. Recently, though,

4.1   Looking north from the acropolis of Cebren over the sort of terrain in which Achilles captured Trojans "pasturing sheep on the flanks of Ida" (Il. 11, 104–6).

a detailed reassessment of his work has led to a better understanding of the relationship between the two men and of the significance of the investigations that Calvert had made before Schliemann's arrival.[1]

Frank Calvert was a quiet, unassuming man who devoted his life to scientific and antiquarian exploration of the Troad. He had correctly identified the site of the Classical Greek city of Cebren in 1860 (fig. 4.1). By 1863 he had acquired land at Hisarlik, had sunk a small exploratory trench into the summit of the Pergamos, and had unearthed significant remains of the temple of Athena from the Greco-Roman city of Novum Ilium. His finds convinced him of the potential of the site, and he sensed that it was probably the location of Homeric Troy, as Maclaren had claimed.

His next move was an attempt to persuade the trustees of the British

Museum to finance and support him in a fuller excavation. He made his approach through Charles Newton, who was then keeper of the Museum's Department of Greek and Roman Antiquities. Newton had visited the Troad some ten years before and had made a rather guarded assessment of the Hisarlik site. He had been shown around by Calvert, and the two men had kept up a correspondence in the intervening years. Calvert generously offered to put his Hisarlik property at the Museum's disposal for an excavation. He was prepared to allow the Museum to keep all finds and asked only that his name should be associated with any discoveries made. Unfortunately, Newton had unfounded doubts about Calvert's abilities and did not present his proposal to the trustees in as full and supportive a way as it merited. The trustees turned it down, and a golden opportunity for British involvement at Troy was missed.

In 1865 Calvert himself started a more extensive excavation at Hisarlik, but he soon realised that he lacked the resources needed to tackle such a rich site, and in particular to penetrate down through the Greco-Roman levels to the Bronze Age strata beneath. He decided to suspend work on the hill, but continued his field surveys around the Trojan plain and farther inland. By now his fund of local knowledge and his publications had established him as the leading resident authority on the antiquities of the Troad, and that reputation must have prompted Schliemann to seek him out. They met on August 15, and this was a most fortunate conjunction for Schliemann. Calvert possessed a promising site and the local expertise that Schliemann lacked, and Schliemann, the successful entrepreneur, had the money that Calvert needed. Calvert warmed to Schliemann and at once proposed that they work together. Nothing was formalised, but late in December 1868 Schliemann wrote to thank Calvert for his help and to announce that he intended to excavate the stratified mound of Hisarlik from top to bottom. His travels had encouraged him to think that he could make a name for himself as a field archaeologist. To this end he was working on his first book, *Ithaque, le Péloponnèse, et Troie,* which was published early in 1869 and earned him a doctorate at Rostock University. In it Schliemann wrote: "After having twice thoroughly examined the entire plain of Troy, I completely shared Frank Calvert's conviction that the plateau of

Hisarlik marks the site of ancient Troy and that on this very hill stood its Pergamus fortress."[2] It was the only time that Schliemann gave such an open acknowledgment of his debt to Calvert. Once the excavation started, under his direction and financed by his money, he came more and more to regard and proclaim himself as the sole discoverer of Homer's Troy. Like a cuckoo in the nest, he greedily claimed the full credit and had no compunction in displacing the diffident Calvert from any share in the limelight.

A year went by before Schliemann was ready to begin work. He had family business that involved a trip to New York. There, in March 1869, he succeeded in finalising the grant of American citizenship to which he had first laid claim during the California gold rush in 1851. He resided for more than three months in Indianapolis in order to secure a divorce from his Russian wife—Indiana was thought to be the easiest state in which to dissolve a marriage. After years devoted to successful business operations, he was now convinced that he could make a new career for himself as a scholar and explorer of Homeric sites. The divorce would signal the transition from his commercial past, but he felt that he also needed the companionship and inspiration of a Greek wife if he were to succeed in his new quest. Accordingly, he wrote to his Greek friend Theokletos Vimbos, who had become Archbishop of Athens, asking him to find a suitable partner. The archbishop sent back some suggested names, accompanied by photographs, and from these Schliemann selected "Sophie" as his bride to be.

Schliemann had an extraordinary capacity for making his hopes and aspirations come true. After securing his divorce, he arrived in Athens early in September 1869, carried through his courtship, agreed on a financial settlement with the family, and married Sophia Engastromenos before the month was out. Despite their age difference—he was forty-seven and she seventeen—the marriage turned out well; Sophie became a loved and respected companion and a skilled excavator in her own right. Indeed, Schliemann's childhood sweetheart Minna told him years later that Sophie was the greatest treasure he had ever discovered.

Early in 1870 he was back again in Athens impatiently awaiting his *firman* (permission to excavate) from the Turkish authorities. The firman had still not arrived by the beginning of April when Schliemann decided to start without it. His trial trenches were sunk on a portion of the hill not owned by Calvert. The peasant proprietors protested against his illegal invasion of their property, the authorities in Istanbul were taken aback, and even the mild-mannered and complaisant Calvert wrote to tell him that he thought his actions "injudicious." Schliemann was not to be deterred. Intensive lobbying at the Ottoman court, and the assistance of the American embassy at Constantinople, eventually produced the desired firman, which came through in August 1871.

The first major phase of Schliemann's work at Hisarlik took place over three seasons:

1. Six weeks of excavation from October 11 to November 24, 1871, in the course of which he unearthed a baffling mass of artifacts, which neither he nor anyone else could interpret. This was hardly surprising, as most of his finds were new to the archaeology of the day.

2. A more extended campaign from April 1 to August 14, 1872, during which he penetrated deep into the heart of the mound and cleared part of the circuit wall of the settlement now known as Troy II, an achievement that he at once proclaimed as the definitive discovery of Priam's citadel.

3. A third extended campaign from February to mid-June, 1873, which laid bare the paved ramp of Troy II that is still one of the most striking features of the citadel area. The ramp led up to a gate in the circuit wall of Troy II that Schliemann naturally saw as Homer's Scaean Gate (figs. 4.2 and 4.3).

The culminating moment of the third campaign was the discovery of the famous hoard that Schliemann identified as "Priam's Treasure." The hoard was indeed a major find, comprising thousands of precious objects, including gold cups, gold diadems, gold jewellery, and silver vases.[3]

It now became Schliemann's overriding objective to get the Treasure out of Turkey and to Greece as soon as possible, and with the aid of Calvert's brother Frederick he soon achieved this goal. Publication of the find brought Schliemann worldwide fame and greatly reinforced his claim to have found Homer's Troy.

4.2   An informative illustration from Schliemann's *Ilios* (35). For the present appearance of the sloped pavement in the left foreground, see fig. 4.3. The "Samothrace view" is visible in the background through the cut.

4.3   The paved ramp leading down from a gate in the walls of Troy II.

He had not in fact done so. The structures he had unearthed belonged to a far earlier epoch, but he can hardly be blamed for such an error when no firm chronology of the Mediteranean Bronze Age existed. He had always assumed that Homeric Troy would be on or close to the bedrock of the hill. Hence his plan of excavation was simply to dig down as far and as rapidly as he could. He prided himself on having removed more than a quarter of a million tons of earth in the process. His faith in Homer was indeed a faith that moved mountains, but it also resulted in the destruction of important stretches of the higher strata without proper recording of the levels and find-spots of their artifacts. We now know that he went down through the "Homeric" layers (Troy VI and VIIa) without recognising them. These layers now are dated to the second half of the second millennium B.C., whereas the cities that he revealed, essentially Troy I, Troy II, and Troy III, were Early Bronze Age settlements covering most of the third millennium B.C. Troy II, the stratum of the Treasure, is now thought to overlap Troy I as a higher or palace culture and to date from c. 2600 to 2450 B.C. (see Appendix 2: Chronology of Troy).

The anger of the Turkish government at his removal of the Treasure prevented Schliemann's return to Troy until 1878. In the interim he published *Troy and Its Remains* (1875), secured Greek permission to excavate at Mycenae, and made there in 1876 an even more astounding discovery. Unlike Troy, the site of Mycenae had never been in doubt. Mycenae had never been built over by a later city, and its massive Bronze Age circuit of walls and Lion Gate had always remained visible. Putting to the test his habitual trust in ancient sources, Schliemann simply followed up the statement of Pausanias (2, 16, 5) that graves reputed to be those of Agamemnon and his companions lay (contrary to later Greek practice) within the circuit of walls. Excavating in the area now known as Grave Circle A, Schliemann found six shafts sunk deep into the bedrock. They contained unplundered interments made with a truly regal wealth of gold and other precious objects. Gold death masks had covered the faces of some of the deceased, and as he studied the imperious features of the occupant of Shaft Grave V, Schliemann felt sure that he was looking on the face of Agamemnon.

As at Troy, Schliemann had no established chronological framework in which to place the finds, and naturally he assumed that he had discovered the remains of the generation that fought the Trojan War. We now know that the shaft graves date from the sixteenth century B.C., at least three hundred years before any such war, but Schliemann's understandable error should not be allowed to detract from the magnitude of his achievement. He had shown that the epic tradition was right to call Mycenae "rich in gold." Even more significant, he had opened up a whole new field of prehistory and laid the foundations for the rediscovery of the major civilisation that flourished in Greece in the Late Bronze Age. His finds provided a secure factual basis for the role of the ruler of Mycenae as leader of the Achaean expedition against Troy. The nature and extent of the Mycenaean world—the term derives from Schliemann's 1876 discoveries—remained to be worked out by his successors, among whom Christos Tsountas, Alan Wace, and George Mylonas deserve special mention. But the glory of the initial discovery belongs exclusively to Schliemann.

Schliemann returned to Troy in September 1878, digging from then to the end of November and again the following year from March to July. He was now operating on Calvert's land with the owner's permission. A formal agreement had been worked out, which, not surprisingly, seems to have been much in Schliemann's favour. Calvert, dominated as usual by his more aggressive partner, had agreed to surrender half of the finds and to allow Schliemann primacy in publishing the results. This second campaign was a more sober and low-key affair, marked by further but more minor finds of "treasure." Schliemann became troubled by increasing uncertainty as to whether he had really discovered Priam's palace. Priam had to be contemporary with Agamemnon, but he could see that the civilisation he was uncovering at Troy was very different from what had emerged at Mycenae.

In 1879 he was buoyed by the arrival of a French scholar, Emile Burnouf, who was honorary director of the French School at Athens. Burnouf had expertise in surveying and cartography and assisted Schliemann with plans and maps. He also worked out a stratigraphical sequence of seven layers which Schliemann used from then on. Schliemann was also encouraged and steadied by the April visit of the eminent German pathologist and polymath Rudolf Virchow. Virchow became one of his firmest friends and was responsible for persuading Schliemann to bequeath his collections to the German Fatherland. The beneficial influence of these experts is evident in Schliemann's next and most substantial publication, *Ilios: The City and Country of the Trojans,* which came out in 1880.

There were still critics who refused to accept the book's central thesis that Homeric Troy had been found, and Schliemann himself was not without his moments of doubt. In *Ilios* he had equated the comparatively humble remains of Troy III with Priam's citadel, but secretly he remained perplexed and troubled by the seeming discrepancy between his archaeological data and Homer's picture of a major fortress containing broad streets, great palaces, and a lofty temple. He toyed with the concept of poetic exaggeration as a way out of his dilemma but was unwilling to go far down that road. He knew instinctively that Homeric historicity can be fatally undermined if one admits the possibility that central facts of the saga could have been seriously falsified in the transmission of the epic tradition. It was in such a frame of mind that he decided on a further campaign to try to silence the critics and resolve his doubts.

The 1882 season, begun on March 1, brought him a far better understanding of his excavation results, and for this he was largely indebted to a new professional adviser, Wilhelm Dörpfeld. Dörpfeld was an architect who came fresh to Troy from the systematic German excavation at Olympia. His trained eye soon succeeded in distinguishing the layers of Troy II and its inferior successor Troy III. He also managed to identify several large buildings, fit to be called monumental or even palatial, that lay within the circuit of the Troy II citadel wall.

Schliemann was comforted, indeed elated, by this reassessment of the site, and at once he dashed off letters to prominent people, including one to Lord Dufferin, the British ambassador in Istanbul:

Troy 3rd May 1882

My dear Lord Dufferin
I am very glad to see that you have delayed your visit to

Troy till the end of May, for by that time my excavations
will have progressed so far as to enable me to show you in
detail the real Homeric Pergamos with its *vast* temples
and houses. It was hidden beneath the ruins of the
succeeding city, which I held to be the Troy of the *saga*,
though its buildings were Lilliputian.

Characteristically, Schliemann corrects his former misapprehensions without
making any mention of the contribution of Dörpfeld. Further correspondence
shows that the Dufferins had not arrived by the end of June. The ambassador was
probably too involved in a diplomatic crisis relating to Egypt to leave his post; he
apparently did not ever see the sights that Schliemann promised him.[4]

Schliemann summed up the results of the 1882 campaign in a pregnant
paragraph in his next book, *Troja,* published in London and New York in 1884:

I have proved that in remote antiquity there was in the
plain of Troy a large city, destroyed of old by a fearful
catastrophe [he had found evidence of a widespread
conflagration], *which had on the hill of Hissarlik only its
Acropolis, with its temples and a few other large edifices, whilst
its lower city extended in an easterly, southerly, and westerly
direction, on the site of the later Ilium,* and that, consequently,
this city answers perfectly to the Homeric description of
the site of sacred Ilios. (*Troja,* 277; my italics)

The general picture of Troy here given is broadly correct in its main outlines, as
the most recent excavations have shown, though Schliemann could hardly have
realised just how far the lower city in fact extended. Nevertheless, the passage
italicised shows considerable prescience on Schliemann's part, even though he
had still not correctly identified the strata of the Late Bronze Age.

He now announced that his work at Troy was "ended for ever," but he was
fated to make one more visit to the scene of his first major triumph. In the

intervening years he successfully excavated the Mycenaean palace complex at Tiryns (1884–85) and unsuccessfully tried to establish an archaeological presence at Knossos.

Schliemann was finally goaded into making a return to Troy by the attacks of a German compatriot, Capt. Ernst Bötticher. In pamphlet after pamphlet Bötticher advanced the absurd claim that Schliemann had found a cemetery rather than a city. Schliemann decided to reopen the excavation and invited Bötticher to come to Troy and contest the issue in front of a commission of specialists. His opponent came and was duly subdued, but not silenced, and Schliemann was now stimulated to look for even more-convincing evidence in his favour.

His plan was to search for a cemetery of royal graves outside the fortification wall of his supposedly Homeric citadel. To this end he installed railways to carry away the excavated soil more quickly, and he began what was to be his last season's work on March 1, 1890. He adopted the sound strategy of working outwards from the southeast gate of the Troy II perimeter, and this gave Dörpfeld the chance to effect a systematic clearance of a well-layered section in the new workface. Schliemann was somewhat impatient at the slowness of the procedure, but knew by now that it was the proper method to follow, and he allowed his assistant to have his way.

The crucial discovery was made in the fourth layer from the top and the sixth from the bottom. Remains of buildings comparable in plan to those at Tiryns appeared, together with pottery that in shape and decoration had to be Mycenaean. Now for the first time the two men were looking at a stratum at Troy contemporary with Mycenae and Tiryns at the height of their power in the middle of the thirteenth century B.C. Troy VI was emerging into the light of day, but what seems obvious to us was not immediately clear to them. Schliemann published a progress report on the discovery at the end of the season but left the dating question open. To do otherwise would have involved too radical a reappraisal of all his previous assumptions and conclusions. He was not psychologically ready to make the inference that his Troy II was far too ancient to be Homer's Troy, and perhaps it is a mercy that he was never

4.4   The longest and best-preserved section of the citadel wall of Troy VI
(see map 4, I6 and K7).

compelled to do so. Weakened by an ear infection and worn out by two
decades of travel and groundbreaking exploration, Schliemann collapsed on a
visit to Naples and died in a hospital there on December 26, 1890.

It was left to Dörpfeld to continue Schliemann's work at Troy in two further seasons of excavation during 1893–94. This he did with great expertise,
uncovering the massive citadel walls of Troy VI (fig. 4.4) and demonstrating
that the settlement they enclosed was contemporary with the power centres of
Mycenaean Greece. He also established the stratification of nine superimposed
cities, an analysis that still provides the framework for all work at Hisarlik.[5]

No further excavation was undertaken at Troy for some forty years. Then
in 1932 a major new campaign was initiated by the University of Cincinnati
under the direction of Professors Carl Blegen and William T. Semple. In seven
consecutive annual campaigns the American team conducted a meticulous new
investigation of the citadel area and surrounding regions. The outbreak of
World War II allowed time for a careful assessment of the new data, and the
results of the excavation were published in four magnificent volumes under the
title *Troy* (1950–58). Dörpfeld's nine-city stratification was refined by appropri-

ate subdivisions to take account of development within the major phases, and the cultural ups and downs of the successive settlements were greatly clarified by the recovery of a mass of new evidence. After the passion and excitement of the Schliemann era, the American excavation was sober and systematic. While not greatly enlarging the field of enquiry, it put our historical understanding of the site on a much firmer basis.

Half a century went by before excavation was resumed at Hisarlik. The current Troia Projekt, which started in 1988, is a long-term multidisciplinary investigation of all aspects of civilisation in the Troad, with its main focus on Troy and its immediate surroundings. The work is being conducted under the auspices of the Universities of Cincinnati and Tübingen and also involves archaeologists from Turkey and other countries. The excavation team is divided into two main groups: one group, under the direction of Professor Manfred Korfmann of Tübingen, concentrates on Bronze Age Troy (cities I–VII); the other, under Professor Brian Rose of Cincinnati, is exploring the remains of Greco-Roman Troy (cities VIII and XI).[6]

One of the most significant results to date has been the revelation that an extensive lower town flourished at the same time as the previously excavated structures of Troy VI and Troy VII. Some of the buildings of this lower town have been located, and its system of perimeter fortifications has been partly unearthed (map 3). The settlement extended southwards from the great Troy VI wall discovered by Dörpfeld, and the area north of that wall must now be viewed as the inner citadel of a much larger city. Blegen had discovered a Bronze Age cemetery on low ground well south of the area then under excavation, and this was an indication that a settlement might lie between it and the citadel wall. To explore this possibility was one of the main reasons for the initiation of the new excavations, and those in charge have every reason to feel proud of their success.

The discovery resulted from subsurface prospection by magnetometer. In 1992 the photographic images produced by this method indicated the outline of what was taken to be a massive new wall running southwards from two points on the perimeter of the known citadel wall. The "wall" appeared to form an

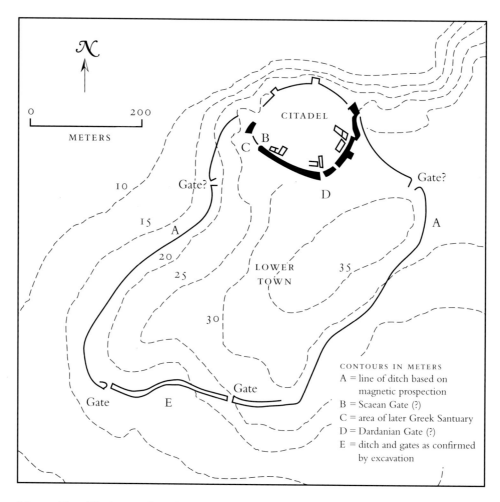

Map 3. Troy: The System of Fortifications in the Late Bronze Age

extended oval enclosure for the inhabitants of the lower town. In 1993 the
magnetic data were tested by an excavation trench sunk at a point about five
hundred yards south of the Pergamos. To everyone's surprise the "wall" turned
out to be a man-made ditch. A subsequent in-fill of assorted debris had given
the impression of a wall (fig. 4.5).

The ditch has a U-shaped profile and is between ten and eleven feet in

4.5   The fortification ditch of the lower town as first revealed by excavation in 1993. The view is taken looking north along the excavation trench. The outer lip of the ditch appears in the immediate foreground, with the sloping inner face some fifteen feet away behind. The thinness of soil coverage over the bedrock is apparent in the upper portion of the trench. (Photograph reproduced by kind permission of Professor Korfmann and the Troia Projekt.)

width. It had been cut into the bedrock, and its sides are up to eight feet in height. The ditch has now been traced over a distance of more than three hundred yards. Its line runs sharply down and across the contours of the slope, and this rules out any suggestion that it could have functioned as a drain or canal. It has to be interpreted as part of the defensive system of the lower town, and it seems to have been designed to keep chariots at least a bowshot away from an inner palisade. Footings for such a palisade have also been found.

In 1995 a break in the ditch was noted well to the west of the initial sounding, and this turned out to be part of a provision for allowing wheeled vehicles to enter the lower city through a defended gateway. The break is eleven yards

4.6   An aerial view of the gate in the southwest corner of Troy's outer ring of defences. The line of the ditch has been interrupted to produce a "bridge" or causeway. (This portion of the bedrock has been overlaid by the stone foundations of later structures.) The narrow incisions in the bedrock, visible on the left of the excavated area, were cut to hold a **V**-shaped wooden palisade guarding the actual gate. The valley of the Çıplak brook is seen behind, extending south to the Çıplak ridge on which stands the Paşa Tepe tumulus (Batieia). The foothills of Ida lie on the farther horizon. (Photograph reproduced by kind permission of Professor Korfmann and the Troia Projekt.)

in width and forms a "bridge" across the ditch to the gate opening, which is six yards in width. Narrow trenches cut in the rock on each side of the gate are interpreted as footings for a wooden palisade to defend the opening (figs. 4.6, 4.7, and 4.8).

A portion of a second ditch similar to the first, and about a hundred yards farther south, has also been found. This outer ditch may be later in date and may represent an extension of the fortified area of the lower town, but the dating of the two ditches and their relation will need further investigation.

One would expect a substantial wall to complement the system of ditches, but any trace of such a wall was slow to appear. Stone-robbing for the fortifications of Sigeum, as noted by Strabo (13, 1, 38), and for Greco-Roman Novum Ilium appears to have depleted it to the vanishing point over most of its length, but in

4.7   A trial trench in the lower town that hit on a section of another palisade incision, possibly part of a large wooden building. The incision has been traced for fifty feet. Note the semicircular cutting (on right between two later foundation blocks) designed to hold a support pillar for the wooden palisade. The circular structure is a Roman-period well.

4.8   A closer view of the "bridge" running between the ditch (rectangular pits on left) and the gate opening (marked by palisade slots on right). The stone footings on the line of the bridge date from the Greco-Roman period. (Photograph reproduced by kind permission of Professor Korfmann and the Troia Projekt.)

1995 a short section was laid bare at the point where it joined the outer bastion of the great Northeast Tower (fig. 4.9). This outer wall was constructed of sun-dried mud-brick on a base of large, shaped stones.

The significance of these discoveries can hardly be overemphasised. The area of the citadel within the previously known walls of Troy VI is 5 acres. The area of the lower town now known to have been enclosed within fortifications

4.9 A stretch of the outer wall of Troy VI/VII discovered in 1995. The wall, which consisted of sun-dried mud-brick on a stone foundation, is seen at the point where it runs in (from bottom right) to join the northeast bastion (top right). The point of contact is just north of the entry gate to the bastion (see map 4, K4). (Photograph reproduced by kind permission of Professor Korfmann and the Troia Projekt.)

is at least 45 acres. The total area of Bronze Age Troy at its maximum extent was therefore on the order of 50 acres. These dimensions make it appreciably larger than Mycenae and put it on a par with such Anatolian residential and trading cities of the time as Kültepe or Alişar. Schliemann, as we have seen, was troubled by the small size of Troy II, which he mistakenly took to be Homer's Troy. He would no longer be worried if he could see the new outline plan of the lower town of Troy VI–VII. Indeed, anyone who believes in the basic historicity of the Trojan War has much cause for satisfaction. It is no longer possible to play down the magnitude of the Achaean enterprise in attacking such a city as we now know Troy to have been. Using now-obsolete archaeological data, scholars had suggested that the scale of the Trojan War had been greatly exaggerated in the poetic tradition and that in fact it was probably no more than a pirate raid on a place of minor importance. In light of the new evidence such a stance is no longer tenable.

Professor Korfmann rejects any suggestion that Homer's picture of Troy is "totally unreal"; on the contrary, he maintains that it is "surprisingly like" the major city that excavation has revealed at Hisarlik. "None of the counter-arguments of archaeology," he states, "retain any countervailing force."[7] He is conscious of the need to maintain the integrity of archaeological methodology, of course, and is careful to state that in his campaigns to date he has not sought the Trojan War, nor will he do so. Yet he is also well aware that our view of Troy has been radically altered by his discoveries, and it may be that the Trojan War will find him.

Korfmann has certainly found strong evidence for *a* war, if not for *the* war, in a burnt stratum of Troy VIIa. The stratum lies close under the Troy VI wall in an area that has become known as the Sanctuary (fig. 4.10). It contained arrow points, abandoned piles of sling stones, and the hastily buried skeleton of a girl. One could hardly ask for clearer evidence of hostile action at a strategic point in the defensive perimeter of the citadel (fig. 4.11).

This new evidence has to be assessed in conjunction with earlier evidence of a similar kind that emerged from the Cincinnati excavation. It also has to be viewed in relation to Professor Blegen's overall view of the relation between Troy VIh and Troy VIIa.

Troy VI was clearly a powerful city that remained intact within elaborate fortifications for upwards of four hundred years. Blegen thought that its final phase, Troy VIh, was heavily damaged by earthquake at a date that he set at c. 1300 B.C. Repairs were made, and the life of the place continued without a major culture break into the phase named Troy VIIa. But this phase exhibited significant differences in the layout of its buildings. Smaller, hastily built houses now adjoined the great walls of the citadel and covered many of its former open spaces. Storage jars for oil and grain were sunk into the floors of many of these

4.10   Structures of the Greco-Roman Sanctuary in the valley to the west of the citadel wall of Troy VI/VII (see map 4, A8). The Hellenistic altar is in the foreground near the notice, with the larger Roman-period altar behind.

4.11   A stretch of paved roadway recently excavated outside the blocked gate of Troy VI/VIIa (see map 4, A7). Arrowheads, piles of sling stones, and a burnt layer were also found in this area below the blocked gate. (Photograph reproduced by kind permission of Professor Korfmann and the Troia Projekt.)

4.12 A Troy VIIa house; the pits contained storage jars sunk under the floor.

houses (fig. 4.12). Blegen inferred that the inhabitants of VIIa felt less secure than their predecessors and had crowded into the citadel for protection. And he argued that their fears were justified, for he found clear evidence that Troy VIIa met its end in a great conflagration. Was this due to enemy action? Yes, said Blegen, pointing to an arrowhead of mainland Greek type found in one of the main streets, together with fragments of human skulls. In view of such finds one could hardly doubt that the city was sacked and burnt by invaders. Blegen dated this disaster not later than c. 1240 B.C., and perhaps as early as 1270 B.C.[8]

This range of dates coincided with the heyday of Mycenae and made it possible to believe that the Trojan War of Greek tradition had been found, with Troy VIIa identified with the city besieged and captured by the Achaeans. Unfortunately, it now seems that Blegen's dates for the fall of Troy VIIa are too early. Fragments of Mycenaean III C pottery found in its strata require, in the view of experts, a down-dating of its end to as late as 1140 B.C. It is similarly thought that finds of Mycenaean III B pottery in Troy VIh may bring the date of its fall down to c. 1250 B.C.

Could the fall of Troy VIh, then, have been due to enemy attack rather than earthquake? Dörpfeld found that it too, like VIIa, had been extensively damaged by fire. Earthquakes cause fires, of course, but Dörpfeld detected human agency also in the destruction. His considered conclusion was as follows: "This city was thoroughly destroyed by enemy action. Not only were the traces of a great conflagration recognisable in many places, but the upper parts of the city walls and the gates and especially the walls of the buildings inside them underwent a violent destruction which can have happened neither through an outbreak of fire alone nor through an earthquake."[9]

If Dörpfeld was right in seeing the hand of man in the destruction horizon of Troy VIh, and if its fall can be dated to the middle of the thirteenth century B.C., then it becomes the most likely candidate for the ill-fated Troy of Priam, whose sack by Agamemnon is central to Greek traditions about the Heroic Age. Given the complexity of the problem, the wisest course is probably to suspend judgment pending the further progress of Professor Korfmann's explorations. It is to be hoped that he will be able to determine the dates and causes of the various destruction horizons with greater precision, as well as elucidate the full implications of the burnt stratum in Troy VIIa.

In general, Homerists are entitled to take the view that archaeological investigation at Hisarlik from Schliemann onwards has found nothing inconsistent with the Greek oral tradition about Troy. This tradition has considerable depth and extends back well beyond the Trojan War. Before the Troy of Priam, Greeks remembered the Troy of Laomedon. Laomedon, legend said, was powerful enough to engage gods in his service, compelling Apollo to tend his flocks and Poseidon to erect great walls for his city. It was part of the tradition that Poseidon was assisted in his work by a mortal hero, Aiakos of Salamis, who built a somewhat inferior section. We shall return to this point in a later connection. Here it is sufficient to say that the walls of Troy VI still excite universal admiration, and it is not surprising that the early Greek imagination should have attributed their construction to divine agency. Homer recounts the legend in considerable detail, making Poseidon say (Il. 21, 446–47): "Indeed I built a wall about their city for the Trojans, a broad and very beautiful wall to make the place impregnable." In the same passage, Homer also makes Poseidon recall how Laomedon refused to pay him the wages agreed for his work, thus ensuring the god's undying enmity against the Trojans.

Legend went on to tell that Poseidon sent a sea monster to plague the king and his subjects, that Herakles, a well-practised monster-killer, also came to work in Laomedon's service, and that he suffered much the same treatment as Poseidon. Laomedon had promised Herakles some of his pedigree horses if Herakles would save his daughter Hesionê from the monster, but then defaulted on the deal. In revenge Herakles brought a force of six ships and sacked Troy (Il. 20, 145–48 with 5, 640–42). In Greek legend, Herakles belongs to a generation earlier than the heroes who fought under Agamemnon, and this tradition of his attack on Troy might reflect Achaean raids prior to the ten-year siege.

These legendary reports of earlier contacts between Greeks and Trojans cohere well with the archaeological record. Commercial contact between Greece and the Troad is attested from c. 1400 on by Mycenaean products found in Troy. These imports include weaponry, ivories, and fine pottery. There is no evidence for Trojan exports in return, but there could well have been a trade in textiles and also in bloodstock to provide a basis for the tale of Laomedon's unscrupulous horse-dealing. Both spindle-whorls and horse bones are very commonly found in the strata of Troy VI–VIIa, and Homer often refers to the Trojans as "tamers of horses."

Some of the stock Homeric epithets for Troy, like "lovely," "holy," "well-founded," and "broad," are also applied to other cities and though appropriate enough are not in any sense distinctive. But five epithets and one short descriptive phrase are used only of Troy and combine to produce a vivid and appropriate image of the place. The phrase is "mighty city," and the epithets are "solidly built," "well-walled," "well-towered," "beetling," and "rich in horses."[10]

Taking these in reverse order, we note that "rich in horses" complements the equestrian activities of the inhabitants documented above. "Beetling" is used once only (Il. 22, 411). It is particularly appropriate for the steep slopes of Hisarlik when viewed from the north or northwest (see fig. 3.3), but the circuit of walls and towers must have looked formidably dominating when seen from any point in the plain. "Well-towered" is fully justified by the massive remains of the towers that may still be seen to flank the Northeast and South Gates. There were also other towers in the circuit. "Well-walled" is the first epithet applied to Troy in the *Iliad* (1, 129) and is still undeniably true of the visible remains of the citadel (see figs. 4.4 and 4.13). It was of course normal for Bronze Age cities to have massive walls, but those of Troy are outstanding for their beauty and durability. "Solidly built," a common enough epithet for walls and towers, is once applied to the whole city (21, 516). It is particularly suitable for the great stretches of the Troy VI wall and also for the palatial mansions that still stand within its circuit. Troy was indeed a "mighty city," and Homer emphasises the point by using this unique description no fewer than five times.[11]

Four other common (but not unique) epithets also call for comment. Troy shares the description "broad-streeted" with Mycenae and Athens. The well-paved road that leads up from the Lion Gate towards the palace is a conspicuous feature of Mycenae, and a comparable street can be seen inside the South Gate at Troy. Also at Troy a section of roadway paved with cobbles has recently been found in the Sanctuary area outside the inner circuit of walls (see fig. 4.11). Neither of these streets is particularly broad, but the epithet is appropriate for a terraced way that ran along the inner face of the citadel wall. This roadway was from twenty-five to more than thirty feet wide and remained unobstructed by any buildings until the Troy VIIa phase. It was a distinctive feature of Troy VI and could well account for the epic description "Troy of the broad ways." Troy/Ilios is also called "windy," "steep," and "holy." Many visitors, and all who have ever excavated at Troy, bear witness to the formidably persistent northerly winds, which can blow for weeks at a time, bringing bitter cold in winter and a merciful alleviation of the pitiless heat of midsummer. It is indeed a windy place. As for the steepness of at least part of the escarpment, this has already been noted in regard to the epithet "beetling." Professor Korfmann also emphasises the steep ascent to the city from a valley below the Northeast Tower, an access route that has been more clearly revealed by his work in that sector. "Holy Ilios" is the commonest phrase of all, occurring twenty-one times. Quite why the city should be deemed holy is not known for certain, but the epithet may derive, as Sir Maurice Bowra suggested, from the prominent position of the temple of Athena. The temple was situated "on the summit of the city," where also stood a temple of Apollo (Il. 6, 88, 297; 5, 446).

Homer amplifies his picture of Troy's acropolis when he reports that Hector

> went to the beautiful house of Alexandros which he had
> built with the help of the excellent craftsmen who then
> lived in the rich land of Troy. They made for him an
> inner chamber and hall and courtyard near the palace of
> Priam and the house of Hector at the summit of the city.
> (Il. 6, 313–17)

Unfortunately, no remains of Late Bronze Age Troy survive on the summit of the Pergamos. The crown of the hill was shaved off in the Hellenistic period to provide an extensive platform for an enlarged temple of Athena with surrounding colonnades. In this reconstruction any surviving remains from the prehistoric period were totally swept away. On the analogy of Mycenae and Athens, though, it is a reasonable assumption that "Priam's palace" once stood there, flanked perhaps by Athena's shrine and one or two mansions of the nobles, as Homer says. The mansions of Troy VI that still stand lower down and closer to the citadel wall give a good idea of what Paris's house may have looked like (map 4, 7C [House VI M]; 8F [Pillar House]). The quality of their cut-stone construction is extremely high. As Kirk says: "Homer's description reflects the late Mycenaean age rather than the intervening centuries down to his own time, in which secular monumental building was virtually unknown."[12]

Book 6 of the *Iliad* provides us with far more information about the architecture and layout of Troy than any other portion of the epic, because from line 242 onwards the action is set within the city. Priam's palace is first described, with its "polished porticoes" and suites of "bedchambers made of well-dressed stone" (242–50). We are given a glimpse of Hekabê's "scented storeroom" with its stock of richly embroidered robes imported from Sidon (288–91). Then comes the passage about Paris's mansion, and finally Hector and Andromachê traverse the "well-paved streets" of the citadel to meet on the walls by the "great tower of Ilios," close to the Scaean Gate (386–93). The Scaean Gate, we are told, was Hector's usual exit point on his way to the plain, and so it is natural that Andromachê should soon start to talk about the danger of a Greek assault at precisely that point (431–39). It is typical of Homer's method that all this information is provided, not in a single scene-setting passage, but piece by piece as the movements of his characters need to be spatially located. His descriptions are primarily related to the requirements of the narrative rather than designed for ornamental effect. The resulting picture of Troy is entirely credible and can be effectively related to the realities of the site as revealed by excavation.

The city described in the *Iliad* is essentially the noble fortress city we call Troy VI, with its lofty gates and paved streets leading to a spaciously planned inner citadel. As noted, this city came to an end c. 1250 B.C., whether by earthquake, or enemy action, or a combination of both. Life went on into the next phase, Troy VIIa, without any major culture break. The survivors patched up the walls and continued to live in their ancestral capital, though in meaner and more crowded conditions. This phase lasted, it is now thought, to c. 1140 B.C., when barbarian invaders took control of the site. Life in Troy VIIb appears culturally much impoverished, with crude handmade pottery supplanting the finer wheelmade wares of older Troy. Occupation finally petered out c. 1020 B.C., and the site then lay ruined and abandoned for upwards of two centuries until the modest beginnings of Aeolian Greek colonisation, now placed as early as c. 800 B.C.

Many scholars, myself included, date Homer to the second half of the eighth century. It is a plausible speculation that Homer's deep interest in the traditional story of the Trojan War would have brought him on a visit to the area, where he

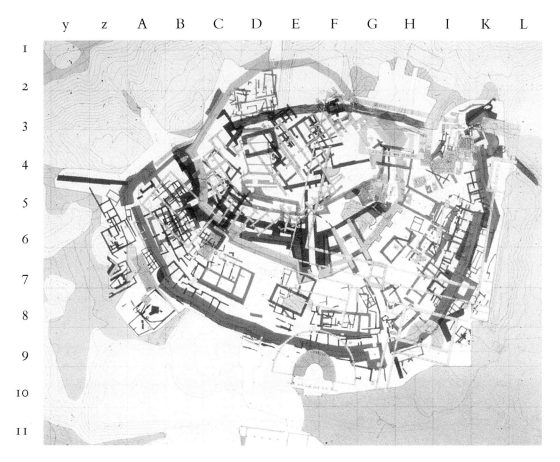

Map 4. Troy: Plan of the Citadel

could survey the scene, inspect the ruins, and talk to his Aeolian kinsmen in their humble village located on the site of former greatness. If he were living in Smyrna or Chios, it would have been an easy matter to secure a passge on a ship making for the Hellespont. Under favourable conditions the voyage of some 150 miles need not have taken more than a few days to complete. He would have seen the area of the lower town perhaps still roughly outlined by shattered fragments of mud-brick walls. Local farmers could have indicated the run of grassed-in ditches from seasonal

4.13 On the left, a recently excavated stretch of the Troy VI citadel wall (see map 4, D9). The wall was left exposed for several centuries after the end of Troy VIIb and could have been seen by Homer rising to a height of more than twenty-five feet. The upper portion is a new stone facing superimposed on the Bronze Age wall in the fourth century B.C. The portion of the older wall below this shows the effects of weathering, and stones have been removed by stone-robbers. (Photograph reproduced by kind permission of Professor Korfmann and the Troia Projekt.)

changes of vegetation, and may have commented on the problems of ploughing with so many ruined buildings lying so close to the surface. Professor Korfmann's recent excavations near the South Gate of the citadel have confirmed that Homer could also have observed a stretch of the great Troy VI wall there, still visible up to a height of twenty-five feet (fig. 4.13). I can imagine the poet nodding with approval as he surveyed the scene and recalled the traditional epithets of "holy Ilios."

The supposition that Homer took ship to view Troy finds some support in a passage of the *Iliad* where the poet, in effect, distances himself from the action to picture how the terrain would look to men of a later generation. Hector is the speaker. He has just challenged the Achaeans to nominate a champion to meet him in single combat and promises that, if he wins, he will return the corpse of his victim for proper burial:

> I shall return the body to the well-benched ships so that the
> long-haired Achaeans may give him solemn burial, and may
> raise a funeral mound for him near the broad Hellespont.
> And in time to come a man of a generation yet unborn may
> utter such words as these, as he comes sailing across the
> wine-dark sea in his many-oared ship: "Yonder lies the
> tomb of a long-dead hero, who perished bravely in battle at
> the hands of noble Hector." Thus will he speak, and my
> glory shall never die. (Il. 7, 84–91; cf. Od. 24, 80–84)

The scene is vividly imagined, and the experience it embodies may still be had by anyone who approaches the mouth of the Dardanelles by ship from the south. When one is off Beşika Bay the huge tumuli now known as Sivri (Beşik) Tepe and Üvecik Tepe are predominant on the skyline. Midway along the Sigeum Ridge the conical outline of Kesik Tepe also looks very like a burial mound (though close examination has shown it to be a natural hillock). Üvecik Tepe has nothing to do with the Trojan War, being a monument raised by the Roman Emperor Caracalla to commemorate his favourite companion Festus. But Festus is in good company, for Sivri Tepe, though Hellenistic in its present form, may well be associated with the memory of Achilles. As he sees these tumuli, a modern seafarer will not find it hard to believe that Homer travelled this route before him, and that the reflections of the poet himself underlie the words he puts into Hector's mouth.

Hither and thither the tide of battle set straight over the plain.

—Il. 6, 2

FIVE

SIGNPOSTS TO THE COURSE OF THE FIGHTING

THE ACTION OF THE *ILIAD* is closely circumscribed in time and space. The whole story unfolds in less than two months, with armed conflict measured in days rather than weeks. When the forces clash in battle the fighting fluctuates rapidly on the plain between Troy and the Greek camp, locations that must be envisaged as lying within a few miles of each other. Four main phases of the struggle may be distinguished. In the first phase (books 2–8) much of the fighting takes place close to Troy, but the Trojans eventually gain the upper hand, and Hector is emboldened to camp overnight in the plain, ready to press home an attack on the Greek ships the following day. In the second phase (books 11–15) Agamemnon counterattacks successfully, but after he and other Greek leaders are wounded, the Trojans force the Greeks back, break through the wall and ditch that fortify the ship station, and set fire to one of the ships. This Trojan success precipitates phase 3 (books 16–17), in which Achilles allows Patroklos to lead the Myrmidons into battle. At first the Trojans are flung back in disorder, and Patroklos, against Achilles' orders, pursues them to the walls of Troy and attempts to storm the city. He is then killed by Hector, and the Trojans surge back to renew their attack on the camp. In phase 4 (books 20–22) Achilles finally enters the fray, slaughtering many of the enemy along the banks of the Scamander and driving the rest in panic back into the city. Hector alone waits outside the walls and is killed in single combat.

The aim of this chapter is to examine how Homer sets the scene for these engagements, and how he charts the changing course of battle with a limited number of precisely envisaged landmarks that serve as recognisable signposts to the action. These signposts, I shall argue, are not fictional but can be topographically located. The picture that emerges makes military sense and is consistent with the nature of the terrain and the archaeology of Troy itself.

The first phase of the fighting is initiated when Agamemnon issues a call to arms and the Achaeans pour out from their camp into the "Scamandrian plain" and gather in their thousands in the "flowery Scamandrian meadow" (Il. 2, 465–68). The designation of the plain as "Scamandrian" occurs only here. In the case of recurrent features of the landscape, Homer normally has a stock of descriptive epithets at his command, but the Trojan plain, where so much of the action takes place, is nearly always referred to simply as "the plain." The only exceptions that I have noted are two passages where the plain in general is called "Trojan" (Il. 10, 11; 23, 464), the present passage, and a later passage where the epithet "Ileian" is used (Il. 21, 558). These epithets are geographical rather than ornamental. "Trojan" is appropriate for the whole plain on which the capital city stands; the other two epithets appear to designate particular parts of the plain. I have given reasons for supposing that "Ileian" designates the upper portion of the plain on the right bank of the Scamander (see Chapter 2). Similarly, I suggest that "Scamandrian" is here used to indicate the part of the plain lying close to the Greek camp on the left bank of the river.[1]

The muster is followed by the detailed Catalogue of the Greek forces that fills most of the rest of book 2. The Greek army then advances swiftly over the plain towards Troy (Il. 2, 785). The Trojan Assembly is notified of the Greek advance, and Hector leads his forces out by all the gates of the city and assembles them on the hill of Batieia. The contingents of the Trojans and their allies are then listed in a shorter Catalogue.

The forces are now arrayed in the field, and a major clash seems imminent. But this is postponed for a short time when Paris declares his willingness to do battle for Helen in single combat with Menelaos. Homer envisages the battle lines as drawn up very close to Troy, for Helen is able to point out the leading Greek champions to Priam from the vicinity of the Scaean Gate, here mentioned for the first time (Il. 3, 145). Priam then drives down to the plain in his chariot to conclude a solemn truce with Agamemnon and to set the terms on which the duel is to be conducted. The result of the duel is inconclusive, and the truce is treacherously broken by Pandaros, who shoots an arrow and wounds Menelaos. A general engagement begins, raging on for a considerable time with varying fortune for both sides as gods intervene and then withdraw. As Homer puts at the start of book 6: "The dread conflict of Trojans and Achaeans was left to itself [by the withdrawal of the gods from the scene], and as each side aimed their bronze-tipped spears, the tide of battle set now this way now that across the plain between the streams of Simoeis and Xanthos [Scamander]" (Il. 6, 1–4). We have previously been told that the two rivers converge near Troy (Il. 5, 773–74), so this second mention of the rivers confirms that the battle still continues to be envisaged as fought close to the city walls.

Apollo and Athena then decide to return to the scene of the fighting. They meet at the oak tree (Il. 7, 22), which, we learn elsewhere, stands close to the Scaean Gate.[2] The line of movement of god and goddess as they rush to their meeting is precisely specified by the poet and can be used to fix the position of the Scaean Gate in the circuit of the walls. The relevant information is contained in the following passage (Il. 7, 17–22):

> Now when the grey-eyed goddess Athena saw the
> Trojans slaughtering the Argives in the violent fighting,
> she came down from the heights of Olympos and rushed
> towards holy Ilios. And Apollo, looking out from the
> Pergamos, rose up to confront her, wishing victory to the
> Trojans. And the two met each other at the oak tree.

The meeting is clearly envisaged as a head-to-head confrontation, with both parties moving to meet each other along the line that joins their starting points. Athena comes from Mount Olympos, which is due west of Troy, and Apollo comes from the Pergamos, and presumably from its highest part, which lay in the east of the citadel. So their rendezvous at the oak tree may be taken to lie just outside and to the west of the citadel wall. It follows that the Scaean Gate should be thought of as located in the western part of the circuit. This is an important topographical point with a bearing on Patroklos's later attempt to scale the walls.

Athena and Apollo agree to put a stop to the fighting by arranging another duel, this time between Hector and Ajax. Neither champion can gain a decisive advantage, and, at the approach of night, they agree to suspend the contest with a chivalrous exchange of gifts. Both sides then retire back to base, the Achaeans to their ship station and the Trojans to their city.

Next day at dawn the Trojan herald Idaios is sent to propose a truce to allow for the collection and burial of the dead, and this proposal is accepted. The Achaeans, meanwhile, on the motion of Nestor, have decided to improve the defences of their camp with a wall and a ditch, and this work is speedily accomplished.

Book 8 tells how fighting is resumed the following day, with Zeus determined to tilt the balance in favour of the Trojans. He forbids any more intervention by the Olympians and takes his seat on the peak of Gargaron to oversee the course of events. Battle is once more joined on the plain, for a time with no advantage to either side. But then Zeus thunders from the mountain and terrifies the Greeks. The fighting still fluctuates, but the Greeks are gradually forced back behind their new fortifications. At nightfall the Trojans have the upper hand, and Hector holds a council of war "by the eddying river," which must be the Scamander (Il. 8, 490). He proposes that the Trojan army should camp on the plain through the night and be ready to storm the camp the following morning. The plan is approved, and the book ends with one of the most memorable passages of description in the whole poem (Il. 8, 553–61):

> Thus all night long they sat, across the corridors of battle,
> thinking great thoughts and keeping their many fires
> alight. There are nights when the upper air is windless
> and the stars in heaven stand out in their full splendour

round the bright moon; when every mountaintop and headland and ravine starts into sight, as the infinite depths of the sky are torn open to the very firmament; when every star is seen and the shepherd rejoices. Such and so many were the Trojans' fires, twinkling in front of Ilium midway between the ships and the streams of Xanthus.
(trans. E. V. Rieu)

The Trojans have now crossed the Scamander and are encamped on the plain quite close to the Greek ship station. Their location is described as astride the "corridors of battle," a vivid rendering of an epic formula that means literally "bridges of war" (*ptolemoio gephurai*). These "bridges of war" are usually taken to be no more than a poetic way of referring to the scene of conflict or battlefield in general. But if one takes a look at other occurrences of the phrase, one can see the possibility of a more concrete and specific meaning. Chariots that have lost their riders are described as rattling along the "bridges of war" (Il. 11, 160), and later also in the epic these same "bridges" are envisaged as possible escape routes for chariots (Il. 20, 427). Just as bridges provide raised and firm pathways over water, so these "bridges of war" might refer to more elevated parts of the plain, natural rises or even artificial embankments, where chariots could run without fear of getting bogged down in waterlogged ground. This suggestion brings the usage into line with a simile in an earlier book (Il. 5, 87–89) where *gephurai* clearly means levees or embankments that are overwhelmed by a winter torrent. The part of the plain on the left bank of the Scamander, where the Trojans are now encamped, is more marshy than that on the right bank, but there are some firmer rises in it, and Hector would naturally seek the aid of these in pressing home his attack on the Greek camp.

Troy is now a fixed point on the map, but where is one to place the Greek camp and ship station? Like many before and after him, Schliemann supposed that the ships were drawn up in lines along the extensive beach that now borders the Hellespont to the north of Troy. Some two to three miles of plain now lie between the city and the sea, and this seemed to answer well to the Homeric picture of a comparatively short intervening space of level ground easily and rapidly traversed by chariots and infantry. A camp on the Hellespont between Cape Sigeum and Cape Rhoeteum was also envisaged in the ancient topographical accounts, notably in Strabo (13, 1, 36) and Pliny (*Natural History* 5, 33). Homer does not use the place names Sigeum or Rhoeteum, but he has been understood to imply a location in their vicinity with his many references to the camp "on the shore of the sea," and more explicitly in a thrice-repeated formula that has the Greeks retreating "to the ships and the Hellespont."[3]

Schliemann's view was endorsed by Virchow and powerfully reinforced by the identifications made by Walter Leaf (map 5). Some difficulties remained, notably the problem of finding anything on the alluvial flats corresponding to the "swelling of the plain," a feature three times mentioned as lying between Troy and the camp. The first mention of this swelling comes when Nestor rouses Diomedes from sleep with the words: "Have you not heard that the Trojans are encamped on the swelling of the plain near the ships, and only a short stretch of ground still holds them back?" (Il. 10, 160–61). The emphasis here is on the nearness of the swelling to the ships, but no such elevated ground can be identified with any plausibility in the lower Scamander delta near the Hellespont. Two other mentions of the swelling come in what looks like a formulaic line (Il. 11, 56; 20, 3 [identical lines]): "And the Trojans [mustered] on the other side, on the swelling of the plain." Both contexts imply close proximity to the ships. The identification of the swelling is further discussed below.

Another difficulty for the Schliemann-Leaf view arose from Homeric mentions of a ford on the Scamander, apparently lying between Troy and the camp. Such a ford is both mentioned and implied in Homer's account of Priam's journey to the Greek camp to intercede with Achilles for the return of Hector's corpse. This culminating episode of the *Iliad* is described in considerable detail. Homer says that Priam on his return journey to Troy was escorted by Hermes as far as the "ford of the fair-flowing river, eddying Xanthos, offspring of immortal Zeus" (Il. 24, 692–93). A ford is also implied on the outward journey,

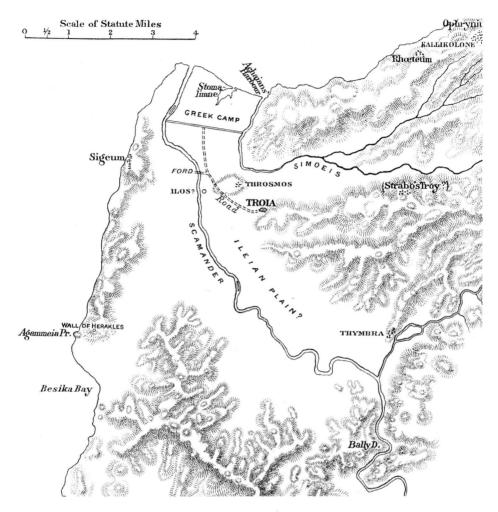

Map 5. Walter Leaf's "Plain of Troy according to the *Iliad*"

as we are told that Priam and Idaios halted their animals "to let them drink in the river" (Il. 24, 349–51).

A glance at map 5 will show that, in Leaf's topography, the course of the river Scamander does not lie between Troy and the Greek camp. In his edition of the *Iliad* Leaf adopted the ingenious, even rather desperate expedient of

5.1 The present-day ford over the Scamander (see map 5). The scene suggests the Homeric epithet "with silvery eddies."

arguing that Priam may have come to the ford, but "in neither of these cases is it said that the ford is crossed." But why then is it mentioned at all?

Leaf appeared to be on stronger ground when he pointed out that the fighting sometimes fluctuates rapidly across the plain without any mention of the river's being crossed by chariots or infantry. Two points may be made in reply to this argumentum ex silentio. First, the Scamander in summer can easily be crossed on foot and has been reported as drying out into disconnected pools. Second, it is not in Homer's manner to mention landmarks like the ford every time the action approaches them. He is economical with such details. But one must emphasise that he *does* mention the ford when the context requires it. At the beginning of the "battle by the river," for instance, the ford is mentioned because it is the escape route of those Trojans who are not trapped and slaughtered in the river itself (Il. 21, 1). In the case of Priam's journey, as Maclaren pointed out, the ford is mentioned because its low banks would have provided easy access to the crossing for his wheeled vehicles.

Over much of the Scamander's course through the lower plain, its present banks are high and sheerly cut, but there is still a ford with low banks on the line between Troy and Beşika Bay. Members of the Troia Projekt have told me that this route is practicable for jeeps and is used by the excavation team (fig. 5.1).[4] One cannot, of course, be sure that the present-day ford corresponds precisely to that envisaged by Homer, but the need for an ancient line of communication with the Beşika Bay coastline and routes to the south establishes a presumption that it must have lain here or hereabouts.

Leaf's quandary about the ford did not arise for Schliemann, who followed what is sometimes known as the "eastern" theory of the course of the Scamander. According to this view the Scamander in ancient times flowed much closer to Troy, following the line of the overflow channel now known as the Kalafat Asmak. The lower part of this channel is also used as an overflow by the Simoeis. The Asmak reaches the sea by a deep inlet near Cape Rhoeteum, which is probably to be identified with Strabo's "harbour of the Achaeans," where some in his day wished to locate the ship station (13, 1, 36; see fig. 2.10). Such a course would bring the river between Troy and a Greek camp on the Hellespont. The "eastern" theory has a certain plausibility because of the existence of many disused flood channels on the lower plain, a feature mentioned by Achilles (Il. 16, 71) and also exploited by Homer in his graphic account of the course of the chariot race at the funeral games of Patroklos (Il. 23, 420–21) (fig. 5.2). It is also a fact that the main outlet of the Menderes is now less close to Kum Kale (Cape Sigeum) than it was 150 years ago, so the river there has swung back somewhat to the east. Leaf, however, refused to regard the Kalafat Asmak as anything more than a flood channel cut in the past few centuries, and modern scientific opinion supports him in this view. The Menderes may have made minor alterations of course in its lower delta in recent centuries, but it seems that north of Troy the river has always followed much the same line roughly midway between the low ridges to east and west.

The parameters of the problem of the location of the ship station were radically altered by the publication in 1980 of new and revolutionary scientific data

5.2 Winter flood damage to the road leading to the ford. "There was a cleft in the surface where the pent-up water of a winter torrent had broken away part of the road and lowered all the ground" (Il. 23, 420–21). It was at just such a narrow and dangerous section of the course that Antilochos forced Menelaos to give ground in the chariot race.

about the evolution of the plain. In the late 1970s a Turkish–American team sank a series of boreholes at various points along the course of the two rivers. The bores penetrated the alluvium, which is more than twenty yards thick in the upper plain, and went well down into the marine deposits that lay below. The cores of sediment secured by this work provided the evidence necessary for a reconstruction of the geomorphology of the plain throughout the Holocene epoch. In particular, the timescale for the progressive alluviation of the area could be determined with much improved accuracy. It became clear that the Schliemann-Leaf assumptions about the position of the shoreline at the time of the Trojan War were no longer sustainable, for the filling in of the lower Sca-

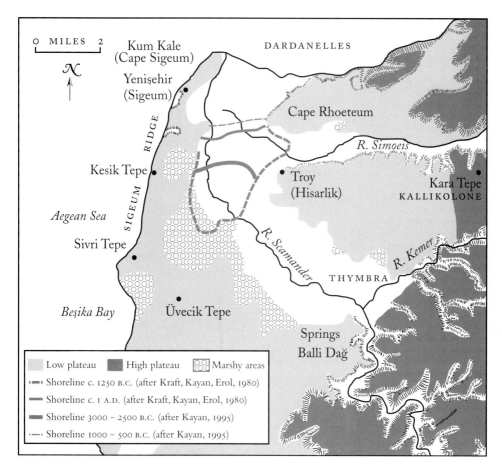

Map 6.   The Plain and Bay of Troy: Recent Geomorphic Reconstructions

mander valley has been completed much more recently than they supposed. In this respect the Scamander valley has been shown to be comparable to that of other major river valleys of western Asia Minor, like those of the Maeander, Kaÿstrios, Hermos, and Caicos, where the extent and rapidity of alluviation over the past three millennia had been much more adequately recognised.[5]

The scientists concluded that in the time of Troy I/II, about four and a half thousand years ago, a broad marine embayment extended south for about six

5.3   An artist's impression of Troy and its bay in the Late Bronze Age. (Photograph reproduced by kind permission of the artist, C. Haussner.)

miles from the present line of the Hellespont, with an arm running up the valley of the Dümrek Su (Simoeis). One must therefore envisage the earliest settlement at Troy as having been established on a sea-girt promontory. Progradation of the plain went ahead steadily down the centuries, but at the time of the transition between Troy VI and Troy VIIa, c. 1250 B.C., the shoreline, in their view, still ran somewhat southwest of the city, and the inhabitants looked across water to the Sigeum Ridge (map 6 and fig. 5.3).

It was immediately obvious that these findings were totally at odds with the Schliemann-Leaf view of the antiquity of the lower plain. In the first preliminary publication of their findings, the American-Turkish team recommended that Homeric scholars "reconsider some of their interpretations in the light of the geological and geographical analysis presented here." I attempted to do precisely that in an article published in 1984.[6]

The problem was to find an alternative site for the Greek camp and ship station. A location on the Hellespont to the north of Troy was ruled out by the

5.4   The "swelling of the plain" on the eastern flank of the Sigeum Ridge. Imbros on the horizon behind.

new data. A site to the east or south of the city would have been a strategic impossibility. The only remaining possibility was to look west across the plain to the Sigeum Ridge and Beşika Bay. It followed that the fighting described in the *Iliad* could not have adhered to a north-south axis, as Schliemann and Leaf had supposed, but must have followed an east-west course. Indeed, with the shoreline of the bay in the position assigned by George Rapp and his colleagues, any Greek assault on Troy must have approached the city across the inner part of the floodplain from the southwest.

If one rethinks the matter in this way, Homer's account of how the fighting fluctuated from one side of the Scamander to the other begins to look much more like an authentic tradition of a real conflict. The "swelling of the plain" can be envisaged at the point where the level alluvium ends and the ground begins to rise to form the Sigeum Ridge (fig. 5.4). Nor is there any problem about the details of Priam's journey. The narrative in *Iliad* book 24 is perfectly in accord with the topographical realities of the area.

Other aspects of the Homeric narrative also fit much more easily into the revised picture of the environment. In particular, there is a passage in *Iliad* book 10 where the Trojan spy Dolon has been captured by Odysseus and Diomedes and is pressed into giving a fairly detailed account of the disposition of the Trojan forces, particularly that of the allied contingents (Il. 10, 427–31):

> I will answer your questions truly and exactly. *On the wing*
> *towards the sea* are Carians, Paionians with their crooked
> bows, Leleges, Kaukones, and divine Pelasgians. *On the*
> *wing towards Thymbra* lie Lycians, proud Mysians, and
> Phrygian and Maeonian charioteers.

The crucial topographical information is contained in the italicised words. The right wing of the Trojan battle order rests along the sea; the left wing extends towards Thymbra. The name Thymbra is associated by Strabo (13, 1, 35) with the southern portion of the Trojan plain and in particular with the junction of the river Thymbrios with the Scamander some fifty stades (approximately six miles) from Ilion. Strabo also refers to a sanctuary of Thymbraean Apollo in the neighbourhood. These indications serve to fix Thymbra to the inner recesses of the Trojan plain southeast of Troy, where the modern Kemer Su joins the main river (see map 6). It is uncertain whether there was an ancient town there. That point, however, is immaterial. What matters is the very good military sense made by a Trojan line of battle covering the southwestern approaches to Troy itself, given that on the north and northwest the city was protected by an embayment running south from the Hellespont, and that any Greek attack would be coming across the plain from the general direction of the Sigeum Ridge.

The Homeric indications point clearly to just such a disposition of forces,

5.5 View from the southernmost section of the lower town of Troy looking across the valley to the ridge that runs from Çıplak to New Kalafat. Trees lining the Scamander are visible in the plain to the right, with Üvecik Tepe on the horizon behind.

deployed with their right flank resting on the inner shore of the bay near the city and guarding the edge of the plateau that runs southeast from the modern village of New Kalafat (fig. 5.5). An east-west rather than a north-south axis for the fighting is here supported by topographical details that appear to be an ancient part of the tradition. In particular, the placing of two chariot detachments well away from the coastline, and so on a firmer part of the plain, rings true. I would suggest that the passage under discussion could be a very ancient piece of saga material deriving from the actual Trojan War. The mention of Thymbra is really more appropriate to a defensive posture of the Trojan forces and does not so well suit the picture developed earlier in the book of the Trojan forces already on the left bank of the river, poised for attack "on the swelling of the plain" close to the Greek ships.

The picture of Trojan forces deployed to cover the southwest approaches to the city also helps to elucidate two topographical problems that arise in connection

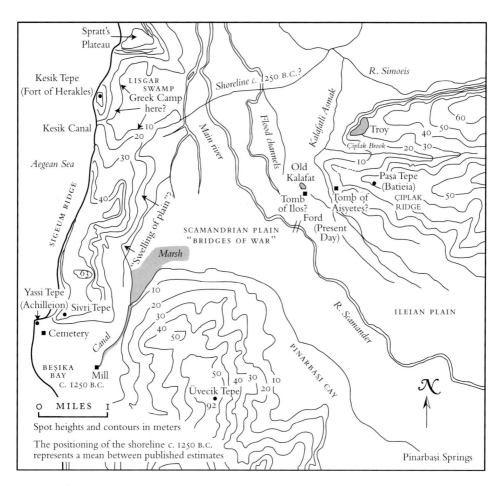

Map 7. The Environs of Troy

with the first mustering of these forces as described towards the end of *Iliad* book 2. The problems concern the location of the tomb of Aisyetes, from whose summit the Trojan scout Polites kept watch on the Greek forces, and the location of the hill Batieia (alias the tomb of Myrinê). The places are named and described in the short piece of bridging narrative that links the Greek and Trojan catalogues. In such a highly traditional context any suggestion that Homer could have invented the landmarks seems most unlikely. It is also to be observed that the military proce-

5.6　Paşa Tepe on the Çıplak ridge, identified with Homer's "Tomb of Myrinê," alias Batieia ("Thorn Hill").

dures associated with them make good sense in relation to a defensive strategy for Troy (map 7).

　　I shall first consider the identification of Batieia. Homer describes its location in some detail (Il. 2, 811–15):

> Outside the town and some way off in the plain, there is a
> high mound, with open ground on every side, which
> men call Thorn Hill [Batieia], but the immortals know as
> the tomb of dancing Myrinê. It was here that the Trojans
> and their allies now formed up in battle order. (Trans.
> E. V. Rieu)[7]

There is one area only that answers well to all the points in this description. This is the low spurlike ridge to the west of Çıplak village on which stands the large tumulus now known as Paşa Tepe (map 7 and fig. 5.6). The ridge is separated from the projecting apron of the lower town of Troy by a small valley down which flows the Çıplak brook, so it is indeed "outside the town and some way off in the plain." The ground rises gently on the northern flank of the ridge, but

5.7   The steep outer edge of the Çıplak ridge running from New Kalafat to the vicinity of the Batieia tumulus (Paşa Tepe).

considerable sections of its southern side fall quite steeply down to the main floodplain (fig. 5.7). A chariot could easily drive around its perimeter, a point that agrees well with the phrase "with open ground on every side." Its spreading slopes afford ample ground for the muster of many thousands of men in battle array. Their ranks facing out across the plain from the ridgeline would present a suitably defiant front to an enemy coming across the plain from the southwest. The position is only a few hundred yards from the newly discovered South Gate in the lower part of Troy, a fact that answers well to Homer's statement that "all the gates of the city were opened" when Hector led out his forces (Il. 2, 809).

The Paşa Tepe tumulus is an impressive defining feature rising roughly halfway along the ridge. It is still surrounded by dense thorny thickets that make Thorn Hill (Batieia) an appropriate name for the whole area as well as the actual mound. "Tomb of dancing Myrinê" would have been an alternative name for the tumulus itself. Schliemann and his wife excavated the tumulus in 1873 and

5.8 Paşa Tepe under excavation by Sophie Schliemann (after *Ilios,* fig. 1514).

again in 1890 and recovered potsherds that they described as both archaic and prehistoric (fig. 5.8). There is a good probability that the "prehistoric" are those now in the Schliemann collection in Berlin and wrongly labelled as coming from the "Tumulus of Priam" (at Ballı Dağ). Experts think that these sherds date from Troy VI/VII, which means that the mound, unlike most of the other tumuli around the plain, would be old enough to figure in a bardic tradition going back to the Late Bronze Age.[8]

If Hector mustered his forces on Batieia to meet an expected attack from the southwest, his scouts must have been keeping watch in the same direction. This is what we find if we look at the account of the activities of Polites, which comes in the same stretch of narrative shortly before the mention of Batieia (Il. 2, 792–94):

> He [Polites], trusting in his fleetness of foot, used to sit as
> a scout for the Trojans on the top of the funeral mound
> of old man Aisyetes, watching for any Achaean advance
> from the ships.

5.9   The view from Paşa Tepe across the Çıplak valley to Hisarlik (the low ridge on the right). Imbros appears on the horizon.

Schliemann took Paşa Tepe to be Homer's Batieia and also Strabo's tomb of Aisyetes. This will hardly do. Defining data for the location of the tomb of Aisyetes are given by Strabo in his statement that it was five stades (about 3,000 feet) from Ilion on the road to Alexandria Troas (13, 1, 37). Paşa Tepe suits the distance given but lies well off the line of the road to Alexandria Troas. This road must have headed out into the plain from Ilion in a southwesterly direction, making for the Scamander in the neighbourhood of the present-day ford and then running on past Üvecik Tepe (fig. 5.10). It probably skirted the western point of the spur where Kalafat village now stands. The spur terminates here in a steep little brow overlooking the plain, which would have made a very suitable lookout point, with an uninterrupted view across to the Sigeum Ridge and Beşika Bay. No ancient tumulus is now to be seen in or near modern Kalafat, but a possible location is pictured in fig. 5.10.

5.10   A possible location for the tomb of Aisyetes and the lookout post of Polites. The mound in the foreground marks the end of the Çıplak ridge. The dirt road in the plain beyond it on the left indicates the probable direction of the ancient road to Alexandria Troas. Above the road, on the horizon, Üvecik Tepe is visible on its low plateau. Farther to the right, the peak of Tenedos appears over the plateau at the point where it dips down to Beşika Bay.

In these proposed locations for Thorn Hill (Batieia) and Polites' lookout post (the tomb of old Aisyetes) the reader will again recognise a situation appropriate to an east-west rather than a north-south axis for the fighting. There must have been a strong local tradition for placing Aisyetes' tomb by the road to Alexandria, for Strabo and his authorities saw that this was inconsistent with the then-current supposition that the Greek camp lay on the Hellespont to the north of Troy. Strabo records the argument that it would have been much more sensible for Polites to have kept watch for Greek sorties from the Pergamos itself, for it was both higher and also nearer to the ship station (13, 1, 37).

The context in Strabo has considerable interest for the history of Trojan topography because of its mention of two local authorities, Demetrios of Scepsis and a woman called Hestiaea, an antiquarian from Alexandria Troas. Demetrios, a prolific author, was clearly Strabo's main source, for he is mentioned at the outset of the whole section on Ilion (13, 1, 27). Here we get the interesting additional information that Demetrios in his turn relied, at least to some extent, on Hestiaea (13, 1, 36). We learn that she wrote a treatise (not extant) on the *Iliad* in which she enquired into the question of whether the Trojan War was fought around New Ilion. She also raised questions about Homer's conception of the plain of Troy, pointing out that "the plain now visible in front of the city" was not then in existence, an insight for which she deserves much credit.

It is clear that neither Demetrios nor Hestiaea accepted the view of the people of Ilion that their city was built on the site of ancient Troy. Demetrios, who flourished in the first half of the second century B.C., was partly motivated by civic pride. As a citizen of Scepsis, in the heart of ancient Dardania, he despised the upstart population of Hellenistic Ilion, which had been a place of no consequence before the patronage of Alexander the Great. He could not bring himself to accept that Ilion had a more glorious past than his own city. But he also had some interesting arguments, based partly on strategic considerations and partly on Homeric passages. Obviously he recognised a debt to Hestiaea, but it is no longer possible to apportion credit between them, and I shall not attempt to do so.

If one reads between the lines in Strabo, one can get some insight into contemporary tourism. When visitors came to Hellenistic Ilion to view the scene of the Trojan War, the inhabitants used to point down to the shore of the Hellespont and to the mouth of the Scamander, then only twenty stades (a little more than two miles) away, indicating that the ship station lay on the beach "in the direction of Sigeum" (Strabo 13, 1, 36).[9] Demetrios recognised that this location was a strategic impossibility, particularly in light of the fact that the shoreline would have come much closer to Ilion at the time of the Trojan War. No general, he argued, would have been so foolish as to put his unfortified base down on the shore within a mile or so of his objective. Such a position would have been militarily untenable. But instead of looking for a different campsite, Demetrios decided that the site of Homeric Troy must be sought farther inland. His solution, which Strabo adopts, was to place ancient Troy some thirty stades (three to four miles) east of Ilion, at the site of a modest Hellenistic settlement known as the Village of the Ilians.

Demetrios's theory is in some ways analogous to the "false Troy" theory of modern times. It appealed to the academic mind because it seemed to suit various indications in Homer. In particular, it offered a good solution for the problem of Polites' lookout post. A scout positioned at Aisyetes' tomb at the western end of the Çıplak-Kalafat ridge could detect movement around the shores of Troy Bay in good time to report it back to "Troy" at the Ilian village site some three or four miles to the east. It was an ingenious theory, but it must be rejected for the same reasons as the Ballı Dağ theory: the absence of adequate Bronze Age remains on the proposed site.

It is time to leave these Hellenistic speculations and return to the Homeric narrative. Odysseus and Diomedes also extract another important piece of information from Dolon. He tells them that "Hector is holding a council of war with his advisers by the tomb of Ilos well away from the din" (Il. 10, 414–16). The word for "din," *phloisbos*, is elsewhere in the *Iliad* used of actual fighting, but in the compound form, *poluphloisbos,* is strongly associated with the roar of surf on a beach. Here it could refer either to the distant sound of the sea or to the confused murmur of the encamped host. Either sense would suit the location of Hector's command post in the rear of his army and some distance south of the shoreline of the bay. The passage contains the first mention of the tomb of Ilos, which is quite a notable landmark, receiving three more mentions in the *Iliad*.

At the start of the next day's fighting, as described in book 11, the Trojans are routed by the fierce onslaught of Agamemnon and stream back past Ilos's tomb towards Troy (Il. 11, 166–68). But then Agamemnon is wounded in the hand by a spear thrust and has to retire from the fighting. The tide of battle sweeps back again to the tomb, and we find Paris using the grave marker on top of it to steady his aim as he shoots an arrow and wounds Diomedes (Il. 11, 369 ff.).

In his account of Priam's journey, Homer gives us a final indication that the tomb of Ilos lay close to the ford of the Scamander (Il. 24, 349–51): "When they [Priam and Idaios] had driven past the great tomb of Ilos, they halted their mules and horses to let them drink from the river." This happened on their outward journey, so the tomb must be envisaged as situated on the right bank of the river.

The now-deserted village of Old Kalafat lay in the plain in this area (see map 7). When Charles Newton visited it in the middle of the nineteenth century, he noted the presence there of a structure that sounds as though it might have been a burial mound: "North of the pavement is a small mound, the top of which forms a level area; its north side is a steep bank running down to the plain below. Here fragments of black Hellenic pottery are found." A small steep-sided mound with a levelled top in this part of the plain would almost certainly have been a man-made tumulus, but unfortunately no trace of it now seems to remain. Cook looked for it without success, remarking that "this mound seems likely to have lain close to the road leading from Ilion to Alexandria Troas." This is an important topographical point, for that road, as noted, would have been making for the Scamander ford, near which Homer locates the Ilos tomb with its funerary pillar. One wonders whether the levelled top of Newton's mound once carried a stone marker. Cook thinks that Newton's mound might answer to Homer's tomb of Aisyetes, but I would prefer to regard it as a candidate for the as yet unidentified tomb of Ilos.[10]

The tomb of Ilos was clearly an important landmark for the Trojans, enshrining as it did the memory of Priam's royal grandfather, after whom the city of Ilios was named (see Appendix 1). It may well have given its name to the Ileian plain. Paris was Ilos's great-grandson, and his successful shot at Diomedes from his ancestor's tomb puts a second Achaean champion out of action. Odysseus and Eurypylos are soon also wounded, and by the end of book 11 the Greeks have been forced to retire back behind the wall and ditch that guard their camp.

5.11   The present shoreline of Beşika Bay leading around to the headland formerly known as Cape Troy (Beşika Burnu), now Yassi Tepe.

Following Homer's indications we have traced the line of Trojan advance from their city past the end of the Çıplak ridge and then out into the plain past the tomb of Ilos to the Scamander. The problem of the precise location of their objective, the Achaean camp and ship station, must now be considered in more detail.

The hypothesis that the ship station was situated at Beşika Bay was first advanced by Alfred Brückner in a lecture in Berlin in 1912.[11] Brückner had collaborated with Dörpfeld in excavation at Troy and in the publication of *Troia und Ilion* in 1902. He now won Dörpfeld over to the Beşika Bay theory, which had also been independently suggested by a Bavarian businessman named Oscar Mey. In October 1924 Dörpfeld and Mey conducted a joint operation at Beşika Bay, with Mey trenching the foreshore and Dörpfeld working on the two tumuli that overlook the area (Sivri Tepe and Üvecik Tepe). Their short campaign did not produce any conclusive results, however, and they were unable to resume work because of intensified military security in the area.[12]

In the 1930s a French scholar, Charles Vellay, attacked the Beşika Bay hypothesis with arguments based on Homeric texts and, in Cook's opinion, won the battle "according to the rules of the game." Thereafter the hypothesis lay dormant until revived by the new geophysical findings about the Trojan plain, as well as renewed archaeological work in the area itself.[13]

As in the case of the plain fronting the Hellespont, geomorphological surveys have shown that Beşika Bay was much more deeply indented at the time of the Trojan War. At c. 1200 B.C. the inner part of the bay lay well to the east of the present shoreline and afforded a commodious anchorage for sailing vessels coasting up from the south and delayed from entering the Hellespont by wind and current. They could wait in a bay that then had a sandy beach and was well sheltered from the prevailing northerly winds by a low ridge running out to a small but prominent headland formerly known as Beşika Burnu, but recently renamed Yassi Tepe (fig. 5.11).

The headland of Yassi Tepe (Cape Troy in older maps) fronts the sea steeply on three sides, and its landward access is also steep. It has a flat-topped oval summit, making it a small but easily defensible stronghold commanding the approaches to the harbour. The site stands about ninety feet above sea level, and inland from it the ground rises gently to about 165 feet. Here rises a great tumulus, formerly Beşik Tepe, but now called Sivri Tepe (fig. 5.12).

Yassi Tepe had long been recognised as an ancient site from the presence of surface sherds but had not been systematically explored until Manfred Korfmann commenced work there in 1982. He continued to excavate in the area until 1988.[14] Korfmann's excavations have shown that Yassi Tepe was inhabited at three widely separated epochs: first, at the time of Troy I, and perhaps even earlier than 3000 B.C.; second, for a brief but significant period in the thirteenth century B.C.; and third from c. 600 B.C. on into the Hellenistic Age. In regard to the third phase of occupation, his findings confirm Cook's well-judged conjecture that the previously unidentified site of Achilleion was to be found at Yassi Tepe.[15]

5.12   Sivri (Beşik) Tepe, a Hellenistic reconstruction of a tumulus probably venerated as the burial mount of Achilles.

Achilleion was a small fortified settlement founded from Mytilenê in Lesbos in the early years of the sixth century B.C. Its importance for the present study lies in its name, and in the fact that Strabo (13, 1, 39) says that the tomb of Achilles lay in its vicinity. So the identification of the Yassi Tepe site as Achilleion makes it virtually certain that the nearby tumulus of Sivri Tepe was anciently regarded as the hero's grave monument. Korfmann's exploration of the great conical mound has shown that in its present form it dates from the Hellenistic period, but there are indications that it is an elaborate reconstruction of a much earlier barrow. It stands on a rocky hillock, and, in its Hellenistic form, measures more than 250 yards in circumference, with a height of nearly 50 feet. It was faced with white limestone and must have been a very prominent landmark, "far-seen from the sea," as Homer says (Od. 24, 83; fig. 5.13).

5.13   An excavated area on the eastern flank of Sivri (Beşik) Tepe, showing the
layered construction, with some of the white limestone facing visible.

Earlier travellers identified the tomb of Achilles with a smaller tumulus near
Yenişehir at the northern end of the Sigeum Ridge. But two separate excava-
tions, the first by an agent of Choiseul-Gouffier in 1787 and the second by
Schliemann in 1882, showed that it could not be earlier than about 500 B.C.[16]

If there was a Late Bronze Age monument to Achilles it must be looked for
in the vicinity of Beşika Bay, and that may well be considered a point in favour
of that site as the location of the Achaean camp and ship station. A Mycenaean
presence in the area is confirmed by Korfmann's findings from the second phase of
occupation on Yassi Tepe, and also by his discovery in 1984 of an important but
enigmatic cemetery nearby. The cemetery was located on level ground between
two and three hundred yards southeast of the summit of Yassi Tepe and within
twenty yards of the ancient shoreline. It was surrounded by a single wall and contained in all about two hundred graves. Many of the burials were in large *pithoi*
(storage jars) whose mouths were covered by stone slabs. Remains of men,
women, and at least two children were identified. Some of the dead had been cre-
mated, but most had been inhumed.

One remarkable finding was that a number of the graves appeared to be cenotaphs. Korfmann suggested that these may have been constructed to do honour to persons lost at sea. Another possibility is that they were temporary repositories for the remains of warriors fallen in combat, whose ashes were later removed and brought back to their relatives. Nestor proposes just such a course for battle casualties when he tells the Achaeans (Il. 7, 333–35): "Let us consume them with fire a little away from the ships, so that each of us may bring home their bones for their children, whenever we return to our native land." This passage has been condemned as a later Attic interpolation, a verdict that must now be reconsidered in the light of Korfmann's findings.

The most elaborate sepulchre was a substantial gravehouse in *megaron* form, measuring more than four by three yards, and situated at the centre of a group of associated burials, if not of the entire cemetery. In its inner chamber stood an urn containing remains of three separate cremations. Fragments of one or two partly melted bronze objects that could have been swords or daggers were also recovered, along with the remains of a bone or ivory comb. The grave goods included a fine Mycenaean mixing bowl and dishes, together with fragments of jewellery made of precious stones and gold. A large *pithos* in the porch, probably an intrusive interment, yielded the first Mycenaean seal to be found in situ in Asia Minor. The seal is a black lentoid with a carving of a human head. It was missed by the tomb robbers, who otherwise seem to have systematically rifled the cemetery.

Present indications are that the cemetery is to be dated somewhat later than the second phase of occupation at Yassi Tepe. It seems to have been in use for a comparatively short time during the period when Troy VIh was in transition to Troy VIIa. This preliminary finding, if confirmed, may well provide significant support for the view that the Trojan War of Greek tradition was a protracted siege of Troy VIh. The cemetery on the ancient shoreline of Beşika Bay was an elaborate, homogeneous, and short-lived assemblage of interments, unrelated, so far as is known, to any permanent habitation centre in the neighbourhood. As such, it could be explained as resulting from a temporary concentration of

5.14   The view eastwards from the top of Kesik Tepe. The ploughed field below the mound leads down to the Lisgar swamp area, now well cultivated. On the far side of the plain (near centre) the yellow line is a field of corn growing where the lower town of Troy once stood.

Mycenaean mercantile activity in the area when Beşika Bay was being used as a supply base for a military expedition against Troy.

Leaf called Beşika Bay the sea gate of the Trojan plain, and its harbour could have been not only a supply base but also the site of the Achaean camp and ship station, as Brückner supposed. This location would suit the concept of an east-west axis for the course of the fighting described in the *Iliad*. But there are other specific indications in the text which do not agree so well with Beşika Bay. Chief among these is a thrice-repeated formula that brings the retreating Achaean forces back from Troy "to the ships and the Hellespont" (Il. 15, 233; 18, 150; 23,

5.15   Kesik Tepe seen from the east.

2). A number of recurrent formulae like "silver-studded sword" or "shield like a tower" can be shown to embody information derived from the Late Bronze Age, and it is a reasonable supposition that this formula is also an ancient part of the tradition. Advocates of the Beşika Bay location argue that "Hellespont" in Homer can refer to the sea outside the straits as well as to the waterway now called the Dardanelles. But detailed examination of Homeric usage rules out this possibility (see pp. 41–44). The Homeric formula describes a campsite opening directly onto the actual Hellespont in a way that Beşika Bay can never have done. Because we now know that an arm of the Hellespont lay between Bronze Age Troy and the northern part of the Sigeum Ridge, the camp, I suggest, should be envisaged as lying on the east-facing slopes of that ridge.

A possible location exists in the area below the prominent mound known as Kesik (Demetrios) Tepe (see map 6 and figs. 5.14 and 5.15). Here as elsewhere the seaward side of the ridge is formed by a line of low cliffs fronting the Aegean, but to the east the ground slopes gently down to an expanse of level ground known as the Lisgar (Ilica) swamp. The swamp has been drained since the 1960s, but it is marked as a marsh or even a lake on earlier maps, like that of William Gell, the early nineteenth-century topographer (see fig. 3.13). The area is partly enclosed by two arms of the ridge that run out for about a mile until they too merge into the main floodplain. Brückner thought that the Lisgar swamp may have provided a south harbour for Sigeum. I believe that in the Late Bronze Age it could have been a well-sheltered lagoon opening off the larger bay in front of Troy. Professor Ilhan Kayan recently sank five boreholes in a line across the swamp from its inmost point to its outer limit, and the one in the middle yielded marine shells with a radiocarbon dating of c. 1400 B.C.[17]

The slopes around the Lisgar swamp would have provided ample space for the beached ships and living quarters of a large force, and the area is well supplied with fresh water. The epic tradition about the Greek encampment contains two features that suit this proposed situation very well: first, that it was on rising ground, and second, that it looked directly onto the main battlefield on the plain.

Homer follows his usual practice in giving his most detailed picture of the camp at the moment when it is about to become the main scene of the action. At the start of *Iliad* book 14, Nestor from his hut hears the din of battle close at hand. He decides to go to a lookout point (line 8), and from there he sees that the Achaeans have been routed and their fortification wall breached (13–15). Next he meets Agamemnon, Odysseus, and Diomedes "coming up from the ships" (28).[18]

The arrangement of the ships is then described (30–36):

> The ships had been beached on the shore of the surging
> sea well away from the fighting. They dragged the first
> ones inland and built a wall at their sterns. For the beach,
> though broad, could not contain all the ships, and the
> force was cramped. So they ranged them in rows, and
> filled all the long mouth of the shore between the
> enclosing headlands.

Aristarchus, as we learn from ancient comment on this passage, compared the rows of beached ships to "seats in a theatre" and to "rungs of a ladder." Both comparisons strongly imply that in his opinion the ship station was on rising ground. Such a location must be sought on the Sigeum Ridge rather than the alluvial plain, and the "theatre" effect is much more marked at the Lisgar swamp than at Beşika Bay.

That the camp looked directly onto the plain and across to Troy is clearly implicit in Homer's picture of the sleepless night spent by Agamemnon before the second engagement (Il. 10, 11–12): "Whenever he looked towards the Trojan plain, he wondered at the many watch fires blazing before Ilios, at the sound of flutes and pipes, and at the murmuring from the host of men." Similarly, Achilles, standing on the stern of a ship to watch the progress of the fighting, catches sight of Nestor's chariot leaving the fray (Il. 11, 596–601).

Troy is in full view from the slopes surrounding the Lisgar swamp, but it is not possible to see the city from the shoreline of Beşika Bay. Furthermore, considering the strategy of the situation, one must surely suppose that the commander of the Achaean expedition would have looked for a secure and easily fortifiable base for his warships. Beşika Bay does not fulfill these requirements. A camp there would have faced onto the Aegean with its back turned to its objective. It would have had no natural features to protect it and would have been particularly open to attack from the low plateau that backs the bay on the south and southeast. A force of Trojan chariots swinging around from the upper plain would have had unlimited opportunities for penetration here along an extended front.

Beşika Bay offered commercial rather than military advantages to an invading force. Korfmann's excavations at Yassi Tepe (Beşika Burnu) indicate that a Mycenaean trading post was located there during the latter years of Troy VI, so there must have been some harbour facilities close under the tepe. These could have been defended by a garrison there and could have served as a supply point for the main fighting force encamped farther up the Sigeum Ridge. The ridge, with the Aegean on one side and the Bronze Age bay on the other, has been well compared to a Gibraltar at the northwest corner of Asia Minor. Homer mentions ships bringing wine for the troops from Lemnos (Il. 7, 467), and one can easily imagine them putting in below Yassi Tepe (Beşika Burnu), with wagons bringing goods on to the camp by road. A local road is mentioned in the night reconnaissance of Diomedes and Odysseus (Il. 10, 274).

5.16 The V-shaped cut in the Sigeum Ridge that is now called the Kesik Canal.

If the main war camp was located farther north on the Sigeum Ridge near Kesik Tepe, it could have been approached only on a comparatively narrow front. Further protection would have been afforded by marshes in the plain and the generally more rugged nature of the adjacent flanks of the ridge. The break line along the western edge of the floodplain and the rising ground between it and the Aegean supply a natural feature that answers well to Homer's "swelling of the plain." As noted, this feature is consistently represented as lying close to the Greek camp.

Attention may also be drawn to a striking natural feature called the Kesik Canal (fig. 5.16). This is a natural depression that appears to have been enlarged by human agency, though there is no evidence that it ever carried water. It now appears as a V-shaped cut connecting the seashore with the innermost southern recess of the Lisgar swamp. Over much of its length it would have formed an impassable barrier for any chariot attempting to reach the rear of a ship station in the area. The defensive potential of the Kesik Canal could have been readily enhanced by earthworks extending down to the shore of the Bronze Age bay (see map 6).[19]

The ship station that I am proposing could have been attacked by land only on its comparatively short southern flank. When I first made the suggestion, it was criticised as being "incompatible with two major Homeric assumptions: first, that the Trojans attacked the camp frontally and not from one end; secondly, that the ships were drawn up along the shore of the Hellespont itself."[20] But from the point of view of the inhabitants of Troy, any hostile base on the shores of their bay could be described as on the shore of the Hellespont. Nor can I find anything in the text of the *Iliad* that rules out the notion of a side attack on the Greek camp. Indeed, I would regard the notion of a frontal assault as a modern rather than a Homeric assumption, based as it is on an untenable view of the siting of the ship station on the present shore of the Hellespont. The notion of a side attack has positive merits in relation to Homer's account of Hector's assault on the ships. The narrative of *Iliad* book 15 focuses on the tenacious resistance of Ajax in his sector of the ship station, while Achilles and the Myrmidons remain detached and uninvolved on the other wing. I submit that this situation is militarily more understandable if the Trojan attack was concentrated on a narrow front on one side only of a camp at the Lisgar swamp.

One other natural feature in the area calls for comment. This is the flat-topped conical mound named Kesik (Demetrios) Tepe that stands on the ridge overlooking the sea abut four hundred yards north of the Kesik Canal (see fig. 5.15). The mound rises to a height of about forty feet and has all the appearance of being a man-made tumulus. Most of the earlier travellers identified it as the tomb of Antilochos, but it is in fact a natural limestone outcrop or butte. This means that we can be sure it was in existence at the time of the Trojan War, which is more than can be said for most of the tumuli that ring the Trojan plain.

Choiseul-Gouffier identified Kesik Tepe with the "lofty earth-mounded wall" (or "fort") mentioned in the *Iliad* as the place where Herakles used to take refuge from a sea monster that plagued Troy in the time of Laomedon (20, 144–48). This identification has much to commend it. Legend associated Herakles with the Sigeum Ridge, placing there his rescue of Laomedon's daughter Hesionê from the monster's clutches. Kesik Tepe is a natural lookout point, commanding good views of the whole coastline from Beşika Bay to the mouth of the Hellespont. When Homer says that the fort was made for Herakles by the Trojans and Pallas Athena, this need have involved no more than a levelling of the top of the mound and the provision of the earth rampart implied by the Homeric epithet "earth-mounded." Professor Kayan takes it to be "a natural hill which has been shaped artificially by man."[21]

Homer's main purpose in introducing the fort of Herakles at this point in the narrative is to provide a clearly recognisable fixed point from which the gods supporting the Greeks can watch the developing battle in the plain below. Kesik Tepe fulfills this function admirably. It is a distinctive landmark and does indeed provide an excellent vantage point overlooking the whole plain, with Troy in full view three miles to the east (Il. 20, 144–52):

> With these words the dark-haired god led them to the
> mounded and lofty fort of godlike Herakles. The
> Trojans and Pallas Athena had fashioned it for him as a
> refuge from the monster whenever it should chase him
> back from the beach towards the plain. There Poseidon
> and the other gods [those supporting the Greeks] took
> their seat, with unbroken cloud wreathing their
> shoulders. And they [the gods supporting the Trojans]
> sat down on the other side [of the plain] on the brows
> of Kallikolonê with you, Phoebus Apollo, and Ares,
> sacker of cities.

The topographical indications are clear and emphatic. Antithetical viewing points are named on either side of the Trojan plain, and the rival groups of gods look down from them on the city soon to be sacked by Ares. Homer is not merely setting the scene but also deftly concentrating our attention on the theatre of war that lies between the heights on either side. The fort of Herakles forms the scenic and dramatic counterpart to the hill of Kallikolonê, whose identification with Kara Tepe has been documented earlier. Like modern sports fans, both groups of gods get literally behind their sides to support them from their respective vantage points. Map 6 shows that Kara Tepe is exactly opposite Kesik Tepe in the sense that a line drawn from one to the other passes through Hisarlik. The reader will also note that the line passes through the area that I have proposed for the Greek ship station (see map 7).

I find the same alignment implicit also in an earlier topographical passage in the same book (Il. 20, 47–53):

> When the Olympians began to mingle with the throng of
> men, violent Strife who rouses hosts to battle lifted her
> head, and Athena raised the war cry, now standing by *the*
> *dug ditch outside the wall*, now shouting loud and long on
> *the resounding headlands*. And Ares like a dark stormcloud
> shouted back from the other side, now urging on the
> Trojans with sharp cries from *the highest point of the city*,
> and now running back along the Simoeis to *Kallikolonê*.

The later "fort of Herakles" passage introduces a lull in the action; here all is tumult, noise, and movement. At one moment Ares is in the Pergamos of Troy; then he is dashing back along the line of the river Simoeis to Kallikolonê. At one moment Athena is standing by the fortifications of the Greek camp; then she is up on the "resounding headlands," presumably moving along them.

Where are we to imagine these "resounding headlands"? I suggest that they should be identified with the line of sea-beaten cliffs that front the Aegean on the western side of the Sigeum Ridge (fig. 5.17).[22] This suggestion brings the passage just cited into close association with the "fort of Herakles" passage. They are topographical doublets. Homer has the same scene in mind in both passages, but his point of view has moved, as Poseidon puts it, "from beaten path to lookout point" (Il. 20, 137). "Beaten path" is appropriate to the frantic movement noted in lines 47–53, whereas "lookout point" is the theme of the much less turbulent lines 144–52. The mention of Kallikolonê in both passages helps to tie them together. Pergamos and camp are explicitly mentioned in the

5.17   A view of the Sigeum Ridge looking north from Yassi Tepe.

"movement" passage and must be thought of as in the line of vision of the watching gods in the "lookout point" passage.[23]

Each passage supports and amplifies the other as they depict the same scene with interlocking detail. The "lookout point" associates the Simoeis with Kalli-kolonê; the "movement" passage adds the detail that the vantage point is on the "brow" of the hill. One names the fort of Herakles (Kesik Tepe), whose presence in the other is implied by the mention of "resounding headlands" near the Greek camp. These resounding headlands answer well to the steep outer escarpment of the Sigeum Ridge, whence, as the "lookout point" passage informs us, the sea monster used to chase Herakles back from beach to plain. As fig. 5.17 shows, there is indeed a narrow beach below the cliffs on which Kesik Tepe stands.

Something must now be said about the highly contentious question of the wall or walls that protected the Achaean ship station. Homer clearly depicts the erection of a great wall and ditch, as proposed by Nestor, in the tenth year of the war (Il. 7, 336–43):

> Let us heap up one single mound over the pyre, bringing
> out [the soil] from the plain. And let us build near it a lofty
> fortification as a protection for the ships and ourselves. In
> it let us make well-fitted gates so that chariots may drive
> through it. Outside it, but not far away, let us dig a deep
> ditch to hold back horses and fighting men so that the
> stout Trojan battle line may not overwhelm us.

The carrying out of the proposal is later recorded in virtually the same words (Il. 7, 435–41). This elaborate defensive system then becomes the focal point for the fierce fighting described in book 12.

It is hard to believe that the Achaeans would have left their camp without any protection during the earlier years of the war, and in fact the account of the setting up of the ship station mentions the first beaching of the ships and the building of a wall at their sterns as part of the initial establishment of the bridgehead on Trojan soil. Common prudence would have required that the camp be fortified at once, and I agree with those who regard this first wall as a separate and earlier structure, standing very close to the ships, and not superseded by Nestor's later and more elaborate fortification.[24]

Presumably the building of this first wall formed part of the wider bardic tradition about the earlier phases of the war, and as such receives only cursory mention in the *Iliad*. Nestor's wall, by contrast, though described in considerable detail, has features which may incline us to think that it is an imaginative addition to the saga made by Homer himself. It appears overnight, provides a dramatically effective backdrop for the fierce struggle for the camp, and is totally obliterated after the end of the war by divine agency. Homer claims to know that Poseidon disliked it because he feared its fame might eclipse the walls of

Troy, which he and Apollo had built (Il. 7, 451–53). In this passage Homer is in effect comparing Nestor's wall to the walls of Troy, and thus perhaps indicating the materials on which his imaginative construction is based.

At the beginning of book 12 the poet temporarily suspends the onward march of the narrative to give what amounts to an excursus on the later fate of the wall. The passage reads as though it might have been designed to forestall objections. One can imagine a contemporary saying to Homer: "Where was this great wall around the Greek camp? I've been to Troy and could see no trace of it." So we read (Il. 12, 24–30):

> Phoebus Apollo turned all the mouths of the rivers
> together, and sent the flood against the wall for nine days.
> Zeus poured down continuous rain the quicker to
> submerge the fortifications. Trident in hand, the
> earthshaker himself uprooted all the footings of stone and
> timber that the Achaeans had laid with such toil,
> consigned them to the waters, and made all smooth
> beside the swift-flowing Hellespont.

This passage is realistic in its physical details and could be based on personal observation of the wholesale flooding that used to be commonplace in the lower Scamander plain before dykes and water abstraction introduced better control of the waters. But with regard to Nestor's wall, Homer's overall purpose in composing the excursus was, in my opinion, correctly summed up by Aristotle in the pithy comment: "The man who imagined it made it disappear."[25]

There is a good case, then, for supposing that Nestor's wall existed only in Homer's imagination, but in design and construction it can be seen to bear a strong resemblance to the outer fortifications of Troy as revealed by recent excavation. The Trojan system was designed in relation to chariot warfare as practised in the Late Bronze Age. The outer ditch was constructed some distance in front of the wall and was clearly intended to hold up the advance of chariots and render their occupants vulnerable to attack by arrows or sling stones. This is exactly the picture we find in Homer. He clearly envisages a considerable space between ditch and wall, for an advance guard of seven hundred men is able to bivouac there (Il. 9, 79–88). When the Trojans attack the next day, Hector's horses are brought up short on the edge of the ditch and stand whinnying in fear, unable to jump it or pass through it (Il. 12, 50–54). Most of the Trojans then dismount and muster for an infantry assault, but Asios with his chariot tries to rush one of the gates, which is still open to allow the routed Greeks to retreat to safety. Here he meets determined resistance from two Greek champions who hold their ground in front of the gate while their comrades hurl missiles from the bulwarks behind.[26] It is easy to envisage just such a contest taking place at the newly discovered outer gate of Troy (fig. 4.6).

The Greek wall itself was made partly of stone and partly of wooden beams (Il. 12, 29) and had "timbered towers" (Il. 12, 36). Homer also relates that the attackers "tried to lever up the jutting pillars which the Achaeans had set first in the ground as supports for the ramparts" (Il. 12, 259–60). Presumably these jutting pillars were also of wood. As noted in Chapter 4, excavation has revealed that a gate opening onto a causeway over the ditch at Troy was protected on each side by wooden palisades, while a wooden bulwark farther back was supported on the inside by pillared offsets just as in the Homeric account.

The convergence between the findings of archaeology and the epic account is remarkable and can hardly be fortuitous. A recent study, to which I am indebted, has deployed the case for supposing that the actual fortifications of the lower town at Troy provided a prototype for the fictitious fortifications with which Homer endowed the Greek ship station.[27] Some details could have been preserved in the broader tradition that formed the epic cycle, but again one must seriously consider the possibility that Homer was able to gain some comprehension of the scope and design of the fortifications from personal observation of the site.

The Trojan assault on the Greek camp reaches a climax when Hector forces Ajax to retire, and one of the ships is set on fire (Il. 16, 112–23). Achilles then permits Patroklos to arm and lead the Myrmidons into action, and the tide of battle turns once again in favour of the Achaeans. Hector and his forces are repelled from the ships and driven back across the ditch with heavy losses. The perils of this obstacle for chariots are emphasised: "For many a team of swift horses snapped their poles at the head of the shaft and left charioteer and chariot behind" (Il. 16, 370–71). A topographical fix is then given as Patroklos manages to cut off the leading ranks of the Trojans and pin them back against the wall. The ensuing slaughter takes place "between the ships and the river and the lofty wall" (Il. 16, 396–97). The killing ground must be envisaged as lying on the stretch of plain near the Greek camp on the left bank of the Scamander. The routed Trojans have been making for the river to cross back to their side of the plain when some of their number are cut off and driven back towards the "lofty wall." Confusion about the location of this action has been caused by the fact that this phrase is often used to describe the walls of Troy. But here, as in some other passages, "lofty wall" must refer to Nestor's wall, not that of Troy itself.[28]

Achilles had given Patroklos very explicit orders not to pursue the Trojans back to Troy itself (Il. 16, 83–96), but in the heat of battle and the flush of victory over Sarpedon, Patroklos disobeys his friend's instructions and tries to storm the city wall: "Three times Patroklos mounted to the angle of the lofty wall and three times Apollo flung him back" (Il. 16, 702–3). Apollo warns him that Troy is not destined to be captured by him, or even by Achilles, and he pulls back from the rampart in fear of the god's anger.

Next we are told that Hector is in his chariot at the Scaean Gate, considering whether to plunge back into the fray or recall his troops back inside the city (Il. 16, 712–14). As previously noted, the Scaean Gate is to be pictured as situated on the western side of the Pergamos, so this must be the area in which Patroklos launched his assault.

This was not the first time the Achaeans had attacked there, as we learn from an earlier passage in which Andromachê is made to give some timely advice to Hector. Andromachê, we learn, has gone out to the "great tower of Ilios," and the pair have met close to the Scaean Gate (Il. 6, 386–93). Andromachê then makes a moving plea to her husband to remember the vulnerability

of his young wife and infant son and not to risk his life in foolhardy fashion outside the walls. Her final words are (Il. 6, 431–39):

> Come now, pity me and remain here on the tower, lest
> you make your child an orphan and your wife a widow.
> Post your troops by the fig tree, where the city is most
> approachable and the wall may be scaled. Three times the
> bravest of our enemies came there to test the defences...
> whether advised by one who knew the prophecies, or
> whether aroused and spurred on by their own bold hearts.

The scene is set on a tower near the Scaean Gate, and it is a reasonable assumption that Andromachê's fears relate to defences in that area. She mentions an
approach route recently used by the Greek leaders and a vulnerable segment of
the walls. Now it is a remarkable fact, first noted by Dörpfeld, that an older and
narrower sector of the Troy VI wall is located in the western sector of Troy's
fortifications.[29] Map 4 shows that the great Troy VI wall, fifteen feet in width,
sweeps round from the Northeast Tower (K 3, 4) to the area of the Sanctuary
(A, 7). There it gives way to a section of inferior masonry only ten feet in width
(fig. 5. 18) that runs north for some forty yards to a small sally port flanked by a
larger bastion (A, 5). This bastion stands at the point where the Bronze Age wall
turned to the east along the steep northern flanks of the citadel.

Close study of the structures at the southern end of the weaker section has
revealed that there was once a gate here that was blocked up in the latest phase
of Troy VI. Before that time one of the main internal roads of Troy ran out
through the gate and down through the small valley in which the altars and
other buildings of the later Greek Sanctuary are now to be seen. Part of the
paving of this road has recently been uncovered (see fig. 4.11). Was this the
Scaean Gate? I like to think so. "Scaean" in Greek signifies "on the left," and
this gate would be on the left of the citadel from the point of view of the
advancing Greeks. The road leading to it would have afforded attackers the easy
approach of which Andromachê speaks, and the older and narrower stretch of

5.18 In the foreground the great wall of Troy VI crosses from the right. The older and weaker stretch of walling turns away from it at an angle, past a leaning tree. To the right of the tree, and behind it, stood one of the mansions of Troy VI (see map 4; A6 and B6). The mound to the left of the weaker segment has been built up artificially and consists mainly of excavation spoil.

wall would have provided a promising target for an assault party with scaling ladders. This sector would be easier to rush and overrun because the blocked gate had no flanking tower and because fewer defenders could be accommodated on the narrower stretch of walling to the north.

And what of the "great tower of Ilios" that also figures in the Homeric account? We are told that Andromachê first went there to view the progress of the battle (Il. 6, 372–73 and 386–87). Might not the massive bastion by the sally port have supplied the vantage point needed, perhaps with the addition of a wooden superstructure of which no trace now remains? The bastion is strategically placed high up at the westernmost point of the defences and would have provided Andromachê with the best possible view of the area below the walls where the Greek attack was developing. It is no farther from the blocked gate than is tower VI H from gate VI S. If this suggestion is acceptable, the saga tradition begins to look impressively authentic at this point. Homer puts a reference to "prophecies" into Andromachê's mouth in the warning to Hector quoted above. She suggests that the Greek leaders may have been guided by some seer or diviner in their assault on the weak sector of the wall. Homer does not elaborate further on the prophecies, but they would obviously have been to the effect that Troy could be entered at this point. It is therefore of great interest to find that Pindar reports just such a prophecy, probably drawing on the broader Cyclic tradition that would have been known also to Homer.

The passage comes in an Olympic Ode glorifying the family of Aiakos in Aegina. Pindar (Ol. 8, 30–46) recalls the tradition that Aiakos, who was grandfather of both Achilles and Ajax, had helped Apollo and Poseidon to build the walls of Troy for Laomedon. The scholia on the passage inform us that most of the circuit, being of divine workmanship, was of superior quality, but Aiakos, being a mortal, built a stretch that was comparatively weak. Pindar then proceeds to put the following very explicit prophecy into Apollo's mouth: "The Pergamos, O hero [Aiakos], is taken through the work of your hands." This tradition must have been known to Homer. His comparative reticence about it in the *Iliad* could be due to a preference for the story of the Wooden Horse as the agent of Troy's downfall. That exciting story of Greek cunning and Trojan credulity bears all the marks of being largely fictional, inspired perhaps by the irony implicit in "horse-taming" Trojans being tamed by a horse. On the other hand, the obscure tradition of a weak section of wall accords with the archaeological evidence and could well be historically true. As we have seen, any Greek attack must have come eastwards across the plain from the direction of Beşika Bay and the Sigeum Ridge. It would have made good military sense to follow the line of the outer defences of the lower town to the point marked West Gate (?) on map 3. The contours indicate that this would have been a likely point of exit for the road coming from the Scaean Gate. A breakthrough at that point would have led the attackers to the weakest sector of the inner citadel wall. The junction point between the broad Troy VI wall and the older and weaker sector with its blocked gate could have entered the tradition as the "angle" or "elbow" of the wall attacked by Patroklos at the limit of his advance (fig. 5.19).

5.19   The point of junction between the newer and wider stretch of Troy VI walling, right, and the older weaker segment, left. Immediately to the left of the junction can be seen the hastily laid courses that blocked up a gate opening, possibly that of the Scaean Gate. Behind, mansion VI M.

Once Patroklos has been repelled from the wall, his death at Hector's hands soon follows. This leads to reconciliation between Agamemnon and Achilles and brings Achilles into furious and revengeful action on the battlefield. For the last time the Trojans are reported "on the swelling of the plain" close to the "beaked ships" (Il. 20, 1–3). From there Achilles drives them back in disorder to the line of the Scamander, and at the start of book 21 the ford receives emphatic mention as the river itself begins to take centre stage (Il. 21, 1–11):

> But when they came to the ford of the fair-flowing river,
> eddying Xanthos [Scamander], begotten of immortal Zeus,
> there Achilles broke the Trojan line, and sent half of the
> enemy flying in rout across the plain towards Troy.... But
> the remainder were pinned back against the deep stream
> with its silver eddies. In they tumbled with loud splashes,

and the din resounded from the depths of the pools and
from the banks on either side. With piteous cries they
swam here and there, whirled round by the current.

As Achilles moves in to slaughter the trapped and helpless victims with his
sword, Homer adds one of those vivid touches that appear to be studied from
life. He tells us that Achilles left his spear on the bank, "leaning it against the
tamarisks" (Il. 17–18). Dense thickets of these shrubs, with their handsome
feathery fronds, are still a conspicuous feature of the riverside scene. So are the
steep banks formed as the river cuts deep into the alluvium. These, too, figure
vividly in Homer's imagination as he pictures how the Trojans in the pools
"cowered below the overhang" (Il. 21, 25–26) or describes how a spear cast by
Achilles misses its mark, and the shaft buries half its length in the "lofty bank"
(Il. 21, 171–72). Nor is the predominantly sandy bed of the stream forgotten as
yet another corpse is left "lying on the sand" (Il. 21, 202).

When the river god tries to overwhelm Achilles with his waters, Homer gives
us another realistic piece of narrative (Il. 21, 240–46): "A fearful wave rose foam-
ing over Achilles, and a weight of water came pressing down on his shield. Losing
his footing, he grasped a large and shapely elm tree in his hands. But the tree was
uprooted and brought all the steep bank away with it. So it fell, bridging over the
flood, and its leafy branches checked the fair flow of the stream." The river is getting the better of Achilles as it floods over the plain, but he is finally saved by
divine intervention when Hera sends Hephaistos to his aid and arouses the winds
to fan the fire god's flames. The whole plain is scorched, and then the flames are
directed against the tree-lined banks of the river itself, whose vegetation is accurately described (Il. 21, 350–52). "The elms were on fire, and the willows, and the
tamarisks. And burning too were the celandine, rush, and galingale, herbs that
grew in lush profusion by the beautiful streams of the river" (fig. 5.20).[30] Homer's
synmpathetic gaze even rests for a moment on the suffering inhabitants of the
waters (Il. 21, 353–55): "The eels were in distress and the fish in the pools, as they
leaped and tumbled helter skelter in the beautiful streams, worn down by the

5.20 "Achilles, son of a goddess, left his spear on the bank, leaning it against the tamarisks..." (Il. 21, 17–18). Elms, willows, and tamarisks growing along the steep banks of the Scamander.

searing blast of crafty Hephaistos." Even so the rich natural environment of the Troad is made to share in the tribulation of its human inhabitants.

The final contest of the *Iliad* is played out close to the walls of Troy, where "ruinous destiny shackled Hector to remain at his post in front of Ilios and the Scaean Gate" (Il. 22, 6–7). Disregarding passionate appeals from Priam and Hekabê, he remains firm in his resolve to confront Achilles in single combat. But as the deadly menace of his adversary's spearpoint comes closer and closer, his nerve fails him, and he takes to his heels.

Swift-footed Achilles dashes after him in hot pursuit, and before the duel even begins, Homer gives us a highly wrought account of the chase which extends for eighty-eight lines in all (Il. 22, 136–223). The narrative is embellished with four extended similes and a discussion among the watching gods about Hector's fate. This degree of elaboration should alert us to expect heroic endeavour over a long course—a marathon rather than a sprint, as I intend to argue.

Achilles, son of a goddess, is particularly noted for his prowess as a runner. If anyone in the audience wonders why Achilles cannot overtake his opponent, Homer has his answer ready: "Apollo was at Hector's shoulder for the last time, increasing his strength and the swiftness of his knees" (lines 203–4). The situation takes on a nightmarish quality as tiring limbs will not respond, and "the pursuer cannot overtake nor the pursued escape" (199–201). Only divine intervention at the highest level can resolve the impasse as the runners continue their protracted contest. Finally, after due debate among the immortals (167–85), Zeus holds up the golden scales of destiny, Hector's lot sinks, Apollo leaves him, and Athena is allowed to intervene decisively on the side of Achilles (208–23).

The divine assistance given to the heroes raises their endeavours to a more than mortal pitch. They are performing, as it were, at Olympic level, and on the basis of the topographical indications given by Homer I shall suggest that he intends us to envisage the race as run over a much longer circuit than is usually supposed.

On the received view, the chase is confined to the immediate vicinity of Troy, with the runners circling the walls three times. The walls are taken to be those of the citadel rather than the lower town, and their circumference would have measured about six hundred yards. A triple circuit of these would amount to little more than a mile, something well within the capacity of any reasonably fit young man.

This is undoubtedly at least part of the picture intended by Homer, for he states explicitly (Il. 22, 165–66): "Even so they whirled on swift feet three times round the city of Priam." But if one supposes it to be the whole picture, one is faced with the problem of the location of the hot and cold springs that the heroes also pass three times. The walls are real enough, but where are the springs? Nothing corresponding to them now exists on or near the hill of Hisarlik. Nor was there any trace of them in Hellenistic times.

Two main ways out of this difficulty have been suggested. First, one might suppose that springs answering to the Homeric description existed close to the city walls in the Bronze Age, and possibly also in Homer's time, but ceased to run after strata in the limestone were altered by earthquake activity. This seems to have been the view taken by Demetrios of Scepsis.[31] Second, one might follow Leaf's suggestion that what Homer describes is "very characteristic of the Troad at large, though not of the immediate surroundings of Troy."[32] This amounts to saying that the springs, even if reality-based in their general nature, are a fiction so far as the topography of Troy itself is concerned.[33]

I suggest that there may be another way of looking at the problem based on the totality of detail supplied by Homer himself. Hector, he says, left the gate behind him and set off in panic-stricken flight hotly pursued by Achilles (Il. 22, 137–38). The gate here is the Scaean Gate, as we are told at the beginning of the book (line 6). Then, after an extended simile in which Achilles is compared to a hawk chasing a dove, the scene of the chase is further set with elaborate topographical detail in a passage that must be quoted in full (145–57):

> They rushed past the *lookout post* and the wind-swept *fig tree*, always following the *wagon road* out from under the walls, and they came to the fair-flowing *fountains*. It was the place where twin sources of the eddying *Scamander* spring up. One flows with warm water, and smoke rises from it as from a blazing fire. The other flows out in summer cold as hail, or snow, or water turned to ice. There at these twin springs are broad and beautiful stone-built washing troughs where Trojan wives and their fair daughters used to wash the bright garments, formerly, in a time of peace, before the sons of the Achaeans came. This was the place the two men passed in their race, the one in flight, the other in pursuit behind.

Great emphasis is laid on the twin fountains as a notable landmark on their route. This is partly for the sake of the pathos engendered by the recollection of their former use in peacetime. But Homer also mentions them a second time to mark the point at which Hector's doom is finally determined (Il. 22, 208–9): "But when they came for the fourth time to the fountains, then Father Zeus held up the golden scales..." It would be strangely anomalous if they alone were topographical fictions in a context that brings together lookout post, fig tree, and Scamander, features previously mentioned and capable of identification in the environs of Troy. Account should also be taken of the wagon road, mentioned only here but presumably indicating a main route leading away from the city.

The history and present state of the famous springs near Pınarbaşı have been described in Chapter 3. They are copious enough to rate as "sources of the eddying Scamander." Their peculiar features have generated a widespread, if unfounded, perception that they differ in temperature. They have been in use down to our day as washing places by the local women, and one at least still has a stone-built surround. "Of all the curiosities of the Troad," wrote J. M. Cook, they are "perhaps the most celebrated." And he ended his account of them with the well-judged comment: "and if we are disposed to look for a natural feature that could have inspired the poetic description [by Homer], only inveterate prejudice can deny that honour to these springs" (p. 145).

The Pınarbaşı springs lie at the southern edge of the Trojan plain, about six miles from Troy. Some may feel that their distance rules them out of consideration as a landmark in what they regard as a race around Troy itself. But is this perception well grounded? Did not Achilles chase the phantom of Agenor out onto the Ileian plain as far as the Scamander (Il. 21, 601–4)? There are, I believe, sufficient indications in the Homeric account to sustain the view that the poet visualised the course of the chase as an extended ellipse rather than as a circle. One of these comes in the simile in which the runners are compared to racehorses swiftly and repeatedly rounding the "turning posts" at either end of their course (lines 162–64). The comparison reminds us that ancient stadia, like ancient hippodromes, were long and narrow, with straight sides, and (in longer races) very sharp turns for the runners around posts at either end of the track. On this model one could envisage

Hector and Achilles running south across the plain on a heroically long lap to the springs, rounding them, and then returning on much the same course to the fortified city, which is then rounded in turn before the pursuit returns to the plain. Such a course would match the heightened circumstances of the culminating moment of the *Iliad,* with all the gods looking on.

Further indications to the same effect come in the extended scene-setting passage quoted above. There the heroes are said to follow a "wagon road" (*hamaxitos,* line 146), a word that occurs nowhere else in Homer. In later Greek it signifies a main road or paved highway, and there is no reason to suppose that it means anything but that in the present passage. One recalls the paved road that has recently been found leading down to the plain from the gate on the west of the city (see fig. 4.11). Its further course is not known, but it would surely be nonsense to suppose that it turned back to make a complete circuit of the city. If a nearby gap in the outer circuit (see map 3) is confirmed by excavation, that would have been its likely point of exit on to the plain. Alternatively, one could think of the road that must have issued from the recently found South Gate in the outer circuit of fortifications. Roads from either exit point would probably have run on to the Scamander ford, and thence to some such destination as Larisa or the Smintheum in the southern Troad. Homer indicates as much when he says that it went "out from under [that is, away from] the wall" and ran past "the lookout post and the wind-swept fig tree." It is natural to assume, in agreement with the ancient scholia, that this lookout post is the same as that earlier assigned to Polites and located at the tomb of Aisyetes. I have already presented the case for locating Aisyetes' tomb some distance away to the southwest of Troy on the Hellenistic route to Alexandria Troas. The fig tree can also be visualised as having stood on the ridge now occupied by the village of Kalafat. Unlike the oak tree, which was close to the Scaean Gate, Homer's other references to it are consistent with a location some distance outside the walls (Il. 6, 433; 11, 167).

If I have correctly identified the lookout, the heroes when passing it are already more than a mile from the Scaean Gate. Hector, like Agenor, may then have had thoughts of escaping into the densely wooded foothills of Ida surrounding the upper Trojan plain. This could be indicated in the next simile, which compares Achilles to a hound relentlessly tracking its prey through broken wooded ground (lines 189–93). The simile is fully consistent with the idea of a long chase across the plain and over the river as far as the Pınarbaşı springs that are in part at least "sources of the eddying Scamander."

Realising that his pursuer is still close behind him, Hector decides to turn sharply back by the springs to seek the safety of Trojan covering fire from the city walls. The Dardanian Gate, which, pace Aristarchus, must be distinct from the Scaean Gate, is the next landmark mentioned (line 194). This could be an indication that the runners are now to be imagined as approaching the fortified area on its eastern or southeastern side, where two other gates certainly existed in the inner circuit, with corresponding exit points through the outer ditch. But Achilles forestalls this manoeuvre by running closer to the walls and forcing Hector once more out "towards the plain" (line 198).

There is one final point that needs to be made about the washing troughs fed by the Scamander springs. If they had lain close to the citadel walls, as is usually supposed, they could still have been used in the war years, for Troy was never closely invested by the Achaean forces. The discontinuance of their use implies a location far enough away from the city for the women to be at risk from raiding parties. It may be of relevance to remark that the word for "washing troughs" (*plunoi,* line 153) is rare in Homer, occurring only here in the *Iliad* and (twice) in the brilliant episode in the *Odyssey* where Nausikaa and her attendants use a wagon, and presumably a wagon road, to take the palace laundry out into the countryside (Od. 6, 71 ff.). Nausikaa is prompted to this action by a dream visitation from Athena, whose final remark is: "The washing troughs lie a good way off from the city" (line 40). In the *Odyssey* the washing troughs mark the point where Odysseus's fortunes at last take a turn for the better. In the *Iliad,* when Hector comes to them for the fourth time (line 208), his fate is finally sealed by Zeus. The two scenes are similar in their location, but sharply antithetical in their outcome. Was Homer himself, I wonder, aware of a certain resonance between them?

A rugged land, but a good nurse of its young.

—Od. 9, 27

SIX

HOMERIC ITHACA

GEOGRAPHY AND ARCHAEOLOGY

THE *ODYSSEY* REFERS TO THE SACK of Troy in its opening sentence, a clear indication that the poem is designed as a sequel to the *Iliad*. All the other survivors of the war, as Homer proceeds to tell us, have reached their homes; only Odysseus is still a wanderer abroad, detained by the goddess Calypso in a remote island in the western seas. Calypso wants him to stay and become her husband, but he is pining for wife and home. At the start of the *Iliad,* Homer had emphasised the destructive wrath of Achilles as the theme to unify his richly diversified account of heroic conflict. He begins the *Odyssey* in a similar way with no fewer than three references to homecoming in the first fifteen lines. This is the leitmotif that will give point and direction to the whole complex plot, and home is Ithaca.

The *Odyssey* was anciently classified as a *nostos* poem, a Greek root familiar to English speakers in *nostalgia,* which literally means "heart-ache for homecoming." Odysseus has an intense longing to return home to Ithaca, and if Troy is the first place to be named in the *Odyssey,* Ithaca is the second (line 18). The action of no fewer than fifteen of the poem's twenty-four books is located in Ithaca itself (books 1, 2, and 12–24). It is not, therefore, surprising to find that the story includes a wealth of topographical material about the island and that a picture of Ithaca is developed that is comparable in detail and consistency to the *Iliad*'s account of Troy and the Troad. The object of this chapter is to examine the general account of the island given in the *Odyssey* and to try to assess how far the overall picture is confirmed by the findings of archaeology. In the following chapter the details of the internal topography will be more closely scrutinised and the case made that Homer's grasp of the terrain is so good that his knowledge probably derives from personal acquaintance with the island.

Homer's genius has elevated Ithaca into a potent and enduring symbol for hearth and home, and the description of it that he puts into Odysseus's mouth will provide an appropriate starting point for the discussion. Odysseus is addressing the Phaeacians assembled at a banquet in the palace of Alkinoos. As he rises to speak, the company is still ignorant of his true identity, so he begins with the dramatic announcement that he is indeed the great and famous Odysseus, son of Laertes. He then continues (Od. 9, 21–28):

> My home is in *clear-seen* Ithaca. In it rises a mountain,
> Neriton, conspicuous, with quivering foliage. Around lie
> numerous inhabited islands, very close to one another,
> [including] Doulichion and Samê and wooded Zakyn-
> thos. Ithaca itself is *low* and is set *farthest out* in the sea
> towards the *dark quarter.* The other islands lie away
> towards the dawn and the sun. It is a rugged land, but a
> good nurse of its young. For me there is no place sweeter
> to the sight than my native land. (Fig. 6.1)

This description is the most geographically detailed that Homer gives us, and also the most disputed. Almost every item in it has been the subject of prolonged discussion and controversy from antiquity onwards. In particular, the meaning of the Greek words corresponding to those I have italicised is not universally agreed, and it is necessary to consider the alternatives before attempting a more general interpretation of the passage.

Eudeielos, which I have rendered "clear-seen," is a stock epithet for Ithaca but occurs also in a more general context in a later book where islands are contrasted with peninsulas (Od. 13, 234–35): "Is this place [asks Odysseus] one of the clear-seen islands, or is it a sea-girt promontory of the fertile mainland?" This passage makes it virtually certain that *eudeielos* is not, as some ancient scholars supposed, a merely decorative epithet meaning "fair in the afternoon sunshine";

6.1　A view of Ithaca looking north from the flanks of Mount Merovigli. The island appears both "low-lying" and with a "conspicuous mountain," as Homer says. The peaks of Lefkas running away to the east can be seen in the background.

rather, it describes the essential nature of Ithaca as a distinctly apprehended island with clear water all around it. It can be seen to be such when one approaches it by sea, and particularly when one surveys it from higher ground within it. There is hardly any spot in Ithaca from which the sea is not visible. *Eudeielos* then expresses much the same truth about Ithaca as another of the island's stock epithets, *amphialos,* meaning "sea-girt" (fig. 6.2).

Chthamale must mean "low" or "low-lying." Strabo agreed with the scholars of his day who thought it could mean "close to the mainland" (10, 2, 12),

6.2 A view of Ithaca looking north from the summit of Aetos on the central isthmus. As Homer says, Ithaca is a "clear-seen island," and "not broad."

but there are no parallels for such a usage. The epithet should not be taken as implying that Ithaca is flat—it is in fact very hilly. It is, however, comparatively low-lying when viewed beside the larger and much more mountainous islands of Kephalonia (Kefallinia) and Lefkas (ancient Leucas).[1]

This interpretation of *chthamale* as "fairly low-lying" receives support from Homer's application of the same epithet to another (but imaginary) island, that of Circe (Od. 10, 196). From other parts of the Circe episode we learn that Circe's island had elevated crags and well-wooded glens (lines 148–50 and 210–11). But like Ithaca, it is envisaged as quite small, for Odysseus from his lookout point can see it falling away to the sea on every side (194–97). Ithaca is divided into two halves by a narrow central isthmus, and both halves of the island fall away to the sea from centrally placed massifs that are not high by Greek standards. Mount Anogi in the north peaks at a little over 2,600 feet and Mount Merovigli in the south at just under 2,200 feet. The Ainos massif in Kephalonia is twice as high (5,200 feet), and Lefkas has several peaks over 3,000 feet, including one of 3,800 feet (fig. 6.2).

Zophos, the "dark quarter," was a directional indication used by ancient sailors and belonged to a system based on observation of solar movement. This becomes clear from the Circe episode, when Odysseus tells his men that they are totally lost and he has no idea where they have come to land. This is how he puts it (Od. 10, 190–92): "My friends, we do not know where lies the dark quarter [*zophos*], nor where the dawning, nor where the sun that brings light to mortals sinks below the earth, nor where he rises." They could obviously see where the sun rose in the eastern sky and where it set in the west. Their problem was that they could not relate these horizon points to any configuration of lands or islands known to them.

If one reads the Ithaca passage with this in mind, one can see that the references to "dawn," "sun," and *zophos* combine to indicate the general orientation of the island group in which Ithaca lies. "Dawn" indicates northeast to east, "sun" south, *zophos* west to northwest, namely, the quarter where the westering sun sinks below the horizon.

The next and related question concerns the identification of the "many islands," and in particular the named group of Ithaca, Doulichion, Samê, and Zakynthos. All agree that Homer's Zakynthos is modern Zante. Map 8 shows that it is the most southerly of the larger islands that lie on the western approaches to the Gulf of Corinth. There has been long-continued doubt and controversy, though, about the identity of the others, for neither Doulichion ("long island") nor Samê remained in use as island designations in the post-Homeric period.

The island now called Kephalonia is the largest member of the archipelago and must be designated by one of the Homeric names. There is a strong case for identifying it with Samê/Samos—both forms are found in the *Odyssey.* The

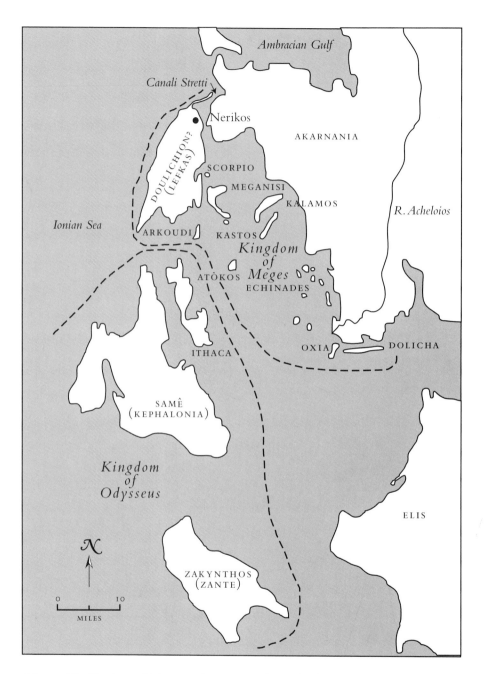

Map 8. The Kingdoms of Odysseus and Meges according to the *Iliad*

case for Lefkas as the former Doulichion will also be considered. As for Ithaca, the ancient world had no doubt that the island still bearing this name was the home of Odysseus. His head appeared on coins of the island, and an athletic festival called *Odysseia* was celebrated there in his memory.

This identification is generally accepted today, even if doubts remain about the total aptness of the Homeric picture. But Wilhelm Dörpfeld refused to accept the almost unanimous verdict of ancient and modern scholarship. In the early years of the twentieth century he mounted a sustained challenge to the view that modern Itháki is the same place as Homeric Ithaca. After completing his work at Troy he worked briefly in Itháki during the spring of 1900 but soon decided that he was looking for Odysseus on the wrong island. He then transferred his attention to Lefkas in the belief that it was the island that Homer really had in mind. His judgment was greatly influenced by the Homeric phrase "farthest out in the sea towards the dark quarter." The inference that he drew from this is neatly summed up by F. H. Stubbings: "If Lefkas is included among the four islands then Itháki cannot be called 'farthest towards the dark quarter,' but Lefkas can. Therefore Lefkas must be the Homeric Ithaca."[2]

Dörpfeld worked for many years on the Nidri plain in the east of Lefkas, hoping to find a substantial Mycenaean settlement as a basis for the saga of Odysseus, but in this hope he was disappointed. Nidri provided evidence for substantial habitation in the centuries before 1500 B.C., but only a very few sherds of Mycenaean pottery were found there, far fewer in fact than were found in the north of Itháki in the course of the British excavations of the 1930s. His case was solidly presented in his *Alt-Ithaka,* published in 1927, but his views have always been strenuously rebutted by Ithakists and in my opinion raise rather than solve difficulties in regard to the *Odyssey.* In the passage under discussion, for example, Homer says that many other islands are situated around Ithaca, and this statement is much more appropriate to Itháki than to Lefkas. Itháki is indeed centrally placed in the archipelago, with Lefkas, Arkoudi, and Meganisi to the north, Kephalonia to the west, Zante to the south, and Atokos, Kalamos, and other smaller isles to the east. Furthermore, all the individual

features of Ithaca as described by Homer can be much more plausibly identified in Itháki than in Lefkas. One critic declared after a visit to Lefkas: "Not a
single feature of the Homeric description of Ithaca corresponds with Lefka-
dian actuality." This verdict, I think, would now be generally accepted by all
who have visited both islands.[3]

Readers will probably have noticed that Homer does not mention Lefkas
under that name, and this leads me on to say something about the identification
of Samê and Doulichion. Zakynthos, as we have seen, is certainly Zante, and
Ithaca holds its ground as Itháki. What of the other two names? Homer twice
speaks of the "strait between Ithaca and rugged Samos [Samê]," where the Suitors planned to place an ambush for Telemachos (Od. 4, 671; 15, 29). This was a
great problem for Dörpfeld because there is no obvious strait between islands at
Lefkas. But there is an excellent candidate in the strait now known as the Ithaca
Channel, the long, narrow passage that runs down the western side of Itháki,
dividing it from Kephalonia. Everything conspires to fix this as the Homeric
strait (see further Chapter 7, fig. 7.15), and so Samê must be identified with
Kephalonia. The older name survives in the modern town of Sami, which is the
terminus of the Itháki-Kephalonia ferry.

As for Doulichion, the best candidate, as T. W. Allen saw, is Lefkas.[4] Strabo
(10, 2, 8) says that Lefkas was not an island until the Corinthians in the seventh
century B.C. dug a canal through the sandy isthmus that now almost joins it to
the mainland. Almost, but not quite, for there is still clear water on the mainland side, and given the extensive silting that has occurred, and still occurs, in
the area, this probably was the case in antiquity also.[5]

The narrow natural channel between Lefkas and the mainland, the Canali
Stretti, is difficult to navigate, so the aim of the Corinthians may have been to
improve navigation (as the modern ship canal does), not to turn Lefkas into an
island (for it is likely always to have been one). It is hard to fault Col. William
Leake's statement that Lefkas was never "more of a peninsula nor less of an
island than it is at present."[6] In any case, the argument about the insular status of
Lefkas is probably irrelevant in regard to Homeric Doulichion, given that in

ancient Greek usage *nesos* can signify "peninsula" as well as "island" in the strict geographical sense.[7]

The Homeric evidence about Doulichion is quite extensive, and the name occurs nine times in all in the *Odyssey*. The first mention of the island comes early in the first book, where Telemachos is complaining to Athena about the rapacity of the Suitors (Od. 1, 245–48): "All the noblemen who bear rule in the islands, in Doulichion, Samê, and wooded Zakynthos, and those who lord it in rocky Ithaca, all these as suitors for my mother's hand are wasting my household." The theme of Suitors coming from Ithaca and three other islands appears to be a traditional part of the saga of Odysseus. The four lines in which it is here expressed constitute a formula that recurs twice more in the poem (Od. 16, 122–25; 19, 130–33, with a slight variation in the last line because Penelope herself is the speaker). The quartet of island names is thus kept constantly in view, and in yet another passage we are given the numbers of Suitors who came from each island (Od. 16, 247–51). The smallest number, twelve, come from Ithaca. The largest number, fifty-two, are assigned to Doulichion, with twenty-four from Samê and twenty from Zakynthos. The actual numbers can have no historical validity, but the proportions suggest that Doulichion was viewed by Homer as a larger island than Ithaca, which is certainly true of Lefkas. In terms of size the only other possible candidate would be Kephalonia, but, as noted above, the case for identifying it with Samê is very strong. We learn from Strabo (10, 2, 14) that some ancient antiquarians wanted to make Kephalonia do duty as two islands, with the name Samê applying to the larger eastern section, and Doulichion designating the western peninsula later known as Palê, but this surgical solution has not attracted much support.[8]

Doulichion also appears three times in quite a different context. In book 14 Odysseus, posing as a buccaneer from Crete, gives Eumaios a ficticious account of his wanderings. Quite a number of these "lying tales" are scattered through the poem, but they are carefully designed to be plausible, and the geographical information they contain is always recognisably authentic. In this particular tale (Od. 14, 191–359) Odysseus tells of visits to Egypt and Phoenicia. He further says that while passing Crete on the way to Libya, his vessel sank in a storm, and he was eventually washed up on the coast of Thesprotia, a district on the mainland to the north of Lefkas. From there King Pheidon dispatched him on a ship bound for Doulichion, "rich in wheat" (line 335).[9] After the ship had gone well out from the land, the sailors, says Odysseus, laid rough hands on him, intending to sell him into slavery. They stripped him of his cloak and tunic, and when they broke their journey for an evening meal at Ithaca, they tied him up to prevent his escape. But he managed to undo his bonds and swim ashore.

This story functions in the narrative as an explanation of how the speaker comes to be alone and in rags in Eumaios's house. Homer must have designed it to be geographically plausible, not just to Eumaios as an inhabitant of Ithaca but also to any member of his audience who might have sailed in these waters. It has been felt to be a difficulty that the northern tip of Lefkas is really quite close to Thesprotia, and that if Lefkas were Doulichion, there would be no need for a Doulichion-bound ship to go near Ithaca at all. This is to overlook the difficulties and dangers for sailing ships of the inside passage around the north of Lefkas, which have been so vividly pictured in a recent book by Tim Severin.[10]

One should also bear in mind that all the main bays and harbours of Lefkas lie on its southern and eastern coasts. An ancient sailing vessel coming from Thesprotia and making for a grain port in Lefkas in a northwesterly wind would have been well advised to stand far out from the inhospitable west coast of Lefkas. Such a ship might quite naturally have headed on down to Ithaca for a short landing there before beating back up to its destination. Nothing in the narrative, which is later repeated by Odysseus to Penelope in a much abbreviated form (Od. 19, 291–95), seems inconsistent with the equation of Doulichion with Lefkas.

I therefore conclude that the modern quartet of major islands off the Gulf of Corinth—Lefkas, Itháki, Kephalonia, and Zante—seems to answer well to the four that Homer names, Doulichion, Ithaca, Samos (Samê), and Zakynthos. That the Homeric names go back to the Bronze Age is rendered credible by their occurrence in the Catalogue in *Iliad* 2, 625–37, a passage that throws further light on the topography of the *Odyssey*.[11] In it Doulichion and the "holy islands of the

6.3   A view of Vathy, the chief town of modern Itháki.

Echinai" are stated to form part of the Kingdom of Meges, and are not under the
rule of Odysseus. The Echinai, later known as the Echinades, lie close to the
mainland of Akarnania. Some of the smaller islets near the mouth of the river
Acheloios are barely habitable, but two of moderate size close to Lefkas, namely
Meganisi and Kalamos, were well populated in Mycenaean times. Together with
Lefkas-Doulichion (where a scatter of Mycenaean sherds has been found in several locations), they add up to a very credible Late Bronze Age kingdom distinct
from the three larger islands farther off the coast. The Catalogue assigns Ithaca,
Samos, and Zakynthos to Odysseus and says that they were inhabited by "great-
hearted Kephallenians." This piece of ethnic information provides a ready explanation for the later change of name from Samos to Kephalonia (Kefallenia).

    In the Ithaca entry the Catalogue gives what appear to be the district names
of Neriton, Aigilips, and Krokuleia. Lord Rennell of Rodd argued convincingly

that Krokuleia was the region around the modern capital Vathy (fig. 6.3) and that "rugged Aigilips" was the lonely upland region in the southwest of the island from the Aetos isthmus down to Port St. Andrew.[12] Mount Neriton (now Mount Anogi) is the main massif of the island north of the isthmus and obviously gave its name to the whole of that area. That leaves Ithaca as a district name for the comparatively well-watered and fertile quarter at the northern extremity, as well as the name for the whole island.

In modern times serious topographical study of Ithaca began with a visit by William Gell, whose work on Troy has already been mentioned. His beautifully illustrated *Geography and Antiquities of Ithaca* appeared in 1807. He offered this work to the public "not entirely without hopes of vindicating the poem of Homer from the scepticism of those critics who imagine that the Odyssey is a mere poetical composition." He was struck, as most visitors are, by "the numerous coincidences, and general similarity to the ancient kingdom of Ulysses" (2), and he wrote with particular vividness about the Raven's Crag and Fountain of Arethusa in the south of the island (for which see Chapter 7). Some of his other identifications are not so successful, and one cannot but feel that Byron was right to describe him as "rapid" Gell. In particular, he was too easily convinced by local opinion that some ancient walls on the impressive peak site of Aetos were the remains of the palace of Odysseus. Schliemann shared this opinion, but to adopt it is to create major difficulties in regard to Homeric topography.

Schliemann was in Ithaca for a little more than a week in July 1868, a visit that preceded his arrival in the Troad. Most of his time was spent in identifying Homeric locations with the aid of Murray's *Handbook for Travellers in Greece,* a useful work that had been published in 1854 and contained a full account of Homeric features in the island. But he did hire some workmen and conduct his first excavation on the summit of Aetos. In two days' work he claims to have recovered painted vases containing human ashes; he was prepared to believe that he might have the remains of Odysseus and Penelope in his hands. Caution is needed in regard to the details of this report. As David Traill points out, no other investigator has ever found any evidence for burials on the highly eroded summit

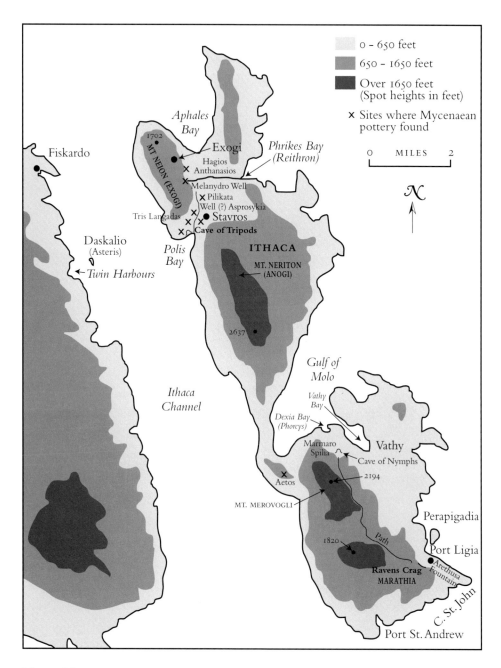

Map 9. Ithaca

6.4   Remains of ancient walling built into more recent terracing on the
Pilikata ridge.

of Aetos, nor anything approaching intact vases, though such have been found
on the saddle lower down. We know that Schliemann purchased antiquities during his Ithacan visit, and the suspicion must remain that his Aetos finds were
bought rather than unearthed.[13]

   No archaeological work of any great significance was done in Ithaca until the
systematic campaigns of the British School in the 1930s. Their main effort was
concentrated in the north of the island and proved that the area around Stavros
and Polis Bay was the main focus of habitation in the Late Bronze Age. Mycenaean sherds were found at six sites from the shore of Polis Bay up to Hagios
Athanasios (map 9).[14]

   These results confirmed that Ithaca formed part of the Mycenaean world and
for the first time provided a firm factual basis for the Homeric tradition. The outline of a substantial circuit wall was traced on the summit of the ridge north of the
modern village of Stavros, and a little Mycenaean pottery was found there (fig.
6.4). The site is known as Pilikata, and W. A. Heurtley, the director of the exca-

6.5   The sight line from the "palace" area (Pilikata) to the harbour of Reithron (Phrikes).

vations, argued for it as the likeliest site for a palace, though admittedly no remains of buildings answering to such a description were found. One would not expect anything on the scale of Mycenae or Pylos, but as one stands at Pilikata at the highest point of the ridge, it is easy to imagine an Odysseus lording it here in a well-timbered hall that has vanished without trace. The summit dominates all the cultivable land north of Mount Anogi—the richest and most productive part of Ithaca. From here one can also look down to the two best harbours in the north of the island, Phrikes Bay to the east, and Polis Bay to the west. Phrikes Bay is still used as a ferry port, and Polis Bay is the most secure haven on the whole of the west coast (figs. 6.5 and 6.6). Aphales Bay to the north is not so favoured by shipping, for it is an exposed and dangerous anchorage. The author of a recent and

6.6   Polis Bay from the hillside west of Pilikata (in the line of sight from the summit of Pilikata).

valuable survey of the archaeology of Ithaca remarks that Pilikata, "commanding as it does the three bays of Aphales, Polis, and Phrikes, has always seemed a likely site for the palace of Odysseus."[15]

No further sustained archaeological work was undertaken in Ithaca until the Odyssey Project of the Greek Archaeological Service under the direction of Professor S. Symeonoglu during the 1980s. Symeonoglu has concentrated his effort at Aetos and maintains that his findings point to it as the site of the Homeric polis. This amounts to a rejection of the main conclusion of the British School, namely, that the Mycenaean occupation of Ithaca was concentrated in the northern quarter of the island. Symeonoglu has found some twelfth-century B.C. Mycenaean pottery and one sherd dating from the previous century. His thorough investigation of the Cyclopean walling in the area also indicates that portions of it may be somewhat earlier than previously thought. Symeonoglu claims his find of Mycenaean sherds as the first from Aetos, but in fact a few such artifacts were found there by his British predecessors. British work in the Aetos area, particularly on the col below the peak, showed that the site was of considerable importance in the immediate post-Mycenaean period. It has the feel of a refugee centre, where survivors retreated for greater security during the progressive decline and fall of the Mycenaean world. The summit could have been garrisoned as a strong point during the heyday of Mycenaean power between 1300 and 1200 B.C., but it does not seem so credible as a palace centre, being deficient in water and far removed from good agricultural land. One must conclude, I think, that Symeonoglu's findings to date are not strong enough to overturn the received view that the Late Bronze Age polis of Ithaca lay in the north of the island.[16]

There is clear evidence in the *Odyssey* to confirm that "Ithaca" could be used as a district and city name as well as an island name.[17] In the vast majority of cases it means the island, but the name is once qualified by the topographical epithet, "[lying] under Neion" (Od. 3, 81). This is a parallel usage to "Thebe under Plakos" (Il. 6, 397) and must refer to a town rather than the island. "[Lying] under wooded Neion" is also the description of a port called Reithron that is visible from the palace but lies "in open country away from the polis" (Od. 1, 185–86). "Wooded Neion" implies a mountain, like "Neriton of the quivering foliage." "Reithron" means a stream, which in Greece implies a winter torrent. It is an inescapable fact that the torrent bed of the most considerable streamlet in the whole of Ithaca may still be seen running through the harbour village of Phrikes on the northeast coast of the island (fig. 6.7). The Phrikes brook takes its rise from the east-facing slopes of Mount Exogi, below which lies the Pilikata ridge, where we have seen reason to place the main centre of Late Bronze Age Ithaca (see map 9). Everything dovetails perfectly: Reithron ("Torrent-Town") is now Port Phrikes; its torrent comes streaming down in winter from the western height of "wooded Neion," now called Mount Exogi; Ithaca as polis rather than island lay on the ridge below Mount Neion. The usage whereby "Ithaca" can designate city or district as well as the whole island

6.7 "Torrent Town": the line of the winter torrent through the heart of the modern village of Phrikes. The name may preserve a memory of the ancient sea god Phorcys.

is fully in line with later practice in the Classical Greek city-states, where the name of the political centre was normally also that of the whole territory, as for example in Rhodes, Cos, or Chios. The unusual survival of the name "polis" in Polis Bay bears significant witness to this fact.

If one pays due attention to all this evidence, one has, I think, the vital clue that explains why Homer can say that Ithaca lies "farthest out in the sea towards the *zophos*." This is certainly the impression one gets in the northern quarter of the island as one surveys the surrounding panorama of sea and mountain. The eastern flank of Kephalonia is seen to run back down the Ithaca Channel, with the towering massif of Mount Ainos (5,310 feet) well to the south. A wide expanse of the Ionian Sea opens up to the northwest with no land between you

6.8   Aphales Bay and the northernmost point of Ithaca, with Lefkas in the background. Seaward viewing from here confirms the impression that Ithaca lies "farthest out towards the dark quarter."

and the toe of Italy. The lighthouse on Cape Dukato at the southern tip of Lefkas is visible ten miles to the north, but from there the mountain spine of the island, with peaks up to 3,500 feet, leads the eye away to the east and the Akarnanian mainland. One seems to be standing on the extreme northwestern rim of all this island world. As Homer says, "the other islands are well away to the east and south," and recourse to the map will do little or nothing to alter the force of the visual impression. Ithaca as a whole, and its northern segment in particular, does seem to lean towards open water, with no conspicuous land mass between it and the quadrant of the sunset (fig. 6.8).

Homer, as has often been suggested, most notably by Victor Bérard, is picturing Ithaca through the eyes of a seafarer (himself, in my view) who has come by ship from the Corinthian Gulf and put in at Polis Bay for a visit to the chief city. To one approaching Ithaca by sea from the southeast (as I have several times done), the island does appear "low-lying" by comparison with the much higher flanks of Kephalonia rising behind and beyond it. It appears low also beside Lefkas to the north. And yet a critic might say it has a mountain 2,637 feet high. Quite so, and Homer takes due account of this fact with his reference to the leafy and conspicuous summit of Neriton. "Ah," retorts the critic, "low, with a conspicuous mountain—the contradiction shows that Homer has only the vaguest conception of the terrain." On the contrary, when one knows a place very well, one can give a lively overall impression of it to strangers by using a series of piquant contrasts. This, I suggest, is the well-judged essence of the description that Homer has put into Odysseus's mouth. Ithaca is rugged, but kindly to its young. It contains a conspicuous mountain, but is comparatively low-lying. Many islands lie around it, yet they are well away towards the east and the south. Many commentators have seen in these seeming inconsistencies proof that Homer could not have possessed firsthand knowledge of Ithaca and its surroundings. I judge the whole passage to be a nuanced and pithy account by an eyewitness, and I venture to suggest that its authenticity is best attested not by studying maps but by paying a visit to one of the most enchanting islands in Greece.

So much for the most important account of Ithaca from book 9. A second set-piece description confines itself to details of the island itself. It comes at the point where Odysseus has been conveyed back to his homeland by a Phaeacian ship. Still in a deep sleep, he has been put ashore at the Bay of Phorcys; when he awakes the island is shrouded in mist, and he does not recognise his surroundings (Od. 13, 187–90). Athena comes to meet him in the guise of a young shepherd, and Odysseus questions her as to his whereabouts. Her reply emphasises the fame of the island and describes its salient characteristics with all the pride of local patriotism (Od. 13, 237–49):

Stranger, you are either a simpleton or come from a far
country if you ask about this land. It is far from being the
obscure place that your questioning would imply. Many
peoples know it well, dwellers in lands to the east and the
south as well as the inhabitants of western lands. I grant
you that it is rugged and unsuitable for horses, but the land
is not poor, even though it lacks broad pastures. It
produces grain in abundance and a rich store of wine.
Rain does not fail to fall, and the dew nourishes. There is
good pasturage for goats and cattle. All kinds of trees grow
here, and springs flow all year long. And so, stranger, I tell
you that the name of Ithaca reaches even to Troy, a city
that they say lies far from the territory of the Achaeans.

The speech shows great artistry in its composition, and the dramatic climax
is beautifully managed. Stress is laid on the island's position on the sea route
from east to west, which has brought many visitors to its shores. In texture the
description shows something of the deliberate contrasts noted in the earlier
account, with the speaker accepting that Ithaca is generally rugged but insisting
that it is not a poor or wretched place. The phrase "unsuitable for horses" is a
deliberate echo of an earlier situation in which Telemachos was offered a present of horses by Menelaos in Sparta, but declined the gift on the grounds that
Ithaca contains "no broad runs nor any meadowland." "None of the sea-girt
islands," he continues, "is suitable for horses or rich in meadows, Ithaca least of
all" (Od. 4, 605–8). This, incidentally, is a telling point against Dörpfeld's identification of Ithaca with Lefkas, which has a certain amount of level and grassy
ground, whereas Itháki has virtually none at all.

Like many a Greek island, Itháki looks rather bare and bleak from the sea, but
such appearances are deceptive. It is true that the higher hills are stony and that
long stretches of naked and deeply fissured limestone cover much of its southwestern corner. There is much to justify its stock Homeric epithets of "rough,"

Homer's four aspects of Ithaca (Od. 13, 195–96):

6.9 "Tracks slanting across the slopes": one footpath leads up across the slope towards the Raven's Crag, the other down towards the ravine and Ligia Bay.

6.10 "Harbours to suit every mooring": the well-sheltered harbour of Port St. Andrew in the southwest corner of Ithaca, with the mountains of Kephalonia behind.

6.11 "Rocks bare of vegetation, flourishing fruit trees": on the Marathia plateau olive trees do well on the nearly naked limestone.

6.12   The village of Platithria in orchard country to the northeast of Stavros. One can easily picture the country estate of Laertes in this area. Ithaca is rugged, but "not a poor place."

"rugged," and "rocky." But even the rockiest region bears its quota of olives, and the sheltered and surprisingly fertile slopes around Vathy and Stavros are rich in orchards and vineyards, interspersed with copses of myrtle and oleander, and the eye-catching cypress. Itháki can feed its population of some five to six thousand inhabitants, produces good-quality wine, and exports olive oil and raisins.

It is excellent goat country and even manages to pasture a few cattle. Bérard was troubled by the phrase "good for cattle" and wanted to emend *boubotos* to *subotos,* "good for swine." Alfred Heubeck thought that "good for cattle" as a description "does not support the supposition of local knowledge."[18] Such comment would be appropriate in an economic survey but fails to take sufficient account of the ethos of the speaker. Homer is evoking the persona of a young and patriotic member of the Ithacan aristocracy (lines 222–23), and such a one must be allowed to indulge in a little pardonable exaggeration when eulogising his native land.

When Homer as narrator throws in a two-line description of the island, he shows exemplary conciseness and objectivity (Od. 13, 195–96):

> Tracks slanting across the slopes, harbours to suit every
> mooring, rocks bare of vegetation, flourishing fruit trees.
> (Figs. 6.9–11)

The antithetical mode of description is again quite marked. Internal communication by land is contrasted with sea travel; barren cliffs alternate with thriving orchards. There are no broad streets or paved chariot roads in Homer's Ithaca, but if you come by sea you can find a haven in any wind. One reads that a hundred years ago there were no roads at all in Ithaca. Even today the road system covers only the centre and north of the island, and the best route from one region to another is often by footpath winding up through the terraced orchards, or by goat track across the open slopes. The car user has problems, but if you own a boat you can come and go much more readily. Polis Bay is well sheltered from the Etesian winds, and the fretted and recessed east coast provides a multitude of anchorages, with Vathy Bay well equipped to handle the seasonal trade of cruising yachts. In the calcareous landscape naked rock is no novelty, but the walker is continually surprised and delighted by secluded villages surrounded by flourishing orchards.

When Odysseus goes to look for Laertes on his farm, he announces his intention to Penelope as follows (Od. 23, 359–60): "I shall traverse the open country rich in fruit trees in order to see my noble father." He finds Laertes alone in his terraced garden-cum-vineyard, breaking the soil around one of his plants. His men have gone off to collect fieldstones to make an outer wall for the cultivated area—a procedure that would be familiar to farmers in the west of Ireland and elsewhere (Od. 24, 222–26). The old man was "wearing a filthy, patched, and disreputable tunic, a pair of stitched leather gaiters strapped round his shins to protect them from scratches, and gloves to save his hands from the brambles" (lines 226–30, trans. E. V. Rieu). The passage has a timeless quality, redolent of the dirt and backbreaking toil of peasant life. The recognition is delayed while Odysseus spins a final yarn, but finally Laertes asks for proof that his son has really returned, and Odysseus cites the list of fruit trees that Laertes had made over to him as a little boy (Od. 24, 340–44): "You gave me thirteen pear trees, ten apple trees, and forty fig trees, and you indicated the fifty rows of vines that were to be mine." It is easy to imagine a location for just such a farm in the orchard country to the east of the Stavros ridge, where still today small vineyards lie interspersed with olive groves, and the trees in autumn are heavy with pear and pomegranate, apple and fig (fig. 6.12).

Come, let me show you the lie of the land to convince you.

—Athena to Odysseus (Od. 13, 344)

SEVEN

HOMERIC ITHACA

THE GENERAL DESCRIPTIONS of Ithaca discussed in the previous chapter come at the point in the story where the wanderings of Odysseus are nearing their end. The account that Homer puts into the mouth of Odysseus serves to define the geographical situation of Ithaca, and that given by the young shepherd summarises the salient characteristics of the island. The scene is thus set for the final trial of strength with the Suitors. As the plot unfolds, Homer throws in many more topographical details, and it will be my task in the present chapter to review these carefully.

Before moving to the palace, Odysseus has to secure his treasure and meet with his faithful servant Eumaios and his son Telemachos. This involves much coming and going in the southern half of the island, where two locations in particular need to be identified. Let us look first at the harbour where Odysseus has been landed by the Phaeacian seamen, and the nearby cave where he stows the valuable presents that he has received from King Alkinoos and his nobles. The security of these goods is crucial if his return home is to be crowned with full success. The harbour is called the Bay of Phorcys, and the cave, sacred to the nymphs, is described with a wealth of detail that testifies to its importance and puts its identification beyond reasonable doubt.

Here is what Homer says (Od. 13, 96–112):

> There is a harbour named after Phorcys, the old man of
> the sea, in the territory of Ithaca. Two abrupt and jutting
> headlands tower over its entrance, sheltering its recesses

from the swell raised by stormy winds. Well-benched ships that come to anchor there can rest without a mooring rope. At the head of the harbour stands a long-leaved olive tree. Near it lies a lovely shadowy cave sacred to the nymphs who are called naiads. Within the cave are mixing bowls and amphoras of stone where the bees store their honey. There are lofty looms of stone where the nymphs weave sea-purple cloaks, a marvel to behold, and ever-running water. The cave has two entrances. The one that faces north is where men descend to the interior. The south-facing entrance belongs to the gods, and men do not enter there, but it provides a way in for the immortals.

7.2   An "abrupt and jutting headland" at the entrance to Dexia Bay.

The Gulf of Molo (see map 9) leads in to the haven of Vathy Bay, where quite large cruise ships can use a well-sheltered anchorage close to the quays of the modern capital Vathy. Vathy Bay could be considered as a candidate for Homer's Harbour of Phorcys: its inner portion lies not far from the Marmarospilia Cave, which, as we shall see, answers extremely well to the Homeric Cave of the Nymphs. On balance, though, I think it preferable to follow the many authorities who have found the Harbour of Phorcys in the smaller and equally well-sheltered cove now known as Dexia Bay (figs. 7.1 and 7.2). My choice is influenced by two of those action details that Homer often throws in for good measure in a context distinct from the initial description of a locality. After evoking cove and cave in picturesque detail, Homer proceeds to describe how the Phaeacian mariners, who "knew the anchorage of old," rowed rapidly in to land and beached the vessel up to half its length, before depositing the sleeping Odysseus "on the sand." They then unloaded his goods and put them

7.3 The narrow entrance to Marmarospilia, the Cave of the Nymphs.

by the olive tree "away from the road" (Od. 13, 113–24). From personal observation I can confirm that the inner part of Dexia Bay is shallow and, for Ithaca, unusually sandy, thus allowing for the landing method adopted. Furthermore, the cave of Marmarospilia, still surrounded by many olive trees, is indeed quite well "away from the road," which then as now would have run close to the shore. The cave is situated some six hundred feet up, at the "head" of the harbour in the sense that there the valley leading up from the beach loses itself in the northeastern slopes of Mount Merovigli.

Caves are extremely common in the limestone mountains of Greece, but the cavern at Marmarospilia has special features that answer very well to the above description. The cavern is easy to reach and explore, for a tolerably good road runs up to it from Vathy, and the interior has artificial lighting. One enters through a

7.4 "Lofty looms of stone where the nymphs weave sea-purple cloaks." Stalagmite formations in the Cave of the Nymphs.

narrow cleft between four and five feet high, and facing north, as Homer says. A little later in the narrative, when Odysseus's treasure has been stowed inside, Athena seals the entrance by placing a stone over it (Od. 13, 370–71). This is another of those interlocking details that shows how clearly and precisely Homer has visualised the scene. The "human" entrance at Marmarospilia is very small in relation to the interior space (fig. 7.3). Having squeezed through the cleft, one finds oneself on a shelf about twenty feet long by six feet wide at a higher level than the main body of the cave. This shelf leads to a broad projecting ledge that could be imagined as a rough altar or offering table. Its saucerlike depressions may have inspired Homer's "mixing bowls and amphoras of stone." Human worshippers, if not bees, might well have placed honey there for the nymphs. Some rough-cut steps lead down to the main body of the cave about fifteen feet below, the place where men "descend." The cave is roughly circular, about sixty feet in diameter, with a comparatively level floor and a large recess opening off to the south. It could serve as a model for a smuggler's cave, with its capacious interior and small, easily concealed entrances. Overhead, the roof narrows in on all sides like a corbelled vault, the "broad and vaulted cavern" of line 349. At the apex is a narrow vent, admitting a glow of daylight from the south, surely Homer's "divine" entrance, accessible only to immortal visitors. No spring is to be seen, but the steady drip and seepage of water has seamed the walls with fluted shafts. In them, and in one freestanding stalagmite column, one can easily visualise the "lofty looms of stone" where the nymphs do their immortal weaving (fig. 7.4).

In a previous account of this celebrated Cave of the Nymphs, I remarked that no evidence of an ancient cult has been found here. Subsequently I learned that sherds picked up in the dump at the cave mouth show that dedications were made to the nymphs in Hellenistic times.[1] These sherds have not, so far as I know, been published, but their finding provides a clinching archaeological footnote to Homer's account, and in particular to the cult which he attributes to his Cave of the Nymphs.

Every detail of his description finds a satisfying analogue in the situation on the ground. One can stand at the mouth of the cave, *Odyssey* in hand, and point, as Athena did with Odysseus, to the main features of the landscape (Od. 13, 344–51):

> Come, let me show you the lie of the land to convince
> you. *There* is the Harbour of Phorcys, the old man of the
> sea. *Here* at the head of the harbour is the long-leaved
> olive tree.... *This* is the broad and vaulted cavern where
> you used to perform perfect sacrifices to the nymphs. And
> *yonder* stands Neriton, the mountain covered in forest.
> (Fig. 7.5)

At this climactic moment the goddess disperses the mists of doubt, a familiar vista of sea and mountain comes into view, and Odysseus stoops joyfully to kiss the soil of his native land and to promise fresh offerings to the nymphs should his venture succeed.

Lines of communication serve equally with localities to fix the details of Ithacan topography. After altering Odysseus's appearance to that of a beggar, Athena instructs him to go first of all to the abode of his faithful swineherd Eumaios, whose pigs "graze by the Raven's Crag and the Fountain of Arethusa" (Od. 13, 407–8). The route he takes is described at the start of the following book (Od. 14, 1–3):

> Odysseus went away from the harbour on a rough
> footpath through wooded ground along the heights, as
> Athena had indicated, to the dwelling of the godlike
> swineherd. (Fig. 7.6)

One of my most exciting experiences on Ithaca was to find and follow just such a path. I could not see any sign of it in the vicinity of the Marmarospilia Cave, but I wanted to go from there to the south of the island to visit the area of the Raven's Crag. Trusting in Homer as my guide I made my way up the scrub-covered slopes behind the cave, and after I had climbed several hundred feet, there was the path! It went exactly as Homer had said it would, "through wooded ground along the heights" (fig. 7.7). The line of it is marked on map 9, and the reader will see that it avoids the lower ground around the head of Vathy Bay, traversing the undulating flanks of Mount Merovigli at a fairly constant height of about a thousand feet. It had the feel of a very ancient route, carefully contoured and designed to join districts rather than villages. There were splendid views over the sea to the east, and in less than an hour and a half it brought me slanting down onto the rocky plateau of Marathia (fig. 7.8).

I had visited the area the previous year so I knew where to find the Raven's Crag. This is a lonely spot without a village in sight, but as I stood there a goatherd came by with his flock, pointed to the cliff, and said: *Stefani tou Korakou.* It is well known that wily Greek peasants readily pick up classical tags from visiting scholars, but I found out later that *stefani* is a local dialect word for "crag" (compare Il. 13, 138), and this lends some support to the supposition that this place-name may have been transmitted down the centuries from ancient

7.5　Neriton (Mount Anogi) in full view from the Cave of the Nymphs. The entrance to Dexia Bay is clearly marked by a small islet.

7.6　A view of Ithaca looking south from Mount Anogi. Dexia Bay opens to the right of the inner harbour of Vathy. The line of the path followed by Odysseus from the Cave of the Nymphs to the Raven's Crag can be traced along the eastern flank of Mount Merovigli. Cape St. John is visible at the southeastern end of the island. (Photograph reproduced by kind permission of Jorge Lewinski.)

7.7   The high path from the Cave of the Nymphs to Marathia.

7.8   The view south over the Marathia plateau; the Raven's Crag is located at the extreme left.

times. The cliff is undoubtedly a very striking natural feature, unparalleled elsewhere in Ithaca. It falls sheer for about two hundred feet to form an unclimbable
barrier above a rugged gorge that runs steeply up from the sea. The cliff face
extends in a gentle curve around the head of the gorge for some six hundred
yards, and only at either end of it will one find a way down to the rough pasturage below. It provides a secure habitat for a colony of ravens, and bird-watch-
ers will be surprised and delighted to see large flocks of this generally solitary

7.9   The Raven's Crag.

bird. One hears their harsh croaking from quite a distance, and every now and then a raven swings out from the edge on its broad wings and goes gliding and tumbling down towards the sea far below. It is indeed the most raven-haunted spot imaginable, and Homerists who visit it will need little urging to believe that Homer, too, was there (fig. 7.9).

My "Eumaios" soon left me to drive his animals down past the cliff into the gorge, and so to the famous Fountain of Arethusa (figs. 7.10 and 7.11). The Marathia plateau is an arid stretch of ground, and a spring as copious and reliable as Arethusa must always have been a magnet for flocks and herds for miles around. The thick scrub in the gorge also provides good pickings for goats. The retaining dam shown in the Maitland print that appears in fig. 7.10 has suffered earthquake damage, but there was still good water to be had in the cave on the right, as I found on a hot September day.

The close conjunction of two such distinctive features as the Raven's Crag

7.10   The Fountain of Arethusa, after Joseph Cartwright in *Views Dedicated to T. Maitland* (1821). Part of the water supply comes from the torrent descending from the Raven's Crag, part from the cave on the right, which is the perennial supply and an invaluable resource in the arid southeast corner of Ithaca. Since the print was made, the masonry surrounds of the fountain basin have been severely damaged by earthquakes, as will be seen from fig. 7.11.

7.11   Looking up from the Fountain of Arethusa to the Raven's Crag. The earthquake-damaged basin of the fountain is seen in the foreground. In September, when the picture was taken, the stream was dry, but there was water to be had in the cavelike openings (centre and right).

and the Arethusa Fountain fixes the location of the homestead of Eumaios to the southeast corner of Ithaca. This is a crucial detail for the interpretation of the narrative, because all of book 14, half of book 15, and all of book 16 are set there. The swineherd's cottage is where Telemachos meets his father on return-ing from Sparta and where their further plan of action is devised. To have the location so pinpointed makes the return voyage of Telemachos fully intelligible.

7.12 The present-day cottage by the Raven's Crag, with its walled courtyard in front. Mount Merovigli rises behind.

As is Homer's manner, he emphasises the narrative importance of the site by an elaborate description (Od. 14, 5–10):

> Odysseus found Eumaios sitting on the porch of his
> house, on elevated ground, where high walls encircled his
> beautiful and spacious courtyard. The swineherd himself
> had built it as an enclosure for the swine of his absent
> master. It lay far from the halls of his mistress and old
> Laertes, constructed from rough fieldstones and topped
> off with a coping of wild pear.

There follows a further description of the exterior stockade and the twelve styes within the enclosure, each housing fifty sows, a passage that to some extent parodies the more elevated account of Priam's palace in the *Iliad* (6, 242–50).

The homestead of Eumaios seems to have been grander than the humble

7.13　The cottage enclosure "constructed from rough fieldstones and topped off with a coping of wild pear," as Homer describes.

dwelling that I saw and photographed in its lonely situation on the plateau above the Raven's Crag (fig. 7.12). But they shared more than the same open and elevated situation with splendid views over sea and islands to the east. In front of the present cottage stood an oval enclosure for the animals, its dry stone walling constructed from unworked fieldstones and topped off with a covering of spiny brushwood (fig. 7.13). I cannot be sure that the dried branches included wild pear. But what is certain is that the isolated farmstead was essentially constructed to the same plan as that described in the *Odyssey,* and its placing was governed by the same need to have easy access to the life-giving waters of the Arethusa Fountain. It was a telling reminder of the perennial patterns of Greek rural life.

Once again interlocking details in other contexts confirm how precisely and comprehensively Homer has envisaged the whole location. Odysseus, still in disguise, encourages the swineherd to believe that his master's return is imminent,

7.14   A rock shelter at the base of the Raven's Crag.

and remarks (Od. 14, 398–99): "If your master does not come as I say, rouse up your servants to fling me down from the great cliff." This is a particularly neat reference to the situation of the homestead in relation to the Raven's Crag.

When the talking is over for the evening, the dutiful Eumaios goes out to spend the night in closer proximity to his herd of hogs, which, as Homer tells us (Od. 14, 532–33), "were sleeping below the overhang of the cliff, sheltered from the blast of the north wind." When I visited the area, I found rock shelters containing animal droppings and answering precisely to this description, under an overhang at the base of the Raven's Crag (fig. 7.14).

Finally, in a summary of how Odysseus won back his kingdom, the suitor Amphimedon tells Agamemnon in Hades (Od. 24, 149–50): "the malign power of the gods brought Odysseus back from some region to *the extreme limit of his land,* where the swineherd had his dwelling." The homestead of Eumaios, as

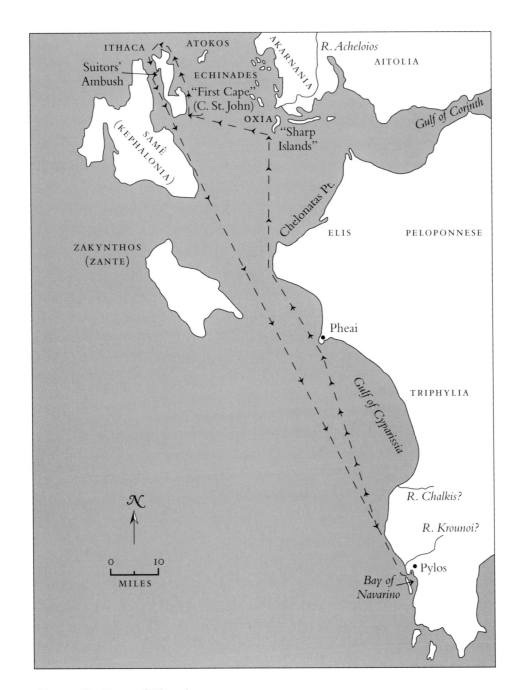

Map 10   The Voyage of Telemachos

7.15 The Ithaca Channel looking south from Fiskardo, with Ithaca on the left and the "windy headlands" of Kephalonia on the right. The islet of Daskalio (Asteris) can be seen in midchannel.

already remarked, is the place where Odysseus first reveals himself to a member of his family in the person of his son Telemachos. If the reader wonders how Telemachos comes to be in that remote spot, the answer lies in a subplot first deployed in the opening books of the poem, and then not resumed until book 15.

Odysseus himself does not enter the action of the *Odyssey* until book 5. In the previous books Telemachos takes the limelight with his enterprising voyage to seek news of his absent father (map 10). His chosen companions make ready a ship in the main harbour of Ithaca, situated in what is still called Polis Bay

7.16　Asteris-Daskalio viewed from Ithaca.

(Od. 2, 382–92). Athena sends a following wind, and with Telemachos at the helm they turn south down the Ithaca Channel for a direct and speedy passage to Pylos, which they reach next morning (Od. 3, 1–5). The spirited nature of Telemachos's undertaking so annoys and alarms the Suitors that they decide to ambush and kill him on his return.

Homer's account of the setting of the ambush is controversial and needs careful examination. The topography is first outlined at the end of book 4 (842–47):

> The Suitors embarked and began to sail over the watery
> ways, plotting brutal murder in their hearts for Telemachos.
> There is a rocky island in midchannel between Ithaca and
> rugged Samos, Asteris, not a large place, and within it are
> twin harbours, good anchorages for ships. There the
> Achaeans lay await in ambush for Telemachos.

We have already been told of the Suitors' plan in outline. Antinoos has proposed to take a single ship and twenty comrades to patrol the Ithaca Channel against Telemachos's return, and all agree that this should be done (Od. 4, 669–74). Now the plan is put into action, and Homer begins to specify more precisely the area in which the ambush is set. He does this neatly enough by the mention of Asteris. In the Ithaca Channel almost due west of Polis Bay lies a small rocky islet now called Daskalio, the modern name being a corruption of Italian *scoglio,* meaning rock or reef. Daskalio is the only island in the whole length of the channel, and the case for identifying it as Asteris is strong (fig. 7.15). Asteris means "little star," an appropriate name, for when viewed from Ithaca its white limestone rocks catch the morning sunshine and make it gleam like a star in the wine-dark waters of the channel (fig. 7.16). "Rocky" is the mot juste for it; it is little more than a reef, though it now bears a small chapel and the remains of a watchtower on its rocky spine (fig. 7.17). It is certainly "not large," being only about two hundred yards in length by thirty yards in width and never rising more than about twelve to fifteen feet out of the water. I once rowed around it in a small boat from Fiskardo, and my boatman refused to attempt a landing as requested even though the day was calm. Its flanks seemed uniformly rugged and inaccessible, and unless its configuration has been totally altered by earthquake action (which geologists say is most unlikely) it can never have provided even one safe anchorage for shipping. It is this absence of "twin harbours" in Asteris that creates the topographical problem. Strabo's account (1, 3, 18 and 10, 2, 16) provides evidence of ancient controversy that anticipates the divergent views of modern scholars. Strabo himself preferred to adopt the explanation of physical change rather than suppose that Homer was ignorant of the locality, or that he created a fictional topography after the manner of a storyteller.

All of these approaches can be documented from modern discussions. Alexander Shewan argued in support of extensive physical change in Asteris-Daskalio, but soundings around the island indicate that this hypothesis is scientifically weak.[2] In pursuance of his Lefkas theory, Dörpfeld identified Asteris

7.17 A close-up of "rocky" Asteris-Daskalio in the Ithaca Channel, with the east flank of Kephalonia rising behind.

with the island of Arkoudi (see map 8). Arkoudi lies in open water between Lefkas and Itháki and is said to have twin bays. But it cannot be said to lie in a strait or channel like Asteris. One problem may be solved, but another is created, and in any case, as we have seen, the Lefkas–Ithaca equation lacks plausibility. Bérard did not believe that Homer ever visited Ithaca, though he accepts that much of the poet's topographical information is accurate. In this instance he thinks that Homer was relying on an ancient *Periplous* (mariner's guide) that provided him with factual information about the Ithaca Channel and that, lacking firsthand knowledge of the area, he transmitted that information in a muddled and inaccurate form.[3] Stephanie West in the *Oxford Commentary* (ad loc.) thinks in terms of a poetic fiction. She writes: "But geographical accuracy was not of first importance to the poet . . . and . . . having set the story in an area unfamiliar to his audience he has created the sort of island required by his narrative."

It has been the constant theme of this book that geographical accuracy was of prime importance both to Homer and to his audience, some of whom may well have visited Ithaca. One also needs to look at *all* the topographical data bearing on any given episode, for these will often interlock to provide a fuller and clearer picture. In this case there is a later account of the ambush, in book 15, that adds detail of crucial importance for the overall interpretation of the topography.

This later account is after the fact and is given by Antinoos in self-justification for his failure to intercept Telemachos. We did all we could, he says in effect, but the gods were on his side (Od. 16, 364–70):

> Alas, the gods have delivered this man from disaster. By
> day we kept continuous watch in relays on the *windy*
> *heights.* When the sun set, we never passed the night in
> sleep on *the mainland,* but we remained all night long sail-
> ing on the sea in our swift ship until dawn came.

The significant extra detail here is in the words italicised. We have previously been told that the ambush was to be set at Asteris, but these words of Antinoos are, I believe, a clear signal that we must broaden our conception of the setting to include part of the adjacent coast of Kephalonia. Only here can we find "windy heights" on a landmass large enough to merit the term "mainland," as opposed to the tiny harbourless island. The initial mention of Asteris-Daskalio served to pinpoint the general area of the ambush, strategically located abreast of Polis Bay. Homer there said that the island lies in midchannel, but this is not strictly accurate. The channel here is a little more than two miles in width, but Asteris-Daskalio lies within half a mile of the coast of Kephalonia. This portion of the coast provided what the Suitors needed to operate their patrol: secure and well-hidden anchorages, and promotories sufficiently high to afford a good view all the way down the channel.

It is a topographical fact of prime importance that "twin harbours" do exist on this stretch of the coast of Kephalonia, lying in close proximity to Asteris-Daskalio (fig. 7.18). I have already published a detailed account of them.[4] They are small coves with sandy beaches, and they lie side by side in the inner part of a broad bay just south of the village of Evreti. The extremities of the bay are marked by bold headlands. Daskalio is in full view from the coves and appears to lie across their mouths (fig. 7.19). They are thus "within" or "inside" the islet in

7.18 The "twin harbours."

7.19 Asteris-Daskalio seen from one of the "twin harbours" on Kephalonia. The entrance to Polis Bay on Ithaca appears behind and just to the right of the islet.

a broad nautical sense. Both coves are invisible from the channel to the south, but a ship moored in either of them would be well placed to dart out and intercept another ship making for Polis Bay. They thus fulfil the conditions required by the Homeric ambush. One can easily imagine the Suitors' ship lying up there by day while relays of sentries on the heights behind kept watch down the Ithaca Channel for the returning Telemachos. When night fell they could launch their vessel to patrol the stretch of water between there and Polis Bay. The ambush failed because Telemachos did not return back up the channel as expected but sent his ship up the east side of Ithaca. The watchers did not see it rounding the Exogi headland to the north of them, and so it slipped into Polis Bay before it could be intercepted. All this makes very good topographical sense.

I would stress the point that only one ship is manned by the Suitors, yet Homer provides twin harbours for it, surely a pointless complication if the description were purely fictional. The mention of this detail strongly suggests that the account is grounded in the topography of the area. The twin harbours do exist, if not exactly in the place that Homer first indicates.

The setting of the ambush is an important element in the plot of the *Odyssey,* and Homer, it may be supposed, felt the need to locate it with precision. The small but conspicuous island of Asteris-Daskalio was as good as a map reference for this purpose. But if the ambush was to be realistic in tactical terms, it needed a hidden anchorage and observation posts that commanded the whole of the Ithaca Channel. These needs were supplied by the windy heights on the mainland of Kephalonia, as the second description indicates. Yet the twin harbours were such a picturesque detail that Homer, it seems, could not resist a mention of them in the first description, thereby giving the impression that they were actually in Asteris-Daskalio rather than "within" or "inside" it in a nautical sense. I judge this to be an understandable piece of compression in a rapidly moving narrative. In the Asteris passage Homer may have taken some slight and temporary liberty with the facts, but it does not amount to the major anatopism that some commentators have found in it and should not be taken as evidence that Homer did not have firsthand knowledge of the area.

One hesitates to resort to emendation to solve a topographical problem, but G. L. Huxley has pointed out to me that the change of a single letter in *Odyssey* 4,846 would produce the broader meaning of "in" for which I have argued. The proposal would be to alter *eni,* meaning "within," to *epi,* meaning "nearby."

Finding Telemachos in Sparta, Athena warns him about the ambush and tells him that he should return at once to Ithaca. Her instructions for his return journey are as follows (Od. 15, 33–38):

> Keep your well-built ship *away from the islands.* Sail on this course by night also. Your divine protector will send you a favouring breeze. But when you reach the *first cape of Ithaca,* urge on your ship and its company to the city, but yourself go first to the home of the swineherd.

Unnecessary difficulties have been raised about the expression "away from the islands." A. Hoekstra, for example, in the *Oxford Commentary* (ad loc.), says that "'Ithakists' who find precise geographical indications everywhere should explain the extreme vagueness of the expression." I would argue that the expression is not at all vague in the whole context of Athena's speech and in relation to the situation of Telemachos. Athena is urging upon Telemachos the need for a quick return home. She knows that on the outward voyage he came down the Ithaca Channel. She has just informed him that the ambush is set in the strait between Samos (Kephalonia) and Ithaca (lines 28–29). He knows that if he were to return by the same route he would come first to the southern tip of Samos and would be trapped between it and Ithaca. Samos must be avoided at all costs, and also the west coast of Ithaca. These are clearly the islands that he is to keep away from, and he does this, as we soon learn, by steering close to the coast of Elis and then heading north to the southwest tip of Akarnania. He avoids the islands (including Zakynthos) by keeping close to the mainland—it is as simple as that. He cannot, of course, avoid Ithaca altogether, for that is his destination, but he approaches it by a somewhat roundabout route from the east. This brings him to the "first cape" of the island, which must be identified with Cape St. John, close

7.20   Cape St. John, the "first cape" of Ithaca at the southeast corner of the island.

to the homestead of Eumaios (fig. 7.20 and map 10). "First cape" is nautical nomenclature geared to the perspective of sailors approaching Ithaca from the Gulf of Corinth, and it has been observed that pottery styles in Ithaca show a very marked influence from Corinth during the eighth century B.C.

Telemachos took Athena's advice. Having driven back by chariot from Sparta to Pylos, he decided to quicken his return by avoiding another meeting with the garrulous Nestor. He did not go up to the palace but took his leave from Nestor's son Peisistratos on the seashore and made haste to embark (Od. 15, 182–219). It is not necessary to spend time considering the older view that Nestor's Pylos should be looked for at Kakavatos in Triphylia. Thanks to the epoch-making excavation of Carl Blegen at Ano Englianos, we now know that the Pylian palace stood on a hillside there overlooking the Bay of Navarino from the north. Telemachos's return voyage must be visualised as starting from one of the sandy beaches below that site. The main landmarks passed are then stated in order as follows (Od. 15, 295–300):

7.21 The "sharp islands" viewed from near the Raven's Crag.

> The ship sailed past *Krounoi* and fair-flowing *Chalkis*. The
> sun set and all the ways were darkened. The ship was
> going towards *Pheai* urged on by a wind from Zeus, and
> past bright *Elis,* where the Epeians rule. Then he directed
> his ship forward to the *sharp islands,* wondering whether
> he would escape death or be captured.[5]

Krounoi and Chalkis, as Strabo informs us (8, 3, 13 and 26), were the names
of small streams. They cannot now be identified with certainty, but they serve
as an indication of the coast of Messenia north of Pylos. Pheai was a place of
some importance, well embedded in the saga tradition and mentioned also in

the *Iliad*. It is plausibly taken to be the Bronze Age predecessor of the Classical town of that name which stood on a bold promontory near the modern town of Katakolo.[6] The ancient city marked the boundary between Triphylia and Elis. Its prominent position near the sea made it a good mark for sailors coasting up from the south through the Cyparissian Gulf. The ship then followed the coast of Elis as far as the promontory of Chelonatas. Then, instead of turning in towards the Gulf of Corinth, Telemachos struck north to the "sharp islands." The name *Oxeiai* (sharp ones) was associated with a group of steep and rugged islands off the mouth of the river Acheloios. Some of them have now been joined to the mainland by the extension of the delta. One is still called Oxia. There is no mistaking the sharply fretted outline of their ridges as they rise to a considerable height above the alluvial plain. One passes close to them as one sails out from the Gulf of Corinth, and they catch the eye on the eastern horizon as one looks across from Ithaca (fig. 7.21). Telemachos has now followed the injunction to keep away from the islands that meant danger to him, and it should not be considered a difficulty that his course has brought him to another set of islands, the Echinades. He now completes the penultimate leg of his journey by sailing almost due west to Cape St. John at the southeastern extremity of Ithaca. There is a convenient landing place a mile or so north of the cape on the small sandy beach of Port Ligia (fig. 7.22). The anchorage is partly sheltered from the north by the island of Perapigadia, whose name means "Over against the spring," an effective reminder of the local significance of the Fountain of Arethusa, where Telemachos could have stopped to slake his thirst on the steep climb up to the homestead of Eumaios.

On landing, Telemachos issues further orders to his crew (Od. 15, 503–7): "You are now to take the ship on to the city. It is my intention to visit the pastures and the herdsmen. After seeing to my lands I shall return late to the city. Tomorrow morning I plan to pay you your wages for the journey, a satisfying meal of meat and sweet wine." The voyage then concludes with the ship sailing on up the east coast of Ithaca to make a safe return to Polis Bay (Od. 16, 321–27) (fig. 7.23). Meanwhile, Telemachos receives a touchingly fond welcome from Eumaios (Od. 16, 11–21).

7.22   Port Ligia, the cove below the Raven's Crag.

7.23   Polis Bay.

Odysseus, still in disguise, is introduced to him as a stranger from Crete. After some discussion of the situation in the palace it is agreed that Eumaios is to go there to inform Penelope of Telemachos's safe arrival at the swineherd's homestead. Telemachos orders him not to linger on his errand and not to make any attempt to contact Laertes, whose farm is clearly envisaged as lying some distance away from the palace (Od. 16, 150–51): "After delivering your message come back here, and do not wander off into the countryside in search of Laertes."

The account of Eumaios's journey to the palace and back shows that Homer has a firm grip of Ithacan topography, in particular of the spatial relationship between the Raven's Crag at one end of the island and the palace at the other. I assume, in accordance with the archaeological findings, that the palace is to be envisaged as situated in the north of the island where the Pilikata-Stavros ridge provides a suitable eminence dominating much good well-watered land. To reach it Eumaios would have to make for the Aetos isthmus and then follow the west coast past Mount Neriton (see map 9). Assuming that he took the most direct route across the hills, one can reasonably estimate the distance at not more than fourteen miles. The round-trip would be less than thirty miles, a long but far from impossible day's walk for a hardy Greek herdsman. And this is the time the journey takes, as we learn from incidental indications in the narrative.

Telemachos arrives at Ligia Bay as dawn is breaking (Od. 15, 495–97). This means that he has been sailing overnight, which is allowed for in Athena's instructions (Od. 15, 34). He finds Eumaios and Odysseus at an early breakfast (Od. 16, 1–2), and Eumaios must be presumed to start on his errand soon afterwards. After delivering his message he starts back at once, as he later informs Telemachos (Od. 16, 464–67), and Homer adds that he does not get back home until evening, when Odysseus and Telemachos are at supper (Od. 16, 452–54). Eumaios's long absence has allowed time for Odysseus to reveal himself to his son and for them to plot their future course of action. It is agreed that Telemachos will return to the palace on his own the following morning and that Eumaios will bring the "beggar" later. This is a particularly good example of a narrative deftly managed and envisaged in full conformity with the topographical realities of Ithaca.

7.24   The broad-backed col, Homer's Ridge of Hermes, that joins Mount Anogi (Mount Neriton) to Mount Exogi. The view is taken looking north over Stavros village. The highest point of the ridge is the area known as Pilikata.

One further point in the narrative needs emphasising because it provides us with another significant Ithacan toponym, and also confirms that Homer envisaged the palace as situated on the Pilikata ridge. As part of his report to Telemachos, Eumaios says (Od. 16, 471–73):

> I was already on my way, walking on the *Ridge of Hermes*
> above the polis when I saw a swift ship coming into our
> harbour.

The ship in question is the Suitors' ship returning from the failed ambush and putting in to "our harbour," a patriotic reference to Polis Bay. Eumaios has just left the palace and is above the houses of the town with a clear view down to Polis Bay. The conclusion, I suggest, is inescapable that the Ridge of Hermes is to be identified with the col that runs south from Pilikata to Mount Neriton (fig. 7.24). The palace, as Heurtley argued, can plausibly be imagined as situated at its highest point (Pilikata), with the houses of the polis occupying the slopes running down towards Polis Bay. A small stream comes down past Asprosykia (where Mycenaean sherds have been found), and this fact coheres well with the detail of the scene setting that marks Odysseus's own arrival (with Eumaios) at the palace.

Telemachos, as agreed the previous day, has gone ahead on his own. Odysseus has resumed his disguise, and Eumaios has been told to bring him to the palace so that he can beg for his supper there. They set out somewhat late in the day and have to hurry. Eumaios is reluctant to leave his steading for the second day running. "The day is mostly gone," he snaps, exaggerating in his impatience to be off (Od. 17, 190–91). Homer makes Odysseus talk in his assumed character as a stranger to the island. "You say that the city is a long way off," he remarks to Telemachos (Od. 17, 25). And in similar vein he says to Eumaios (Od. 17, 195–96): "Give me a stick to support my steps, if you have one cut, since you tell me that the path is treacherous."

And so at last he finally reaches his home (Od. 17, 204–11):

> Walking on a rugged road they drew near to the city and
> came to the fair-flowing fountain with its well-made
> basin whence the citizens used to draw their water.
> Ithakos and Neritos and Polyktor had built it. A grove of
> water-loving poplars surrounded it, and the cold water
> flowed down from the rock above. Over it stood a built
> altar of the nymphs where all wayfarers used to make
> their offerings.

This is a picturesque but somewhat conventional piece of landscaping designed to highlight the hero's long-delayed return. A contrast is implied between the rough and rocky track through the wilder parts of the open countryside and the amenities of city life. The polis, with its civilised drinking fountain, is a human creation in which the citizens take pride, and it is appropriate for the poet to recall the eponymous founding fathers of a former generation. They are royal Achaean predecessors of the king who is about to resume his authority in Ithaca,

7.25   The Stavros-Pilikata ridge (Homer's Ridge of Hermes) seen from Polis Bay. The valley of the stream running down from Mount Exogi is visible on the left.

and it is of interest to note that Neritos is attested as a personal name in the Linear B tablets from Pylos.[7]

No trace remains of the drinking fountain or the altar of the nymphs with which they are said to have adorned the city, but these constructions, if they ever existed, are likely to have been on a comparatively humble scale. Perhaps the works turned the local stream into something like the Fountain of Arethusa in the nineteenth century (see fig. 7.10) and have long since been dismantled by earthquakes or swept away by winter floods. It is possible that Homer saw something of the sort on a visit to Ithaca. A water source of the quality of the Pilikata brook is good by Ithacan standards and would have been well utilised by a nearby settlement. Below Stavros church, where paths converge from Stavros, Tris Langadas (where Sylvia Benton excavated a substantial Mycenaean house), and Polis Bay, the stream cascades down over rocks into a thicket of bushes. The place is about a quarter of a mile from the summit of the ridge at Pilikata. I do not remember any poplars in the area, but I recollect it as a possible place where

7.26 A closer view of the western flank of the Stavros-Pilikata ridge. The ravine of the stream that watered the Late Bronze Age polis is seen in the foreground. Asprosykia, where Mycenaean sherds were found, lies in this area. Part of Stavros village is seen above, with the church on the left.

the water could easily have been trapped in an artificial basin. Such a watering place would have been conveniently located for the inhabitants of a town on the slopes of the Ridge of Hermes (figs. 7.25 and 7.26).

It has already been pointed out that Homer makes the point in the first book of the *Odyssey* that Phrikes Bay is visible from the courtyard of Odysseus's palace. As noted above, he makes Eumaios report the sighting of a ship in Polis Bay from close to the palace. Sight lines from Phrikes Bay on the east coast and Polis Bay on the west coast do indeed intersect at Pilikata on the Stavros ridge, which is yet one more proof of the credibility of Homer's narrative. I hesitate to

say that one could not see both harbours simultaneously from any other location in the north of the island. One could probably do so from higher up on Mount Exogi or from the northern slopes of Mount Neriton. But the view from Pilikata is a telling one and tends to haunt the memory as one recalls also the archaeological arguments for a substantial Mycenaean building there. The sector of the ridge from which the dual view is possible is quite narrow, and as soon as one dips down to either side of the summit, sight is lost of one or the other haven.

An impressive bust of Odysseus stands in Stavros village (fig. 7.27), and there is more than local patriotism to associate his memory with the area. In

7.28   The Cave of the Tripods on the northern shore of Polis Bay.

the early 1930s Miss Benton, working for the British School, explored and thoroughly excavated an interesting and important site close to the sea on the north side of Polis Bay (fig. 7.28). In antiquity it had been a cave shrine, but the roof of the cave collapsed early in the Christian era, a fortunate event that helped to preserve the remarkable series of finds discovered below its floor. Access was also rendered more difficult by a rise in the sea level. Miss Benton was not the first to excavate there. In 1868 and 1873 a local landowner called Loizos dug up some intriguing objects, including a bronze sword and spear-point and a bronze tripod-cauldron. A visiting Dutch archaeologist, Carel Vollgraff, recovered some Mycenaean pottery from the site in 1904, the first to be found on Ithaca. But no thorough exploration was made until Miss Benton's campaigns. Working under considerable difficulty from intrusive seawater, she revealed an important deposit of well-stratified pottery and

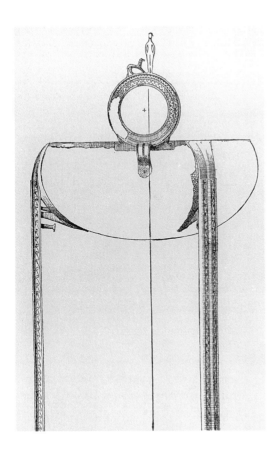

7.29 A bronze tripod dated c. 800 B.C., reconstructed from fragments found in the Polis Bay cave.

votive offerings. These proved that the cave had been continually in use as a shrine over a very long period from the Bronze Age down to the first century A.D. A cult of the nymphs at the cave was proved by inscriptions on some of the sherds. But even more exciting was the recovery of a fragment of a terra-cotta mask dating from the second or first century B.C. and bearing the words ΕΥΧΗΝ ΟΔΥΣΣΕΙ, "MY PRAYER TO ODYSSEUS." This is clear proof that a cult of the hero was associated with the cave in the Hellenistic period. His memory must still have been honoured in the area, and it is very pleasing to have his name documented so close to the conjectured site of his palace and polis.

There was yet another find from the Polis cave of even greater significance for Homeric studies. Miss Benton and her team recovered fragments of twelve magnificent tripod-cauldrons (fig. 7.29). These were massive bronze vessels whose circular basins were supported on legs about three feet in length. I was able to inspect and admire their fine workmanship in the little museum in Stavros. Legs and handles are handsomely chased with linked spirals and other geometric motifs, and some of the handles are surmounted with animal and human figurines. One of the tripods was wheeled in the Cypro-Phoenician manner. Their style and decoration enable experts to date them to the late ninth or early eighth century B.C. They represent opulent dedications in the cave shrine at a date considerably later than the age of Odysseus and the other heroes of the Trojan War, and also appreciably earlier than the probable date of Homer and the *Odyssey*. Yet they have a fascinating link with that poem, and possibly also with a cult of Odysseus in the cave, for they may well have been dedicated in his honour.[8] In view of the unique importance of this find, I feel that the Polis cave should always be called the Cave of the Tripods rather than (as it sometimes is) the Cave of the Nymphs. It is important to avoid confusion with the cave at Marmarospilia.

The link of the tripod-cauldrons with the *Odyssey* derives from Homer's account of the parting gifts given to Odysseus by King Alkinoos and his peers before he left Phaeacia. Homer does not say explicitly that the gifts included thirteen tripods, but this emerges if one takes two passages together. When Odysseus has won the approval of the Phaeacians for his athletic prowess and general demeanour, Alkinoos proposes that he should receive gifts in token of guest friendship and that these should be given by the chief men of the country. His actual words include the following statement (Od. 8, 390–91):

> Twelve noble peers lord it as rulers in the community,
> and I myself am the thirteenth.

The proposal is accepted and carried out, and Odysseus amasses a stock of garments and gold against his departure. After he has further charmed his hosts with his spellbinding account of his wanderings, Alkinoos is moved to propose another parting gift from the Phaeacian elders and leading councillors, who must surely be the same group of thirteen rulers referred to in the earlier passage. The crucial passage in the later book reads as follows (Od. 13, 13–15):

> Come let each of us man by man give him a large tripod
> and cauldron. We shall later levy compensation from the
> community, for it is painful for individuals to make
> bountiful gifts without reimbursement.

These two passages together make it clear that part of the treasure brought back to Ithaca by Odysseus consisted of thirteen large tripod-cauldrons. If one adds the tripod-cauldron earlier found by Loizos to those found by Miss Benton, precisely thirteen of these objects were recovered from the cave on the shore of Polis Bay.

The coincidence between the poem and the archaeological facts gives much food for thought. Was the number thirteen firmly embedded in oral versions of the story of Odysseus current before c. 800 B.C., and did knowledge of this lead some Ithacan leader or other local chieftain to make a commemorative dedication of precisely that number? Or did thirteen similar dedications accumulate over a period of a generation or so, later to be seen and admired by Homer and his contemporaries? Did the locals represent them to credulous visitors as having belonged to Odysseus himself? And was that the reason why Homer, either from personal knowledge or on the basis of reliable information, decided to weave thirteen tripod-cauldrons into the texture of his narrative? Did the number of the dedications in fact determine the number of Homer's Phaeacian leaders?[9]

Such questions are easy to ask and impossible to answer with certainty. I will merely say that intensive study of the text of the Homeric epics tends to make one increasingly conscious of a single mastermind ordering and controlling all the manifold elements of the narrative. Homer's genius appears to me to consist above all in his ability to comprehend the vast and disparate legacy of his tradition and to shape it into a consistent, accurate, and harmonious whole. The topographical material that has formed the staple of this study is just one of the fields in which this ability for monumental composition is exercised. Homer shows such an easy mastery of the geography of Ithaca and moves his characters so realistically through its landscape that personal knowledge of the island seems the most plausible explanation for the factual accuracy of his descriptions and allusions. In keeping with this hypothesis, I would suggest that he had seen the thirteen tripod-cauldrons in the cave by Polis Bay, that he had noted their connection with the cult of Odysseus, and that he took pleasure in working them unobtrusively into the narrative as part of the treasure that his hero brought from Phaeacia.

On the basis of all the evidence presented in the past two chapters, I conclude that the topographical setting for the events of the last twelve books of the *Odyssey* is in full and accurate correspondence with the terrain of the island still known as Itháki. Its four main districts (Ithaca, Neriton, Krokuleia, and Aigilips) receive mention in the Greek Catalogue in the *Iliad,* and in the *Odyssey* Homer names two of its mountains (Neriton and Neion), two of its harbours (Reithron and Phorcys), two distinctive natural features (the Raven's Crag and the Fountain of Arethusa), a ridge near the palace (the Ridge of Hermes), and a small rocky island in the strait between it and Samos (Asteris). He alludes to one of its promontories (the "first cape") and another harbour ("our harbour") and describes a cave sacred to the nymphs in such a way that they can be securely identified with Cape St. John, Polis Bay, and the cave at Marmarospilia. In addition he names three nearby islands, of which one (Zakynthos) can be identified with certainty, and the other two (Samos and Doulichion) with reasonable assurance. He mentions sea routes to Doulichion and to Elis, where Ithacans have property on the mainland (Od. 4, 634–37). He emphasises the rough and rocky nature of much of the island's surface, the fact that it is "not broad" and "not suitable for horses" because it lacks meadows and level ground, but says also that it is not a poor or miserable place, because it has an adequate rainfall and a sufficiency of springs and running water. It produces corn and wine, and has pasturage for goats, pigs, and even cattle. Its "flourishing fruit trees" are specified in the vines, pear trees, fig trees, and apple trees that grow on the farm of Laertes. What more, I wonder, could a modern guidebook tell one, apart from archaeological information about the chief area of

Achaean occupation—which is implicit in Homer's siting of the main town and palace of Odysseus in the north of the island.

The hypothesis of *Homeros autoptes,* Homer as eyewitness of the Ithaca he describes, appears in the ancient *Lives* of the poet and has received strong, if intermittent, support from modern Homerists.[10] One must, however, respect the scholarly caution that deters many from making the leap of faith needed to embrace it. I would not claim that it is proved beyond all reasonable doubt, but on the balance of probabilities I think it is more likely than not to be correct.

It is my earnest hope that some of my readers may be stimulated to visit the island, for in this matter seeing is indeed the surest road to believing. The evidence assembled in this study should at least make it hard to deny that Homer's picture of Ithaca is well grounded in reality and that it relates to the island that still bears the ancient and celebrated name. It then becomes a question of assessing how far charges of vagueness and inaccuracy are sustainable. It would be well if any final verdict were postponed until one has surveyed the panorama of sea and islands from the northern shores of Itháki (in the district the Catalogue calls Ithaca), or examined Asteris-Daskalio and the nearby coastline of Kephalonia at close quarters. The authenticity of Homer's brushwork will then, I think, stand up to the closest scrutiny.

If so, one has then to consider whether such a detailed and accurate picture could have been composed solely on the basis of travellers' reports, without any direct and personal knowledge of the terrain. One should also take account of the important and intimate relation between locality and the narrative. The action of the second half of the *Odyssey* takes place in three distinct settings: the area of the Bay of Phorcys, the area of Eumaios's cottage, and the area of the palace. Homer visualises and describes these locations accurately in themselves but also, and more significantly, exhibits a very firm grasp of the spatial relations that bind them into the overall landscape. He knows, for example, that the Cave of the Nymphs has a small, north-facing opening easily blocked by a single boulder. He is also aware that the chief mountain of Ithaca is in full view from that spot. In the case of the swineherd's cottage, he knows that it is near the "first cape" in the southeast corner of Ithaca, which makes it a suitable landing place for a ship coming from the "sharp islands" on the coast of Akarnania. He also knows that its distance from the palace requires a full day to be allotted if a messenger is to travel there and back. With regard to the palace, which he locates on or near a named ridge (the Ridge of Hermes), he alludes incidentally to the fact that sight lines from the nearest and best harbours on both coasts intersect there. These particulars are not obtruded; they emerge naturally and easily from the course of the narrative. In the same way Homer weaves in a reference to the thirteen tripod-cauldrons, strikingly suggestive of an equal number found in a cult cave at Polis Bay.

One could, I suppose, imagine Homer in Ionia meeting and talking to seamen or merchants who had sailed the western route to Sicily. From such conversations he might progressively have built up a picture of the main landmarks of Ithaca, from "first cape" to Polis Bay. Some of his informants might have visited the Cave of the Nymphs or the Cave of the Tripods to discharge a vow or leave a votive offering, and they could have given him a detailed description of these locations. With the plot of the epic forming in his mind and the movements of the characters already visualised, he could have quizzed them specifically on distances and directions. Merely to imagine such proceedings gives rise to interesting questions about how the poem came to be composed. But how much simpler to suppose that Homer went to Ithaca to see it for himself! Just as we have seen reason to suppose that Homer had viewed from shipboard the burial mounds that ring the plain of Troy and had stood on the plain itself, so the conjecture of a fact-gathering expedition to Ithaca may in the end be the best hypothesis to explain the detailed knowledge of landscape and locality so tellingly deployed in the *Odyssey*.

THE STEMMA OF THE TROJAN ROYAL HOUSE

After Homer, *Iliad* 20, 213 ff.

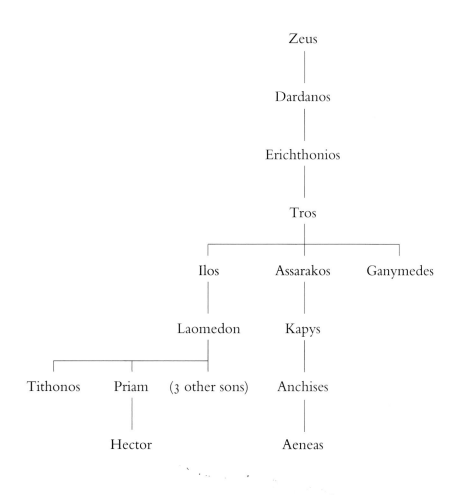

CHRONOLOGY OF TROY

An outline chronology of the successive cities at
Hisarlik, based on the most recent assessments
by the Troia Projekt.

Troy I: 2920–2450 B.C.

Troy II: 2600–2450 B.C.
The civilisation of Troy II is now viewed as that of a dominant class superimposed on the cultural framework of Troy I.

Troy III: 2390–2200 B.C.
This city still belongs to the same line of development that begins in early Troy I.

Troy IV: 2200–2000 B.C.

Troy V: 2000–1870 B.C.
Troy IV and Troy V represent a new phase with a culture more closely related to central Anatolia.

Troy VI: 1700–1250 B.C.
In this phase the layout of the Citadel is remodelled and the fortifications greatly extended.

Troy VII: 1250–1020 B.C.
The cultural features of Troy VIh continue unchanged in Troy VIIa for about a century. Troy VIIb represents a culture break associated with new invaders from the Balkans.

Troy VIII: 800–85 B.C.
This phase is associated with the Greek city of Ilion. It reflects the initial colonisation and subsequent development by Greek settlers. It is taken to end with the sack by the Roman general Fimbria in the war against Mithridates.

Troy IX: 85 B.C. on
The Greek city was extensively rebuilt by the Romans under Augustus because of the supposed descent of the Julio-Claudian dynasty from Aeneas. As Novum Ilium it continued to flourish for at least five centuries but gradually petered out in the late Byzantine period and was never occupied by the Turks.

The Aegean Bronze Age may be taken as lasting for approximately two millennia, from c. 3000 to c. 1100 B.C., with the Late Bronze Age running from c. 1500 B.C. to the end of the epoch. The Early Iron Age (c. 1100–800 B.C.) was a period of cultural impoverishment in both Greece and the Troad. Greek civilisation began to revive again in the eighth century B.C. with a renewal of literacy, expanding trade, and overseas colonisation. The period 700–500 B.C. is known as the Archaic Age of Greece. The heyday of Greek city-state civilisation, the Classical period, may be regarded as running from the successful struggle against Persia (490–479 B.C.) to the death of Alexander the Great in 323 B.C. The Hellenistic Age occupies the next three centuries, down to the victory of Octavian over Antony in 31 B.C. This ushers in the full Roman imperial age.

NOTES

CHAPTER ONE **LANDSCAPE AND THE BARD**

1. See B. B. Powell, *Homer and the Origin of the Greek Alphabet* (Cambridge, 1991), 148–50: "From Ithaca survives a piece of writing of the end of the eighth or beginning of the seventh century. Written from left to right, the fragmentary hexameters run in a spiral around a Geometric jug of local manufacture." There are six "sadly tattered hexameters," of which little can be made out except the phrase "a guest and a friend and a trusty companion." For the last words, compare Il. 15, 331.

2. A. Thornton, *Homer's Iliad: Its Composition and the Motif of Supplication* (Göttingen, 1984), 150. W. Elliger, in his *Die Darstellung der Landschaft in der Griechischen Dichtung* (Berlin, 1975), also held that Homer's plain of Troy related to an artistic not a geographical reality. In general he took the view that the question of "truth to life" is irrelevant in a *Kunstwerk*.

3. *The Iliad: A Commentary,* in six volumes, by various hands (Cambridge, 1985–93), hereafter cited as *Cambridge Commentary.* The quoted comment comes in the note on Il. 11, 166.

4. *A Commentary on Homer's Odyssey,* in three volumes, by various hands (Oxford, 1988–92), hereafter cited as *Oxford Commentary.* The quoted comment will be found in vol. 1, 65.

5. R. Janko, *Homer, Hesiod, and the Hymns* (Cambridge, 1982). The conclusions of his stylistic analysis are summed up in his fig. 4, p. 200.

6. Albin Lesky, *A History of Greek Literature* (2d ed., London, 1966), 40.

7. Aristotle, *frag.* 66 (Rose), from the Plutarchan *Life,* sect. 3; Pindar, *frag.* 264; Aristotle, *Rhet.* B. 23, 1398b, 12–13.

8. I owe the reference to J. Griffin, *Homer on Life and Death* (Oxford, 1980), 6.

9. See G. L. Huxley, *The Early Ionians* (London, 1966), 85–86.

CHAPTER TWO **THE TROAD**

1. R. Janko in *Cambridge Commentary,* ad loc.

2. C. Kinglake, *Eothen* (1844), 65. Cf. Janko in the *Cambridge Commentary* on Il. 13, 10–12: "The poet who placed the god there [on Samothrace] had seen it from the plain of Troy."

3. See G. L. Huxley, "Aigai in Alkaios," *Greek, Roman, and Byzantine Studies* 10, (1969): 10–11. This Thracian Aigai may not be the same as the Aigai mentioned in Il. 8, 203 as a cult centre of Poseidon. Poseidon would have felt at home at any Aigai, for one of his epithets was

Aigaios; the same root appears in the Aegean Sea. See R. L. Fowler, "ΑΙΓ—In Early Greek Language and Style," *Phoenix* 42 (1988): 95–113.

4. The mention of a peak sanctuary is curiously reminiscent of the religion of Minoan Crete, with its many peak sanctuaries. Crete has its Mount Ida (the name is said to mean "forest"), with the great cult cave Kamares near its summit. When the Greeks took over the island they acquired also a strange tale of how Zeus was born in just such another cave on Mount Dicte, while his grave was pointed out on Mount Juktas, south of Knossos. But the concept of a "dying Zeus" is alien to the whole thrust of the religion of the "immortals" as we find it in Homer.

5. Walter Leaf, in his discussion of the Agenor incident, places the "foothills of Ida" therein mentioned at Ballı Dağ. He also locates the "Ileian plain" to the west and south of Troy. (W. Leaf, *Troy* [London, 1912], 163–64, hereafter cited as *Troy* [1912]).

6. J. M. Cook, *The Troad* (Oxford, 1973), 306, hereafter cited as *Troad*. Cook, as always, has much useful information in his section on the Kaz Dağ (304–7).

7. Il. 21, 449; cf. the herds of Aeneas driven off by Achilles from the southern slopes of the mountain during a foray on Pedasos and Lyrnessos, Il. 20, 91–92.

8. Robert Wood, *An Essay on the Original Genius and Writings of Homer* (London, 1775), 321–22, hereafter cited as *Essay*.

9. *Troad,* 306, 227.

10. In the opening chapters of book 13 of his *Geographica,* Strabo discusses some widely differing views on the extent of the Troad. He himself equates it with Priam's realm in its widest possible sense and so takes it to begin at the mouth of the Aisepos and extend as far south as the boundary between Aeolis and Ionia. The *Periplous* of Scylax put its northern boundary at Abydos, and its southern boundary was placed by some writers no farther south than Cape Lekton. As Cook points out, the lack of unanimity in the ancient sources makes it impossible to attach "precise geographical or political connotations" to the term (*Troad,* 1). But in purely geographical terms, the Ida massif does mark a distinct physical frontier on the southeast, just as the Hellespont marks the border on the northwest. D. E. W. Wormell, in *The Oxford Classical Dictionary* (3d ed., s. v. *Troas),* is crisp and to the point: The Troad is "the mountainous north-west corner of Asia Minor forming a geographical unit dominated by the Ida massif and washed on three sides by the sea. Its name derives from the belief that all this area was once under Trojan rule."

That Homer's conception of the Troad is the same as that adopted by Wormell appears clear from his list of the eight rivers summoned by Poseidon and Apollo to obliterate the fortifications of the Achaean Camp (Il. 12, 20–23). Four of these (Scamander, Simoeis, Granikos, Aisepos) can be identified with certainty: see map 2. The remaining four (Rhesos, Heptaporos, Caresos, Rhodios) are more controversial. Strabo (13, 1, 43–44, based on Demetrios) discusses the problem in detail, and I have largely followed his indications in the tentative identifications given on map 2. It will be seen that three of the rivers are marked as tributaries of the Granikos, which is certainly the largest river of the Troad. The Aisepos is also mentioned in the Trojan Catalogue, as is the river

Selleïs (Il. 2, 825, 839). The Selleïs could be the classical Praktios, for it is associated with Arisbê. One other river, the Satnioeis, is three times mentioned, twice in connection with Pedasos (probably the later Assos), and is almost certainly the modern Tuzla Çay (Il. 6, 34–35; 14, 445; 21, 87).

11. G. L. Huxley has kindly allowed me to quote a strong statement of the point from an unpublished lecture on the geography of Sophocles: "Greek myth and legend are firmly set in the realities of Greek land and water. That is one of the reasons why they have so firm a hold upon the imagination, and why they are not directly convertible into the systems of belief held by peoples living in other places. Zeus presides upon Olympos, the god Acheloios is the greatest of Greek rivers; Hesiod saw the Muses on Mount Helikon; and Homer's Agamemnon reigns in the fortress of Mycenae. Myth and legend were ever present to the minds of Greek poets; so when we study Greek poetry we too must try to keep in mind the landscape in which the stories of gods and heroes are placed."

12. J. B. Bury and Russell Meiggs, *A History of Greece* (4th ed., London, 1975), 452.

13. I owe the references to Brooke, Hankey, and Buchan to an unpublished paper by the late Robert M. Ogilvie that he read some years ago at Trinity College Dublin. The Buchan passage is quoted from *Episodes of War*, 206. The Brooke fragment will be found in *The Collected Poems of Rupert Brooke* (London, 1992), 162, and the letter in ibid., 150.

14. Thebê: Il. 6, 415–16; Pedasos and Lyrnessos: Il. 20, 92. Thebê is probably to be identified with a prehistoric site in the plain near Edremit. Leaf (*Troy*, 221–23) followed Edward Daniel Clarke (*Travels in Various Countries of Europe, Asia, and Africa* [London, 1810–23], part 1) in identifying Pedasos with the later Assos, and despite the reservations of Cook (*Troad*, 245–46), this should be accepted. It follows that the river Satnioeis, twice mentioned by Homer in connection with Pedasos (6, 34–35; 21, 87) must be the Tuzla Çay. For Lyrnessos see Leaf (1912), *Troy*, 217–21.

15. See H. Ebeling, *Lexicon Homericum*, s.v. *Hellespontos*. Some commentators have argued that the meaning of Hellespont can be stretched to cover the northern Aegean as well as the Dardanelles (e.g., Janko in *Cambridge Commentary*, vol. 4 on 15, 233–35). Cf. Strabo on the problem, quoted in the *Loeb* edition (book 7, frag. 57 [58]). It is true that there is a certain vagueness inherent in the derivation from "Sea (*pontos*) of Hellê," and those who want to widen its designation in Homer point to the epithets "fishy" and "boundless," which are often used of *pontos* (the sea) in general. But as noted above, "broad" is particularly appropriate for the channel as distinct from the open sea, and in my opinion "swift-flowing" more than counteracts "boundless." I have attempted to account for "boundless" in context as a reflection of the subjectivity of Achilles' perceptions. But it is to be remarked that in a passage in Herodotus (1, 57), "on the Hellespont" means on the shores of the Propontis (Sea of Marmara), and this usage might already be implicit in the Homeric epithet "boundless." As noted earlier in the chapter Priam's kingdom extended as far as Zeleia on the Propontis.

16. For details of the area see Cook, *Troad*, 189–235.

17. Strabo's argument (13, 1, 48 and 63) begins from *Iliad* 1, 366–69, which clearly implies

that Chryseïs was captured at Thebê, which for other reasons needs to be located southeast of the summit ridge of Ida. Therefore, he argues, her hometown of Chrysa must have been near Thebê. This does not necessarily follow, for she might have been on a visit to Thebê as the scholia on 1,366–69 explain. See Kirk's note in *Cambridge Commentary,* ad loc. Strabo's other main argument is that the Smintheum is not on the sea, though in his view Homer indicates that it is. It is true that Chryseis is brought back by ship, and a harbour is mentioned (Il. 1, 30–41), but the narrative does not state that Chrysa lay right on the coast. The Homeric data are quite consistent with its having been situated a short distance inland.

18. Cook, *Troad,* 232, locates it at Göz Tepe.

19. Wood, *Essay,* 131–32. His remarks form a prologue to a good discussion of the geography of the journeys of Neptune and Juno (as he calls them).

20. *Troad,* 257–59.

21. Kirk, in *Cambridge Commentary,* vol. 2 on 8, 47–48, says that the battlefield of Troy is not visible from the Koca Kaya, but my own investigations encourage me to express strong doubts about the accuracy of this statement.

CHAPTER THREE THE PLAIN OF TROY AND THE RIVERS

1. Leaf, *Troy* (1912), 24.

2. The epithet *eribōlax/eribōlos* occurs at *Iliad* 3, 74; 6, 315; 9, 329; 16, 461; 18, 67; 23, 215; 24, 86. When Homer wants to specify the city rather than the district, he often uses architectural epithets like "high-gated" or "with broad streets."

3. Leaf, *Troy* (1912), 30.

4. *Troy,* supp. monograph 4, ed. G. Rapp and John A. Gifford (Princeton, 1982), fig. 3, p. 17.

5. It is much to his credit that Cook saw and stated this clearly before the new geophysical evidence became available: "At the same time, the fact remains that for an army with a thousand ships the north end of the Trojan Plain on the narrows is an impossible camping site, and must surely have been so three thousand years ago" (*Troad,* 171).

6. *Troad,* 23.

7. I owe my knowledge of this poem to a well-documented work, *The Search for Troy, 1553–1874,* by A. C. Lascarides. The publication was made by the Lilly Library of Indiana University (Publication no. 29, 1977) and is the catalogue of a major exhibition of 169 items comprising books, maps, and photographs, prepared and described by the author.

8. *Byron's Letters and Journals,* ed. L. A. Marchand (London, 1973), vol. 8, 21–22.

9. See N. Richardson in *Cambridge Commentary,* ad loc.

10. W. M. Leake, *Journal of a Tour in Asia Minor* (London, 1824), 282–83. Leake was unable to test the water temperature for himself because his thermometer had been broken when his horse fell. He spent some days in the Troad, noting the site of New Ilion on a hill "three miles

from the nearest shore" (275). He did not take it to be the site of Troy, however, but accepted the then-current views of Lechavalier and Choiseul-Gouffier about Ballı Dağ and the Scamander. He seems to have been aware of Maclaren's support for Hisarlik, speaking critically of "some adverse systems recently maintained with great learning and ingenuity, though chiefly, it must be admitted, by those who have considered the question in the closet only" (277).

11. For a typically thorough and judicious review of the archaeological evidence, see Cook, *Troad*, 134–140. Cook is inclined to think that the hilltop may have been the site of a minor Classical Greek city called Gentinos. His work must now be supplemented by recent field surveys carried out by members of the Troia Projekt, which indicate that two nearby heights were fortified in the Late Bronze Age, presumably to guard the route along the Scamander from its middle basin to the lower plain.

12. For a discussion of this difficult problem, see Cook, *Troad*, 92–94. Cook's considered verdict is that Clarke identified the New Ilion site with certainty, but Maclaren, who may have misunderstood Clarke's use of toponyms, attacks his speculations as "the very essence of confusion" (*A Dissertation on the Topography of the Plain of Troy* [1822], 74).

13. "Observations on the Topography of the Trojan Plain," *Journal of the Royal Geographical Society* 12 (1842): 29. It is certainly much larger than any river of the Peloponnese and must on that account have impressed the invading Achaeans with the volume of its flow.

14. For further details see Cook, *Troad*, 291–93.

15. Il. 14, 433–34; 21, 1–2; 24, 692–93; "fair-flowing" Scamander also in Il. 7, 329; "great deep-eddying river," 20, 73, and four other instances; "eddying," 21, 124–25. The formulaic system covering all cases is well set out by Richardson in the *Cambridge Commentary* in his note on 21, 1–2. I observe that there is only one use of Scamander in the dative (Il. 5, 36), and it is there qualified by the unique epithet *eioenti*.

16. Scene in Il. 6, 390–493; name in line 402; prayer in lines 476–81. In Greek tradition Achilles' son Neoptolemos flung Astyanax to his death from the battlements.

17. *Cambridge Commentary*, ad loc.

18. See Cook, *Troad*, 110–13.

19. *Troia*, 281–83, and *Ilios*, 59, 71.

20. The fodder is *ambrosia*, and Kirk, *Cambridge Commentary*, vol. 2 ad loc., comments that "the special food of the gods becomes that of their horses too; nowhere else is it implied to be a kind of plant, though the idea is plausible."

CHAPTER FOUR **TROY, HOMER, AND THE ARCHAEOLOGISTS**

1. For a well-documented and sympathetic treatment of Calvert, see Marcelle Robinson's articles: "Pioneer, Scholar, and Victim: An Appreciation of Frank Calvert (1828–1908)," *Anatolian Studies* 44 (1994): 153–68; and "Frank Calvert and the Discovery of Troia," *Studia Troica* 5 (1995): 323–41.

An important biography of Schliemann by David Traill entitled *Schliemann of Troy: Treasure and Deceit* (John Murray) appeared in 1995, and in Penguin Books in 1996 (hereafter cited as *Schliemann).* By extensive use of Schliemann's diaries and letters, Traill is able to show that many serious discrepancies exist between the "facts" as therein recorded and what Schliemann subsequently published, particularly in the autobiography prefixed to his *Ilios.* Even the diaries were sometimes doctored and are not a completely reliable record of his day-to-day doings. Some of the exaggerations and distortions of fact are trivial enough, but others are more serious and appear to justify the charge that Schliemann sometimes indulged in calculated mendacity. For example, he gives a dramatic account of how his wife Sophie helped him to unearth what he called Priam's Treasure, but it is clear from other sources that she was not in Troy at the time. The Treasure is not a fake, but there are grounds for thinking that not all the items in it were found at the time and place that Schliemann indicates in his published account. Similar doubts attach to his shaft grave finds from Mycenae. Schliemann, it is urged, was a highly manipulative character who did not shrink from using duplicity to achieve business ends, and his consuming desire for scholarly recognition seems, as his detractors maintain, to have led him to be less than totally honest in his archaeological reporting. Supporters of Schliemann have to reckon with these charges and must be circumspect about taking all his statements at their face value. But even as one recognises the elements of selfishness and chicanery in his character, one can still maintain that the pioneering importance and magnitude of his archaeological achievement remain substantially unimpaired.

2. *Ithaque,* 175–76; translation by Leo Deuel, in his valuable *Memoirs of Heinrich Schliemann* (London, 1978), 153. Calvert's own account of the August 15 meeting puts the facts in a very different light: "When I first met the doctor, in August 1868, the subject of Hisarlik as the probable site of Troy, was new to him"; quoted by D. Traill (*Schliemann,* 57) from an article by Calvert published in *The Guardian,* August 11, 1875.

3. Schliemann presented his collection of Trojan antiquities, including the Treasure, to the German people in 1881 on condition that it should remain on view in perpetuity. On the outbreak of World War II the collection was dispersed and hidden at various places in Germany and Poland. Four hundred crates of ceramics and other artifacts were recovered from Schloss Lebus on the Oder and returned to East Berlin in 1946. Some caches in other places in Poland are known to have been destroyed in air raids. At the end of the war the precious objects constituting Priam's Treasure, packed in three crates, were stored in a bunker beside the zoological gardens in Berlin. The crates disappeared in the confusion caused by the Russian advance, and thereafter the Soviet authorities disclaimed any knowledge of their whereabouts. There were fears that the objects might have been stolen and melted down. Fortunately this was not the case, and early in 1994 the Russian Ministry of Culture announced that the Treasure was located in the Pushkin Museum of Fine Arts in Moscow, where it has been made available for inspection by international experts. An exhibition of it was mounted in Moscow in 1996, accompanied by a

finely illustrated catalogue: *The Gold of Troy: Searching for Homer's Fabled City,* by Vladimir Tolstikov and Mikhail Treister, published by the Ministry of Culture of the Russian Federation/A. S. Pushkin State Museum of Fine Arts/Abrams.

4. For further details and the text of the letters, see "Five New Schliemann Letters in Belfast," by J. V. Luce, *Hermathena* 132 (1982):8–13.

5. His results were published in his magnum opus, *Troia und Ilion, Ergebnisse der Ausgrabungen in den vorhistorischen unde historischen Schichten von Ilion, 1870–94* (Athens, 1902).

6. Detailed work reports appear annually in the journal *Studia Troica,* published by Philipp von Zabern, Mainz.

7. In an article, "Hisarlik und das Troia Homers," in *Festschrift* for Wolfgang Rollig (1997).

8. C. W. Blegen, *Troy and the Trojans* (London, 1963), chap. 7, especially 161–64.

9. *Troia und Ilion,* 181. For a judicious assessment of the whole question in the light of historical argument and archaeological discovery up to 1989, see G. S. Kirk's introductory section 4, "History and Fiction in the Iliad," in the *Cambridge Commentary,* vol. 2, 36–50.

10. See the classic article by C. M. Bowra, "Homeric Epithets for Troy," *Journal of Hellenic Studies* 80 (1960):16–23. Bowra concludes that the epithets "go back in part to the Mycenaean age and reflect the sight which the city must have presented to at least one generation of Achaeans."

11. Il. 2, 803; 7, 296; 9, 136, 278; 17, 160; 21, 309. Bowra, "Homeric Epithets," thought it "not very appropriate to the site of Troy if it refers simply to extent." But as noted elsewhere, the size of Troy is now known to exceed that of Mycenae.

12. Note on Il. 6, 316–17 in the *Cambridge Commentary,* vol. 2.

CHAPTER FIVE **SIGNPOSTS TO THE COURSE OF THE FIGHTING**

1. In Il. 16, 79 the temporary Trojan domination in the field is emphasised in Achilles' statement that they control "the whole of the plain."

2. The association is made in a thrice-repeated formula: "When he/they came to the Scaean Gate and the oak tree" (Il. 6, 237; 9, 354; 11, 170). Homer may well have invested the oak tree with symbolic overtones of doom for Hector, as Agathe Thornton has suggested (*Supplication,* 151–52), but this is quite compatible with the one-time existence of such a tree, possibly sacred to Zeus (Il. 5, 693), in a prominent position near the citadel wall of Late Bronze Age Troy. A parallel comes to mind in the "lone pine" that had such direful significance for the Anzac forces at Gallipoli.

3. The ships are associated with the Hellespont in Il. 15, 233; 18, 150; 23, 2; less precise references to the ship station on a wave-beaten seashore occur in Il. 8, 501; 13, 682; 14, 30–31; 19, 40–46; 23, 58–61.

4. Maclaren, *Dissertation,* 212–15. Cook, *Troad,* 393, remarks that the vicinity of the present-day ford is "where we should expect the Roman road [between Novum Ilium and Alexandria

Troas] to have crossed the Scamander." If so, one might expect to find some remains of a Roman bridge in the area, and in fact Wood in the sketch map in his *Essay* (p. 207) marks an "ancient bridge" in the Trojan plain about halfway between Pınarbaşı and Kum Kale. No trace of such a structure is now to be seen, but Wood can hardly have been mistaken about it, for in addition to marking it on his map he printed a sketch of it (p. 326).

5. Herodotus (2, 10) explicitly mentions the vicinity of Ilion as a region where rapid alluviation of a river valley had taken place, filling in an arm of the sea. The same thing, he says, happened in Teuthrania, at Ephesos, and in the plain of the Maeander. References to modern scientific work on the geophysics of the Trojan plain are given in the next note. Robert Wood, *Essay,* showed himself well aware of Herodotus's point when he wrote: "It is evident, both from history, and present appearances, that a great part [of the plain] has been produced since the time of Homer" (p. 332).

6. The fundamental scientific paper "Geomorphic Reconstructions in the Environs of Ancient Troy," by J. C. Kraft, I. Kayan, and O. Erol, appeared in *Science* 209 (1980):776–82. The data on which this paper was based were further assessed by G. Rapp and J. A. Gifford, supplementary monograph 4, *Troy,* ed. Carl Blegen (Princeton, 1982), 11 ff. In response to these publications, my article "The Homeric Topography of the Trojan Plain Reconsidered" was published in the *Oxford Journal of Archaeology* 3 (1984):31–43. Recently the scientific debate has been extended by an important article by I. Kayan, "The Troia Bay and Supposed Harbour Sites in the Bronze Age," *Studia Troica* 5 (1995):211–35.

Kayan's article is based on data accruing from a much more extensive drilling programme and from a series of carbon 14 dates for marine material. Its conclusions about the situation of the shoreline of Troia Bay at selected dates in the past differ quite substantially from those of Rapp and Gifford. Kayan thinks that the alluviation proceeded even more rapidly than previously supposed. In particular, he places the shoreline in the Early Iron Age (c. 1000–500 B.C.) between one and a half and two miles north of Troy. Map 6 shows how much this placing differs from that adopted by Kraft, Kayan, and Erol and by Rapp and Gifford. But even on Kayan's placing, the impracticality of a military base on the plain north of Troy c. 1250 B.C. remains obvious, and Kayan's revised findings cannot, in my opinion, be used to rehabilitate the Schliemann-Leaf view of the Greek camp. Some of the basic scientific issues involved in the problem are mentioned in note 17 below. See also note 9 for the marked discrepancy between Strabo's evidence and Kayan's reconstruction.

7. For examples of similar scene-setting descriptions, all beginning with the formula "There is... *[esti de tis],*" see Il. 11, 711–12 and 722–23; Od. 3, 293–96; 4, 844–47; 13, 96–101. Sophocles has the same formula in *Trach.* 752. S. West, in the *Oxford Commentary,* vol. 1 on Od. 3, 293, calls the introductory formula "a rather stately phrase," and says that the "usage, found also in Sanskrit and Latin, is clearly very ancient." Good parallels in English literature are provided by Shakespeare's "There is a willow grows aslant a brook" and Mrs. C. F. Alexander's famous hymn beginning "There is a green hill far away."

8. This complicated little problem is well discussed by Cook, *Troad,* 107–8 and 133–34. In favour of a Bronze Age date for the tumulus is the scholiast's comment that Myrinê was the name of an Amazon.

9. An alternative site for the ship station favoured by some ancient enquirers was the deep inlet close to Cape Rhoeteum, then known as "the harbour of the Achaeans," now the In Tepe Asmak (well seen in Cook, *Troad,* plate 6b). Strabo says (13, 1, 36) that this inlet lay only about twelve stades from Ilion. He also adds the interesting reflection: "If the distance is now twelve stades, it will have been half as much then." In other words, following his local authorities, he is attempting to measure the advance of the alluvium between the time of the Trojan War and his own day. It is also of interest to note that Strabo's evidence in the same passage on the distance between Troy and the mouth of the Scamander in his time (about two thousand years ago) shows a marked discrepancy with what appears to be Kayan's estimate of the position of the shoreline at that date ("Troia Bay"). Strabo says that the Scamander entered the Hellespont twenty stades (a little more than two miles) from Troy in the direction of Sigeum. This figure enables us to judge that the shoreline in his time followed very much the line indicated by Kraft, Kayan, and Erol, "Geomorphic Reconstructions," and Rapp and Gifford, supp. monograph 4, *Troy.* To judge from Kayan's fig. 8, the shoreline, in his view, had already reached this position between five hundred and one thousand years earlier.

10. C. T. Newton, *Travels and Discoveries in the Levant* (London, 1865), vol. 1, 131–32. Discussion in Cook, *Troad,* 103–6.

11. The lecture was published in *Archaeologischer Anzeiger* (1912):616 ff.; see also *Archaeologischer Anzeiger* (1925):229 ff.

12. The campaign is well summarised by Cook, *Troad,* 169–74; see also O. Mey's *Das Schlachtfeld vor Troia* (Berlin, 1926).

13. *Troad,* 170, n. 2; C. Vellay, *Controverses autour de Troie* (Monaco, 1936).

14. His preliminary reports appeared in *Archaeologischer Anzeiger* 1984, 1985, 1986, 1988, and 1989. The 1984 report begins with an important general survey of geographical and historical data relating to Beşika Bay, which he calls the Port of Troy.

15. *Troad,* 185–86.

16. This finding was a severe blow to the then-current Schliemann-Leaf placing of the Greek camp on the Hellespontine shore between Cape Sigeum and Cape Rhoeteum. In Roman times Cape Rhoeteum was certainly associated with the memory of Ajax, for Pliny says that a harbour town named Aianteion was located there, and the tomb of Ajax was pointed out (*N.H.* 5, 125). But as in the case of the supposed tomb of Achilles on Cape Sigeum, there is no archaeological support for a Mycenaean presence on Cape Rhoeteum at the time of the Trojan War. The large tumulus at In Tepe was deemed to be Homeric by Pococke in 1740, but it is in fact of Hadrianic date. The history of the tumuli in the Yenişehir area is well summarised by Cook in *Troad,* 159–65. For Aianteion and the supposed tomb of Ajax, see ibid., 86–89.

17. See his finely illustrated article "The Troia Bay and Supposed Harbour Sites in the Bronze Age," *Studia Troica* 5 (1995):211–35. The finding from borehole 16 is mentioned on 225. His general conclusion is that what he calls the "Kesik plain" (Lisgar swamp) ceased to be a harbour c. 2000 B.C., but the data from borehole 16 seem to make this less than certain.

As stated in note 6 above, Kayan's conclusions about the advance of the plain and the position of the shoreline at different epochs differ quite markedly from those published by Rapp and Gifford in supp. monograph 4, *Troy*. The Rapp-Gifford conclusions were based on an earlier coring programme in which Kayan collaborated with J. C. Kraft and O. Erol. Kayan offers no explicit critique of the earlier results, which, as pointed out in note 9 above, agree much better with data in Strabo. When one compares the methodologies, one sees that the sea-level curve used by Rapp and his collaborators (fig. 4, p. 18) differs quite markedly from that used by Kayan in his later article (fig. 3, p. 216). The question of eustatic sea level is a difficult and contentious one for science. Kayan also allows that some of his data could be explained by down-faulting in the Trojan plain, though he believes that the hypothesis of a fall in sea level has better support. These are critical issues not yet fully resolved. Until they are I prefer to believe that the Lisgar swamp, which Kayan allows could have been an "excellent harbour" in the third millennium B.C., continued to be usable as such down to the end of the Bronze Age.

On a different issue, one may note that Kayan uses his data to formulate strong scientific objections to E. Zangger's theory that ancient Troy provided the model for Plato's Atlantis (*The Flood from Heaven: Deciphering the Atlantis Legend* [London, 1992]). Zangger holds that remnants of the system of canals and port basins that connected the metropolis of Atlantis with the sea can still be detected around the Trojan plain. Kayan concludes that "from a geomorphological point of view" the theory "does not have the necessary proof" (232–33).

18. In the *Cambridge Commentary*, vol. 4 ad loc., Janko takes the meaning to be "coming inland," but the tradition of rising ground in the camp is confirmed by an earlier passage where Agamemnon says to his commanders: "Let us go down to the sentry posts" (Il. 10, 97).

19. For a fine aerial view and full discussion of the nature and function of the Kesik Canal, see also Kayan, "Troia Bay," 223. Lechevalier is the only topographer, so far as I know, to have attributed a military function to it. He thought of it as a protection of the right wing of the Achaean forces, but in his view they would have been encamped much farther north. See C. G. Lenz, *Reise nach Troas* (Altenberg, 1800), 124 f., a reference I owe to Cook, *Troad,* 166.

20. G. S. Kirk in *Cambridge Commentary,* vol. 2, p. 48.

21. See Kayan, "Troia Bay," 228. For the legendary associations of Herakles with the Trojan plain and the Sigeum Ridge, see Cook, *Troad,* 168–69. Leaf, *Troy* (1912), sketch map pp. 44–45, rpt. here as map 5, identified Beşik (Sivri) Tepe as the fort of Herakles, but he is not correct in saying that that tumulus stands at the highest point of the ridge. Kesik Tepe stands equally high and is an even better lookout point.

22. M. W. Edwards, *Cambridge Commentary,* vol. 5 ad loc., takes them to be "the beach

beside the ships," but does not cite any Homeric parallel for *akte* in this sense. Homeric usage really compels us to take *aktai eridoupoi* here as bold sea-beaten promontories or headlands. Cf. Ebeling, *Lexicon Homericum*, s. v. *akte*.

23. M. W. Edwards, *Cambridge Commentary*, vol. 5, 51–53, notes the repetition, with the remark: "Clearly his invention (?) [Kallikolonê] stayed in the poet's mind." Such an "invention" would assort strangely with the actuality of the Simoeis, not to mention the reference to the Trojan Pergamos in the previous line.

24. See M. M. Willcock, *The Iliad of Homer*, vol. 2 (London, 1984), on Il. 13, 683 and 14, 32. See also G. S. Kirk in the *Cambridge Commentary*, vol. 2 on 7, 327–43.

25. Aristotle, *frag.* 162 (Rose), quoted by Strabo (13, 1, 36).

26. Il. 12, 108 ff., with special reference to lines 152–56, where the word for missile, *chermadion*, literally "hand-held stone," was later applied explicitly to sling stones.

27. Brigitte Mannsperger, "Die Funktion des Grabens am Schiffslager der Achäer," *Studia Troica* 5 (1995):343–56.

28. For "lofty wall" meaning the Greek rampart, see Il. 12, 388; 16, 512. Janko, *Cambridge Commentary*, vol. 4 on Il. 16, 394–98, takes the "lofty wall" here to be that of Troy and says: "The killing ground is between Troy to the S.E., the ships to the N. and the Skamandros to the E." I find it difficult to match this topographical analysis with what Homer says about the Trojans being cut off from retreat and pinned back against the ships.

29. *Troia und Ilion*, 608. The implications for the authenticity of Homer's narrative are well argued by Leaf, *Troy* (1912), 156–58.

30. Richardson, *Cambridge Commentary*, vol. 6 ad loc., quotes Leaf, *Troy* (1912), 10 on the "realism" of this description. Especially notable is Leaf's description of the "tamarisks that spread from the banks in thick copses, making with their young shoots at the end of April conspicuous patches of dull crimson."

31. Strabo 13, 1, 43.

32. *Troy* (1912), 50.

33. A specific variant of the Leaf approach has also been put forward involving springs more than thirty miles away at the source of the Scamander itself. See N. Richardson in the *Cambridge Commentary*, vol. 6 on Il. 22, 147–56.

CHAPTER SIX **HOMERIC ITHACA**
GEOGRAPHY AND ARCHAEOLOGY

1. In Od. 12, 101 Homer uses the comparative form of the adjective (*chthamalōteron*) to characterise the headland by Charybdis, which is low by comparison with the lofty crag of Scylla on the other side of the strait. I owe this point to V. Bérard (*Les navigations d'Ulysse* [Paris, 1927], vol. 1, 217, hereafter cited as *Navigations*). Bérard's long and nuanced account of Ithaca is still

required reading for anyone who wants to go deeply into the topography of the island. He is particularly good at eliciting and illustrating the nautical point of view inherent in much of the Homeric narrative. One of his great merits is to have seen, merely from the Homeric indications and before the archaeological confirmation provided by the British School excavations, that the city of Odysseus must have been at Polis Bay. Lord Rennell of Rodd also reached the same conclusion (in opposition to the earlier views of Gell and Schliemann) in his attractively written account of a fortnight's fieldwork in Ithaca prior to the start of the British School campaigns. See *Homer's Ithaca: A Vindication of Tradition* (London, 1927), 117–21.

2. *A Companion to Homer* (London, 1962), 403–4, hereafter cited as *Companion*. Stubbing's account of Ithaca is particularly notable for its judicious and comprehensive review of all the evidence bearing on the Lefkas-Itháki controversy.

3. H. L. Lorimer, *Homer and the Monuments* (London, 1950), 494 ff., is sympathetic up to a point with Dörpfeld's theory. She thinks that Lefkas in the Bronze Age was indeed called Ithaca and that its geography is reflected in the "crucial passage," Od. 9, 21–26, as well as in Od. 21, 346–47, where Telemachos contrasts Ithaca with the islands "over against Elis." But she also believes that a "double view of Ithaca is presented in the Odyssey," with the poet describing the Ithaca of his own day (Itháki) in almost every other topographical passage. This seems to me to be an overly complex explanation of the Ithaca problem. She accepts that Homer had "personal knowledge" of the island (498) yet also believes that he could have put into the mouth of Odysseus a description that "is in every vital respect inapplicable" to Itháki (494).

With regard to Od. 21, 346–47, the lines are omitted in one manuscript, and the reading in 347 is not certain. The passage can bear very little weight in relation to the problem of the four islands. M. Ferandez-Galliano has a good summary of the various solutions proposed for the general problem in his note on the passage in the *Oxford Commentary*, vol. 3.

4. T. W. Allen, *The Homeric Catalogue of the Ships* (Oxford, 1921), 87. This solution is endorsed by Stubbings (*Companion*, 403) and strongly supported also by R. Hope Simpson and J. F. Lazenby in *The Catalogue of the Ships in Homer's Iliad* (Oxford, 1970), 101, hereafter cited as *Ship Catalogue*.

5. British Admiralty chart 2405 shows clear water at all points between the sandy isthmus and the mainland, even if much of the lagoon is less than three feet in depth.

6. W. M. Leake, *Travels in Northern Greece* (1835), iii, 19, quoted in Stubbings, *Companion*, 404.

7. Homer nearly always classes Doulichion as an island, but in one passage he may refer to it (though not by name) as a peninsula. This is in Od. 24, 377–78, where Laertes recalls his capture of "well-built Nerikos, the promontory of the mainland." Thucydides (3, 7) implies that Nerikos was a town in Lefkas, and a situation on the Lefkas lagoon opposite the Akarnanian coast would suit all these contexts. See also Heubeck in the *Oxford Commentary*, vol. 3 ad loc.

8. See *Ship Catalogue*, 101, where it is called a "brutal bisection." Strabo himself favoured Dolicha in the Echinades, but this will not do either. Bérard argued for Meganisi (*Navigations*, 246–48), which remains a possibility, but its claims are weak compared with Lefkas. The *Oxford*

Commentary comes to no firm conclusion. Hoekstra in vol. 2 on 14, 335 favours the "old hypothesis" of Doulichion as the western part of Kephalonia. West in vol. 1 on 1, 246 sees that the Homeric data "suit Leukas well," but speaks also of the "poet's generally imprecise conception of his hero's homeland," a generalisation that I could not accept.

9. In Od. 16, 396 Doulichion is also called "grassy." The epithets suit Lefkas much better than Itháki. Lefkas is a large and fertile island with extensive plains near its modern capital and at Nidri.

10. *The Ulysses Voyage* (London, 1987), 190 ff.

11. See the concise and cogent account of the Kingdom of Meges in *Ship Catalogue,* 101–2.

12. *Homer's Ithaca,* 104–5. He suggests a derivation from *krokus,* the flock or nap on wool, and refers to "the prevalence in the [Vathy] region of blocks or boulders of white limestone resembling flocks of wool."

13. Traill, *Schliemann,* 42–47.

14. *Annual of the British School at Athens (BSA),* vols. 33 (1933), 35 (1934–35), 39 (1942), 43 (1948), 44 (1949), 47 (1952). Further information in S. Benton, "Antiquities of Thiaki," *BSA* 29 (1927–28), and Lord Rennell of Rodd, "The Ithaca of Odysseus," *BSA* 33 (1933). See also *Companion,* 416–19.

15. Lady Helen Waterhouse, "From Ithaca to the Odyssey," *BSA* 91 (1996):301–17.

16. Symeonoglu has published summary reports of his work in *Ergon* (1984, 1986, 1987, 1990, 1992) and a fuller account in *Praktika* (1986):234–40. For the previous find of Mycenaean sherds at Aetos, see Catling in the archaelogical report of the *Journal for Hellenic Studies* (1986–87):31. In his interpretation of Ithacan topography as given in the *Odyssey,* Symeonoglu cites Od. 16, 138–53 in support of his view. He argues that this passage shows that the polis lay midway between the farms of Eumaios and Laertes. My own account of Eumaios's journey and the farm of Laertes shows that a different interpretation is possible. Symeonoglu also lays much emphasis on his discovery of a votive from Aetos inscribed ΑΠΟ. He links this with Homer's reference (Od. 20, 278) to a "shady grove of far-darting Apollo" in the vicinity of the palace. The new evidence for an Apollo cult at Aetos is of course of considerable interest, but there is nothing per se in the *Odyssey* passage to link it with Aetos. If all the Homeric evidence for the location of the palace is considered, the indications point very strongly to the north of the island.

17. Strabo (10, 2, 11) comments on the ambiguity of Ithaca as city/island, referring specifically to Il. 2, 632 and Od. 3, 81. In addition to Od. 3, 81, see 16, 322–24, where the ship of Telemachos, which has started from the southeast corner of the island, sails around to Polis Bay and is described as coming into port "at Ithaca." The expression "city of Ithaca" occurs three times (10, 416–17; 18, 1–2; 22, 223). Other expressions like "throughout the community of well-built Ithaca" (22, 52), "in the community of Ithaca" (1, 103; 13, 97; 15, 534; 16, 419; 24, 284), "to the rich community of Ithaca" (14, 329; 19, 399) could refer to the whole island but seem to gain in point if restricted to the main settlement.

18. *Navigations,* 265; *Oxford Commentary,* vol. 2 ad loc.

1. As a result of a personal communication from Professor J. M. Cook. For my previous account, see *The Quest for Ulysses* (London, 1974), 90–91, with ill. 82. Lord Rennell of Rodd, *Homer's Ithaca,* mentions finding a squared block, which he took to be an altar, on the floor of the cave (153–54).

2. *Homeric Essays* (Oxford, 1935), 47–48, 76–77.

3. See the full discussion in *Navigations,* 306 ff.

4. "Asteris and the Twin Harbours," *Journal of Hellenic Studies* 96 (1976):157–59. I acknowledge that Bérard did look for the twin harbours in Kephalonia but thought to see them in the Fiskardo inlet farther north.

5. I have followed the readings in the *Oxford Classical Text* (3d ed., Oxford, 1919) of Monro and Allen, which derive from Strabo. There are some minor variants in the manuscripts—e.g., Phera for Pheia—but the general course of the voyage is clear. A similar voyage is described in the *Homeric Hymn to Apollo,* 421–29, with the ship coasting up the western shores of the Peloponnese and gaining a view of the cloud-capped peak of Ithaca in the distance before turning in to the Gulf of Corinth.

6. See Kirk in the *Cambridge Commentary,* vol. 2 on Il. 7, 133–35. Cf. *Ship Catalogue,* 94.

7. According to the scholiast, the Argive historian Akusilaos (fifth century B.C.) reported the tradition that Ithakos and Neritos crossed over from Kephalonia to found the city of Ithaca. The fact that Mycenaean remains in Kephalonia are both older and more extensive than anything yet found in Ithaca lends some colour to this tradition. In recent years a fine *tholos* tomb has been found in the southeast of Kephalonia, dating possibly from as early as 1400 B.C. Such tombs are normally associated with a palatial centre, as at Pylos, Mycenae, and Orchomenos, leading to some otherwise unsupported speculation that the palace of Odysseus may really have been in Kephalonia.

8. Lady Waterhouse, "From Ithaca to the Odyssey," 312, emphasises the use of ceremonial tripod-cauldrons as competition prizes, a use well documented for eighth-century B.C. Greece, and suggests that some at least of the Polis cave tripods could have been prizes dedicated by the victors in a local contest held in honour of Odysseus.

9. This last question is posed in this telling form by Hoekstra in his note on Od. 13, 217–18 in vol. 2 of the *Oxford Commentary.* If the answer is yes, he suggests that "a large part of the *Odyssey* would begin to look more like a historical novel than an epic poem." I have long thought that this is a good way to categorise the second half of the poem.

10. For example, D. T. Ansted, *The Ionian Islands in the Year 1863* (London, 1863), 233; Thomopoulos, *Homeric Ithaca* (Athens, 1908), 235–36 (in Greek, with a German summary); Lekatsas, *Ithake* (Athens, 1933), 62 (in Greek, by a native of Itháki); H. L. Lorimer, *Homer and the Monuments* (London, 1950), 497–98.

General Index

(Maps and figures cited in **boldface**.)

INDEX OF HOMERIC PASSAGES